Writing Children's Books

Everything You Need to Know from Story Creation to Getting Published

Anthony D. Fredericks
www.anthonydfredericks.com

BLUE RIVER PRESS

Indianapolis, Indiana

Dedicated to
Sandy Ferguson Fuller
—devoted friend, consummate colleague,
and exceptional agent!

Writing Children's Books:
Everything You Need to Know from Story Creation
to Getting Published

Published by **Blue River Press**
Indianapolis, Indiana
www.brpressbooks.com

Distributed by **Cardinal Publishers Group**
A Tom Doherty Company, Inc.
www.cardinalpub.com

ISBN: 978-1-68157-081-5
Library of Congress Control Number: 2018943651

Cover Design: Glen Edelstein
Book Design: Dave Reed
Cover Photograph: iStock
Editor: Dani McCormick

Printed in the United States of America

7 6 5 4 3 2 1   18 19 20 21 22 23 24

Contents

About the Author   v

Acknowledgements   vii

Foreword   ix

Introduction   x

The ABCs   **1**

1. Are You Ready?   2
2. Persistent Myths and Honest Truths   12
3. Occupation: Author   21

The Facts of Life   **29**

4. The Biggest Mistake You'll Ever Make!   30
5. Other Common Errors, Blunders, and Boo-Boos   42
6. What is a Good Book?   55

"Where Do You Get All Those Ideas?"   **75**

7. A Plethora of Writing Prompts   76
8. How to Generate Even More Ideas   92
9. Ideas—They're All Around You!   108

Children's Books and the Writing Process   **118**

10. Genres and Formats   119
11. Beginning Your Book: The "How To's"   135
12. Revision: The Author's BFF   147
13. How to Format Your Manuscript   165

Into the Fray   **177**

14. Finding the Right Publisher   178
15. How to Submit Your Manuscript (and impress an editor)   186
16. Do You Need an Agent?: Yes! No!   207
17. What About Self-Publishing?   225

Reality Check   243

18. From the Editor's Desk   244
19. Rejection is Just Another Fact of Life   254
20. Dollars and Sense   265
21. Becoming a Successful Children's Author   277
Postscript   294
Sources and Resources   295
Index   299

About the Author

Anthony D. Fredericks grew up in southern California. After college in Arizona and four years of service in the US Coast Guard, he and his family moved to Pennsylvania where he obtained his MEd and EdD in reading education. He then worked as a classroom teacher and reading specialist for many years. In 1987, he became professor of education at York College of Pennsylvania. For thirty years (he's now retired), he taught undergraduate classes in reading education, elementary science education, children's literature, elementary social studies; as well as several writing courses. A popular and energetic visiting author at elementary schools throughout North America, he is also a dynamic keynote speaker at numerous writing conferences and conventions.

He's a prolific author having published over 450 articles and 160 books. His books include an eclectic array of adult nonfiction titles (e.g. *The Secret Life of Clams: The Mysteries and Magic of Our Favorite Shellfish; Ace Your Teacher Interview: 149 Fantastic Answers to Tough Interview Questions*) and more than fifty children's books. His children's titles have won numerous awards, citations, and commendations (see "Selected Children's Book Awards for Anthony D. Fredericks"). When he's not working at his computer, visiting schools, or leading writing workshops, he can be found paddling his kayak on quiet lakes, camping in wild and wonderful places, or visiting his children (and grandchildren) in England and Colorado. He lives with his wife Phyllis and a (slightly) rotund cat named Tubby in south-central Pennsylvania. Please check out his web site at www.anthonydfredericks.com.

Selected Children's Book Awards for <u>Anthony D. Fredericks</u>

- Bank Street College of Education Best Book of the Year (2007)—*The Tsunami Quilt: Grandfather's Story*

- ForeWord Reviews Book of the Year Honorable Mention (2012)—*Around One Log: Chipmunks, Spiders, and Creepy Insiders*

- Grand Canyon Reader Award Finalist (2015)—*Desert Day, Desert Night*

- International Reading Association Teacher's Choice Award (2004)—*Around One Cactus: Owls, Bats, and Leaping Rats*

- Isaac Walton League Book of the Year (2008)—*Under One Rock: Bugs, Slugs and Other Ughs*

- Learning Magazine Teacher's Choice Award (2004)—*Around One Cactus: Owls, Bats and Leaping Rats*

- Learning Magazine Teacher's Choice Award (2003)—*Under One Rock: Bugs, Slugs and Other Ughs*

- Missouri State Teacher's Association Recommended Reading List (2003)—*In One Tidepool: Crabs, Snails and Salty Tails*

- National Best Books Award Finalist (2009)—*A is for Anaconda: A Rainforest Alphabet*

- Newton Marasco Foundation Green Earth Book Award (2005) —*Near One Cattail: Turtles, Logs and Leaping Frogs*

- New York State Reading Association Charlotte Award (2012)—*A is for Anaconda: A Rainforest Alphabet*

- NSTA/CBC Outstanding Science Trade Book for Children (2018)—*Tall Tall Tree*

- NSTA/CBC Outstanding Science Trade Book for Children (2001)—*Slugs*

- Skipping Stones Magazine Ecology and Nature Award (2002)—*Under One Rock: Bugs, Slugs and Other Ughs*

- Skipping Stones Magazine Ecology and Nature Award (2006)—*Near One Cattail: Turtles, Logs and Leaping Frogs*

- Storytelling World Awards Honor (2008)—*The Tsunami Quilt: Grandfather's Story*

Acknowledgements

I am sincerely indebted to many people who have contributed mightily to this book as well as to a corps of supporters whose council and sage wisdom has made this tome far better than would otherwise be the case. I am fortunate to have such a wealth of friends, colleagues and fellow writers who consistently go "above and beyond" to share their expertise, advice, and insights. Their passion for children's literature is evident on every page and it is to be celebrated in every way.

I am especially thankful for my editor Dani McCormick who has consistently supported my authorial proclivities since her arrival at <u>Blue River Press</u>. She is both a champion and advocate of the highest order; a colleague and a friend whose high standards and editorial acumen resonate on every page of this tome.

Gold stars (and lots of "high fives") go to two incredible ladies in my life! First to my agent, Sandy Ferguson Fuller, who has cheered and supported my career as a children's author for almost twenty-five years. And, to Carol Malnor, whose editorial skills and unfailing support has nourished both my soul and my literary efforts.

A standing ovation (with a plethora of confetti) goes to Aimee Jackson and Demi Stevens whose contributions to this book are to be celebrated and cheered. And, to my dear friend and colleague Lindsay Barrett George, an enormous hug and a crescendo of accolades. She is one of the finest children's authors you're likely to meet and that I am fortunate to know.

My dearest thanks to all the authors and editors (both living and dead) whose wisdom and erudition are sprinkled throughout the pages of this book. Their insights and quotes are testimony to the power of a children's book to change lives, both for the authors who write them and the children who read them.

I am equally thankful to all the editors, agents, and fellow authors I have met on the road these past three decades. Although the names may have faded from my memory, their contributions to my writing career (and ultimately this book) will not. This is, indeed, a most friendly fraternity, and I am privileged to have had an opportunity to tap into that collective wisdom.

Ultimately, my never-ending appreciation goes to my constant morning companion (and all-around "supercat")—*Tubby*. An audience of one, his presence beneath my desk each morning allowed me to vent (when something wasn't working) and sing (when things were "clicking"). The fact that he slept through most of the writing process is completely immaterial.

And, to you the reader, I offer my appreciation for including this book as a valuable resource in your professional library. I wish you the greatest of success on this adventuresome journey towards publication. There will be much to experience and much to learn as you travel down this road. May your travels be filled with exciting discoveries, delightful exploits, insightful vistas, and the joy of truly affecting a new generation of young readers. Cheers!

Expert Quote

"Writing isn't about making money, getting famous, getting dates, getting laid, or making friends. In the end, it's about enriching the lives of those who will read your work, and enriching your own life, as well."

—Stephen King, author

Foreword

Why do you want to write children's books?

Please take a few moments and ponder that query. If your answer is because you want to make a ton of money, own several tropical condominiums, drive an expensive Italian sports car, be seen at all the trendy places in Beverly Hills, and be selected as Time Magazine's annual Person of the Year, may I respectfully make a small suggestion? Please return this book to the bookstore where you bought it, give it back to the friend who loaned it to you, or drive it back to your local public library. This is not the book you need.

I'm frequently asked why I write for children. My response is both simple and complex. I write for the pure pleasure of taking an idea, doing some creative things with that idea, and making that idea exciting and memorable for youngsters. I also write for a more complicated reason: the passion. I want to bring my passion for storytelling into the hearts and minds of young readers. I want them to feel an excitement for words and the ideas they convey. I also want youngsters to be zealous and fervent readers. I want them to experience the emotions that good writing can convey as well as the energy that can create a bond between an author and an audience of readers. For me, writing is all about passion—an opportunity to shape minds, stimulate interests, influence thinking, and foster strong emotional responses.

I believe that crafting a story that can change someone for the better is essential to the writing process. Do I make a little money from this effort? Sure, but that isn't my *raison d'etre*. I write because words can influence people for the better. A story or book offers a unique opportunity to impact the arc of someone's life. That impact is what propels my creative efforts and fuels my linguistic endeavors. It is my passion!

In essence, I write to bring words and ideas alive for youngsters, and for the opportunity to create an emotional and intellectual bond with young minds. Ultimately, I write for the love of language and the love of kids.

Why do you want to write children's books?

Introduction

It was a letter I've never forgotten!

Throughout my professional career, I have been invited as a visiting author to scores of schools throughout the United States, Canada, and Mexico. However, there was one visit, a few years ago, that was, well, truly memorable!

It was almost 100°F (at eight in the morning) as I walked into the elementary school just outside Las Vegas, NV. I was there to share my books and my literary life with some 700 students. The school's air conditioning unit was clearly struggling as I began to set up my props in the gymnasium. Soon after morning announcements, the students began filing in. Row upon row of students sat on the floor and filled up the gym.

The school librarian introduced me as "the author guy we've been talking about for the past four weeks." I shared a little about myself and began to show slides of my books, talk about the research and writing that went into each one, share elements of the writing process, and describe some forthcoming projects. Fifty-five minutes later, amidst laughter, reams of personal questions ("Is it true your wife is an enchanted princess?"), and many anecdotes, the students signaled their appreciation with a thunderous round of applause.

Throughout the remainder of the day, I traveled to various classrooms, doing storytelling programs, sharing several of my books, promoting the writer's life, teaching some valuable writing techniques, and talking about the challenges I face as a children's author. By the end of the day I was tired, but refreshed with the energy of the student body. It was a most satisfying experience—one filled with lots of lessons, lots of inspiration, and lots of magic!

Two weeks later I received a large manila envelope in the mail—the inevitable bundle of thank you letters teachers often ask students to write after an author's visit. Most were the customary "Thank you for coming all the way from Pencil-vania," and "You are my favorite author in the whole world (but don't tell the other authors I said that)," and "I used to have head lice, but now I don't. Can I write a story about that?"

However, at the very bottom of the stack, was one letter neatly printed on blue-lined paper. It immediately caught my eye. I read it over and over and have saved it to this day.

> *Dear Mr. Fredericks,*
> *Thank you for coming to read stories to us. It was very interesting and I loved the slugs and the scary story. Well, I got to go. Oh, are you always that sweaty and handsome?*
> *Love,*
> *Sara Jane*

What more could a slightly-past-middle-aged children's author ask for?

Whatever your age (or propensity to perspire), I am sure you would love to receive a letter (or several letters) just like that one. Indeed, knowing that you have touched the lives of youngsters with your words and with your books is truly one of the greatest thrills in life.

And, that's why I wrote this book!

What do I need to know to write a children's book?

It could be rightly said that those words have become the universal question that has bedeviled every potential children's author ever since the invention of pen and ink. Although frequently asked, it is infrequently answered. Inevitably, whenever I do a school visit, a writing workshop, or a conference presentation, there are several folks who come up and ask me for a resource on how to write and publish a children's book. It became clear that many authors-to-be were looking for a practical, insightful, and complete writing instruction book. With that "guide on the side," they could have a confidence and a commitment to become active participants in the engaging world of children's literature.

And so, for many years, I recommended a few titles I had used early in my writing career. Then, I reread some of those titles and noticed that there was valuable information missing—ideas, tips, and techniques critical to authorial success in the competitive world of children's books. In short, there seemed to be a lot of unanswered questions. In many conversations with prospective authors, I noted a frustration on the part of those individuals simply because the information they really needed wasn't being shared.

So, what is it that this book has that those "Brand X" books left out?

Where can I get some good ideas? Most of those other books describe the need to get good ideas, but fail to show prospective authors *how* to locate and generate viable book ideas. *Writing Children's Books* not only offers a plethora of writing prompts that will get you writing immediately; it also offers strategic writing strategies that will generate thousands (yes, thousands) of wonderful, terrific, dynamic, delightful, incredible, and eye-popping ideas for you to use. In fact, this book devotes three whole chapters to this topic alone.

What is the secret to success as a children's author? Yup, there is a secret to becoming an accomplished and successful children's author! We'll examine that secret in considerable detail in an entire chapter. Make this secret part of your approach to writing and watch some magical things happen!

How much money will I make? I was surprised to discover that there is not a single "Writing Books for Children" book that addresses this question. Not one! In this book, I'll offer you an inside look into my own royalty statements. I'll give you some facts and figures on what you can expect to earn and (of course) what you shouldn't expect.

What are the biggest mistakes new authors make? Many of those "Brand X" books give you lots of information on what you should do to become a published children's author. I will too; but I'll also show you the most common mistakes that will doom any chance you have of ever getting published. These mistakes are made so often that editors can spot them within ten seconds of reading a manuscript. Avoid them and you can move your manuscript to the head of the line. Oh, I'll also spend an entire chapter on the all-time biggest mistake of new writers. This is one "boo-boo" you never want to make.

What are editors and agents really looking for? Many writing instruction books are written by very capable authors. There's lots of good advice from competent and successful writers. But, what if you also heard directly from agents and editors—the people who make the decisions as to whether your manuscript will be accepted and eventually published. Knowing what these folks are looking for can make your job that much easier. In this book I'll share their thoughts and perspectives through a series of eye-opening and informative interviews and quotes.

What about self-publishing my children's book? For many writers, this is brand new territory. It offers some new options as well as new challenges. Unfortunately, most writing instruction books (particularly those published a few years ago) don't address this topic, but this book will. I'll share the opportunities available to you as well as some practical advice you must consider before traveling down this road.

Like most prospective authors, you want to know how to get started: the initial first steps, where to get ideas, how to turn those ideas into a manuscript, how to transform that manuscript into a salable book, and how to get happily published. And, so, based on my own three decades of writing children's books, and my conversations with experts throughout the field, I wrote this book. This book is unique in that it focuses on the basic and essential elements of book authorship tailored specifically for you: the writer looking for down-to-earth answers to your often unanswered questions.

Writing Children's Books is designed as your all-in-one sourcebook of practical ideas: a compendium of proven strategies and practical advice for publishing success. A creative range of "inside information" is offered on every page, providing you with everything you need for a rewarding career as a children's author. This book is for everyone who has ever wanted to craft a tale, spin a yarn, or share a story with children, but were unsure of where or how to start.

Writing for children is the most satisfying aspect of my literary life. As I frequently tell participants in my writing workshops and seminars, it is also the most challenging writing I do. That's simply because children will accept nothing but the best! The same holds true for editors who know that the children's book market is incredibly competitive. Each year more than 6,500 children's books are published in the US—each one competing for limited shelf space in bookstores and limited advertising space in catalogs and online booksellers. Add to that the fact that many of the large publishers of children's books (e.g. Putnams, Scholastic, HarperCollins) will each receive upwards of 20,000 (or more) submissions for potential book manuscripts every year—20,000 from which they may only select twenty-five to thirty books to add to their respective catalogs—and one can quickly see that the children's book market is incredibly competitive and unbelievably demanding.

But, I can't think of a more satisfying and more rewarding professional field than that of children's book authorship. I have met many inspiring children in my travels, some delightful editors, and a whole raft of adults (teachers, parents, and other children's authors) who seek to share with kids the power and joy of a story well told. Each day, as I sit down at my computer, I know that somewhere, somehow, my words may affect a child in a magical way; they may challenge a child to explore a new dimension of his or her world; they may cause a child to laugh, sing, dance, cry, or just think; or (best yet) those words may inspire a child to sit down at her or his computer one future day and transform an idea into a captivating and mesmerizing story for others to enjoy.

What joy!

What possibilities!

What a journey!

—Tony Fredericks

(AKA "That Sweaty & Handsome Author")

Part I

The ABCs

Chapter 1

Are You Ready?

What a great time to be a children's author! Children's literature is an essential component of school reading programs. Teachers and school librarians are integrating more children's books into their respective curricula. And, read-aloud sessions with an adult, a child, and a good book have been treasured moments for countless generations. Despite the onslaught of electronic diversions and social media, children's books remain the number one form of information and entertainment by kids today. Parents and grandparents choose books as the primary gift for children—a gift that keeps giving for a long time (and never needs batteries).

> **Expert Quote**
>
> "There have been great societies that did not use the wheel, but there have been no great societies that did not tell stories."
>
> —Ursula K. Le Guin, children's author

The opportunities to write and publish a children's book have never been greater than they are today. According to *Bowker*, the number of children's trade books published annually in the United States rose from approximately 2,500 in 1975 to over 6,600 in 2015. Publisher's Weekly reports that publisher's sales of children books have multiplied more than twenty times since 1980—from $211 million to $4.27 billion in 2015. Just as significant, there are more than 800 publishers of children books—from super large conglomerates such as Scholastic which releases about 600 original titles each year in the US (Their web site notes that they "sell approximately one out of every two children's books purchased in the US") to small niche publishers such as Dawn Publications which only releases four to five nonfiction nature books each year.

Insider Tip

Fascinating Facts About the Children's Book Publishing Industry

- According to <u>Publisher's Weekly</u>, women purchase approximately seventy percent of all children's books.

- For children under the age of seven, the most influential factors likely to influence what they read include (in descending order): friends and family, bookstore browsing, teachers, online research, book fairs, and mass media.

- The single-most influential media for children in the birth – six years old age group is children's books. Books are followed by children's DVDs, TV, educational websites, board games, children's magazines, video game systems, handheld games, and online games.

- As reported in 2016, the overall book market has grown thirty-three percent since 2004, while the children's book market has grown fifty-two percent.

- As reported by booksellers, the top juvenile fiction categories ranked by unit sales include humorous stories, fantasy, and magic.

- Religious books for children have shown steady growth over the last several years in both the fiction and nonfiction categories.

- Seventy-five percent of children's books are purchased in a physical store (versus online).

Insider Tip (cont.)

- Bookstores are the primary place that parents of children birth to six years old turn to in order to find out about particular titles, followed by "the child tells me," and public libraries.

- For books "read for fun," children get about sixty-eight percent of those titles from the school library. Public libraries come in second (sixty-four percent). Physical bookstores account for twenty-eight percent, and Amazon.com accounts for twenty-one percent.

- Forty percent of children's book purchases are impulse (that's double the rate for adult titles).

- For children ages seven to twelve, the primary criteria for selecting a book is a familiar character or series, followed by "child asked for it in store," and then front cover image.

- Forty percent of children's book purchasing is focused on five- to eight-year-olds.

- As reported by the American Booksellers Association, the two areas ripe for the largest growth in children's books are multicultural literature (people of color accounted for only twenty-two percent of children's books characters in 2016) and "girl power" books.

- Twenty-five percent of juvenile nonfiction is being purchased by adults for themselves.

- Nonfiction, particularly in the area of science and nature, continues to be a "hot" topic—one continually supported by school librarians and classroom teachers.

In reading the data above, you might assume that it's a great time to break into the children's book market. And, you would be right! With the right topic, the right approach, and the requisite level of professionalism, it's possible to make a contribution to the field that will excite kids, delight teachers, and impress parents. Not that you won't face a lot of challenges. Take, for example, Chronicle Books—a publisher that consistently releases a delightful array of children's titles that frequently find their way to the front of "brick and mortar" bookstores and the top of bestseller lists on Amazon.com and barnesandnoble.com. According to the company's blog, they receive approximately 12,000 manuscripts each year. Out of that enormous pile of submissions, they will select about sixty or so for publication. If you're doing the math, that's means that your chances of having a manuscript accepted for publication by Chronicle Children's Books is somewhat less than one percent. Ouch!

Those odds may appear disheartening at first glance. But consider this: the sheer number of submissions present a logistical conundrum for editors and publishers. In simple terms, they can only produce so many books per year; thus, they have no choice but to reject more than ninety-nine percent of the manuscripts they receive. That alone may be sufficient for you to fold up your laptop and seek another line of work (something really fun, like spreading hot asphalt on city streets in the middle of a summer heat wave). But, before you head on over to Walmart to purchase a set of blue denim overalls, let's take a look at those numbers in a slightly different way.

Most editors, many agents, and a host of publishers (and this author) will tell you that more than ninety percent of all those initial submissions that were rejected committed several cardinal sins that doomed their chances of acceptance even before they were mailed to a publishing house. That is to say, most beginning authors commit a common set of writing sins and omissions that virtually guarantee their manuscript a quick and early demise. In fact, those errors are so prevalent and so obvious that most editors can spot them within seconds of reading. They are clearly evident on the first page of a manuscript; so much so that it is often unnecessary to read any of the other pages that follow.

But, you and I are going to change that!

Why? Because we're going to examine some of the most common mistakes and errors novice writers make. We're also going to focus on the elements of writing that delight editors and get them reading not just page one of your book idea, but every page after that. In short, this book will give you a critical edge over your competition. You'll get insider secrets that have taken me more than three decades to master, you'll see inside the mind of an editor and what she wishes she could be reading instead of what she usually has to read, you'll learn what to do as much as you will learn what not to do, and you will create a manuscript that will rise above all those other thousands of submissions as something an editor wants to publish and something a child will want to read.

Expert Quote

"Focus on where you want to go, not where you currently are."

—Demi Stevens, editor

A Self-Exam

Before we set off down that (long) road, I'd like to suggest a self-examination. No, you don't need a PhD in psychology to administer this exam. But, know this—most folks won't take the time or make the effort to do this self-analysis. They think they can plow ahead writing and publishing a children's book. After all, how hard can it be? Well, if you'll re-examine the figures earlier in this chapter, you already know the answer to that question. This exam, on the other hand, sheds light on the dynamics and characteristics of successful children's authors. Your embrace of these factors will ultimately determine the success you will enjoy in this field.

Ready? Here goes:

1. Goals.

   What are your goals for writing a children's book? What do you hope to achieve? Are you doing it because you've always had an affection for children's literature? Were you influenced by a certain author when you were growing up? Do you have unique storytelling abilities that would translate into a published book? Are you in it to improve your writing skills? Or, would you like to make a positive contribution to the lives of youngsters? Please respond to the following statement in <u>exactly six words</u>:

My ultimate goal in writing children's books: _____

_____

Hang that six-word statement over your computer. Make it the first thing you read every day.

Insider Tip

Here's my personal goal for writing children's books: Imagine and create. Inspire and change.

---

2. Hard Work.

Becoming an accomplished children's author (one whose books get published and one whose books are read by children) takes a lot of hard work—LOTS! Are you willing to devote long hours to mastering your craft and improving your skills? Are you willing to put in the time it takes to draft and revise a book manuscript so many times that you actually get ill seeing it for the eighty-seventh time? Are you willing to write through the good times and the bad, for richer or poorer, and in sickness and in health (sorry, that sounds like a wedding vow!)? Are you comfortable in devoting long months (and maybe long years) in crafting a thirty-two-page children's picture book (for example)?

_____ Yes (to all of the above)

_____ Maybe

_____ No (to some or most of the above)

_____ Wow, Tony, you're starting to freak me out!

3. Talent.

Do you have the necessary writing skills to enter the world of children's writing? Have you embraced writing as a fun and exciting enterprise or do you consider writing as one of the seven circles of Hell as defined in *Dante's Inferno*? Are you aware of grammatical conventions? Have you written compelling essays in high school or eye-popping papers in college? Have you frequently read books and said to yourself, "Holy Moly, I can write much better than this hack. How did he ever get this stuff published?" Have your teachers or your friends ever told you that you have a real talent for expressing ideas through print? Simply put, are you a good writer?

_____ Yes

_____ Geez, maybe I should have listened to my high school English teacher.

_____ I'm still working on it.

_____ No

4. Self-Education.

Are you willing to learn new techniques and skills to improve your writing? Are you able to invest the time to read instructional materials (such as this book), attend writer's conferences, pore over stacks of children's books, talk to other writers, and read hundreds of web sites to improve your writing skills? Are you willing to devote much of your free time to your own re-education—learning and mastering the skills necessary to get into this field and stay in this field? Are you devoted to continually educating yourself?

_____ Yes

_____ You mean, I'm still not done with school?

_____ Will I be graded on this?

_____ No

5. Seriousness.

Here's something I absolutely dread. It happens whenever I do a writing workshop or serve as a visiting author at an elementary school. At the end of the presentation, someone will invariably come up to me with a sheaf of papers in her hand and a certain look on her face. I know exactly what is going to happen next. I can see it a mile away. The person, with somewhat sheepish eyes, will come up to me and say something like this, "I've written this little story and was hoping you might look at it and tell me what you think."

I offer the most sincere smile I possibly can. But, there's something I know immediately—this "little story" will never, ever be published—not in a thousand years, not in a million years, not ever! Why? That's simply because kids don't want "little stories."

Expert Quote

"Don't even think about being a children's book writer unless you know why you're writing for children in the first place. This will give you pause—but this is THE MOST important piece of advice I can give you. You write to make a difference in a young child's life. You write for children to let them know that they matter—and that things will be . . . OK . . . hopefully—in your book. Write the book that a child will cherish—forever."

—Lindsay Barrett George, children's author

Kids want enormous stories: big stories with characters larger than life: stories that are packed with grand adventures and incredibly wonderful discoveries: stories that whisk them to faraway places: stories that take their breath away: stories that captivate, enthrall, and delight: and stories they will want to read again and again. They don't want (and certainly won't read) "little stories."

So, here are your questions: Are you serious about becoming a children's author? Have you simply thrown something together (perhaps a story you shared with your children or grandchildren at bedtime), spent a couple of days writing it down, and then printed it out in order to get some feedback from folks like me? Did you just write a first draft and considered your work done? Did you write something with poor character development, the barest hint of a plot, and language that is sentimental, condescending, or didactic (or all three)? Have you done your homework and approached writing children's books as a serious profession worthy of lots of time and lots of effort?

_____ Yes

_____ I think so . . . perhaps

_____ Now, I'm not so sure!

_____ Can I answer this one in a couple of months?

6. Patience.

Here's the big one! Are you a patient person? Do you need immediate gratification in your life, or are you willing to endure all the "hard knocks" of this profession: all the bumpy roads, all the rejections, all the time waiting . . . and waiting . . . and waiting . . . to hear back from editors about a submission you've worked on for over a year? Are you willing to invest the time to educate yourself, train yourself, school yourself, and instruct yourself in all the nuances necessary for successful publication? Are you willing to write draft after draft after draft of a manuscript until it is absolutely perfect— no matter how much time it takes?

_____ You bet I am!

_____ OK, I'm starting to freak out again.

_____ WOW—That's a lot to think about.

_____ No, I think I'll go fold some laundry and drink some wine.

How did you do? Did you have a lot of positive responses to all those queries? Or, did you find yourself wrestling with the answers to many questions - not quite sure if you could respond in the affirmative? Did you discover some questions you've never considered before? Did you see queries that were challenging to read and answer? Did you leave some questions unanswered?

Suffice it to say, there's a lot to consider in your quest to publish a children's book. We'll address all those issues in the pages of this book. I'll hold your hand, stand by your side, pat you on the shoulder, guide your footsteps, cheer you on, applaud your efforts, and help you along the path to publishing success. The journey is a challenging one, but others have started right where you are and succeeded beyond their wildest dreams. They've written and published, not one, but a whole library shelf worth of children's books. And, so can you!

Are you ready?

_____ I'll get back to you. I'm still working on that wine.

_____ I can't wait!

Chapter 2

Persistent Myths and Honest Truths

Please take a look at the following list. All of the items have one thing in common.

- Lightning doesn't strike twice in the same place.
- We only use ten percent of our brains.
- Bats are blind.
- Primitive cavemen (and cavewomen) would often fight dinosaurs.
- The sun orbits the earth.
- Diamonds form from pressurized coal.
- Mother birds will abandon their chicks if touched by humans.

The list of items above are common scientific myths and fallacies. Every one of the statements above is false—completely and totally false! Yet, for some reason, large numbers of people continue to believe these falsehoods.[1] Perhaps it was because of their education (or miseducation), the barrage of information (and misinformation) that often appears on the internet, conversations with friends and colleagues who continue to perpetuate the myths simply because each one sounds plausible, or a myriad other reasons.

The fact of the matter is these myths have been around for a long time, and it is likely they will continue to be perpetuated far into the future.

In the world of children's publishing, there are copious fantasies, tons of fallacies, innumerable myths, and a plethora of falsehoods. I'm not sure where all these misperceptions came from, but in every writing workshop I present and in every conference I attend, I hear these

---

1. A survey (of twenty-two hundred participants) conducted by the National Science Foundation in 2014 found that fully 25 percent of Americans still believe that the sun orbits the earth - a belief disproved way back in the sixteenth century by Nicolaus Copernicus.

statements in one form or another. Friends and colleagues who want some advice on writing for children always pose questions regarding these lies, suggesting that these fabrications are a perpetual fact of life.

Since you obtained this book to get the best and most current information on how to become a successful children's book author, I thought it best that we address these common misunderstandings early on—tackle them and get them out of the way before getting into the tips and techniques that will ensure your success in this very competitive field. It is certain other prospective authors (who don't read this book) will continue to embrace these misunderstandings and, in turn, completely jeopardize their writing career.

Let's take a look:

1. Writing children's books is easier than writing for the adult market because the books are shorter.

   Trust me on this one: writing children's books is much more challenging, demanding, and intense than writing books for adults. I've done both and I can tell you from personal experience that children's writing is considerably more precise, certainly more time intensive, and without a doubt more mentally exhausting. Just because there are fewer words in a children's book versus an adult book doesn't make it easier to write. Quite the opposite. Each word in a children's book must be the best word possible—no exceptions. If a word is there, it's there for a reason—every adjective, preposition, conjunction, adverb or any other grammatical entity you can think of.

   I have spent weeks crafting a four-word sentence only to throw it out later because "it just didn't work." The truth of the matter is the shorter the sentences, the more work is needed to convey an idea or feeling.

2. Picture books are the easiest children's books to write.

   Actually, picture books are the hardest. That's because every word you include in a picture book must convey a rich visual illustration to the reader (initially an editor, later a child). The words you select for your story must initiate visual images in the mind of any reader—images that might later be converted into the drawings or paintings that make it a complete picture book.

For example, try to create a mental image of this sentence: "He didn't look very nice." It's hard to imagine that character because the word "nice," although short, doesn't tell you much. Now, see if you can create a mind picture of this character: "He was damp, muddied, and covered in stink." A little different? Yes! And, it took a lot more effort to create.

3. Stories for children need to teach a moral lesson.

    This myth has its roots way back in the sixteenth century, when almost all of the writing done for children was designed to teach a lesson or impart a moral. In early Puritan days, school lessons evoked religious themes. Teaching children to read and teaching them to avoid the devil (or any other unsavory characters with sharp horns and a bad attitude) went hand in hand. Today's books are quite different. They do not preach, moralize, or end with a significant life lesson (e.g. Always help little old ladies across the street—or off their motorcycles!). Rather, a good children's book explores significant themes that entertain and inform. It does not command, rather it educates.

Expert Quote

"As a child, I disliked books in which children learned to be 'better' children."

—Beverly Cleary, children's author.

4. Writing in rhyme will give my story more appeal.

    They must be easy to write, because there are so many of them. Not true! Here's what you should do. Take a look at the authors who are producing rhyming stories. They're usually experienced authors: authors who have written a number of books, authors who have earned their "chops" in a very competitive field, authors who have the eyes and ears of an editor because they also have the eyes and ears of children. As someone who has written many nonfiction rhyming books, I can assure you that this is a very hard nut to crack.

In all my conversations with editors, they all agree that you will be increasing your chances for rejection by writing your first book in rhyme. Ninety-nine percent of those manuscripts are automatically rejected for the simple reason that first-time authors make classic mistakes. Most of the rhyming manuscripts editors receive promote poor rhyming patterns, inconsistent meter, or imperfect syllabication. One more thing, editors are also looking for books that can be sold on the international market; that is, books that can be easily translated into another language. Rhyming books make this especially challenging, if not impossible.

5. Because my kids love the stories I tell them at bedtime, I'm sure they are good enough to be published.

    Of course, your children or grandchildren love the stories you wrote; they're your relatives and they will tell you what you want to hear ("Hey, Grandma, that was the best story ever. Please read it again!"). The awful truth is the folks who are not your relatives frequently have other thoughts about what you have written. It's also important to remember that your family is giving you an emotional response to your story, not a professional response. They may not know all the elements of good writing or the structure of a well-told story. They may be simply thrilled by the fact that "Grandma wrote a story."

    As a corollary, far too many editors see cover letters with something like this: "Your (kids, grandkids, neighbor kids, some kids I found in the mechanical toys aisle at my local toy store) loved this story and you will, too." Most editors, when they read something like that, don't really read the accompanying manuscript. They just gently slip it into the paper shredder by their desk.

6. I'll need to find an illustrator to create images for my story.

This is one of the most persistent myths of children's writing and is one of the issues I'm asked about most. Here's a short and direct response. **DO NOT HAVE SOMONE** (your cousin, your daughter, your former college roommate who now designs t-shirts for a local grunge band) **DRAW ILLUSTRATIONS AND DO NOT SUBMIT THOSE ILLUSTRATIONS WITH YOUR STORY!** I'm sorry to be so emphatic with the bold capital letters, but I really want to be very clear and direct on this response. The words you craft for your story must evoke clear mental images in the mind of the editor. It is with those images that an editor or art director selects an illustrator to match up with the words.

Insider Tip

It is very rare for an author and an illustrator to ever communicate or confer on a children's book. After more than fifty children's books, I have never had any communication with the illustrators of my books, with one single exception. The artist sent me a brief email inquiring about the precise scientific name for a specific animal in the book so she could draw a scientifically accurate representation. In fact, most editors dissuade any communication between authors and illustrators.

I often tell prospective authors that they will be doubling their chances for rejection if they submit any illustrations with their manuscript. The reader may love the text and hate the illustrations; or they may love the illustrations and hate the text. In both cases, it's rejected. Here's one of the best pieces of advice you need to know: never submit pictures or drawings with a manuscript; let your words do the illustrating.

7. It doesn't take long to write a picture book.

    Many people assume that, because most children's books are
    short, they can be completed in considerably less time than it
    takes to prepare a chicken casserole or watch your kids' after-
    school soccer game. In many cases, just the opposite is true.
    From my own experience, I have crafted adult books (more
    than 250 pages) in less than nine months and taken up to a
    year and a half to finalize a thirty-two-page children's picture
    book manuscript. The length of a book (and its quality) is not
    correlated to the amount of time necessary to craft that book.
    Besides, if you are like most children's authors, you also have
    a day job and, more than likely, some house repairs, dentist
    appointments, social engagements, errands, grocery shopping,
    and a host of other responsibilities to attend to. Time is not the
    determinant of whether a book is ready for publication; craft,
    effort, and dedication are.

8. Vampires are really "hot" right now, so I'll write a book about
    vampires and make a ton of money.

    Many new writers make the mistake of assuming that if they
    write a book that favors a current trend they will have an
    "in" in the marketplace. Not so. Here's something to keep in
    mind: if a trend is "hot" right now, it may not be so in two
    years, which is the minimum amount of time necessary to go
    from story idea to published book. So, just because vampires,
    or pirates, or young British boys who attend an academy for
    future sorcerers may be popular in children's books today,
    doesn't mean they will be around two years down the road.
    The best thing you can do is to start a trend, not follow one.

9. Kids are fairly unsophisticated readers.

    Kids are much more sophisticated than many people give
    them credit for. Some of the most memorable children's books
    have been written on topics as diverse as a gay couple raising
    a child, death of a parent, murder, suicide, drugs, and gang
    violence. Those "cute little stories" of yesteryear are dated and
    passé. Today's kids, exposed to all manner of information via
    the internet and social media, are much more sophisticated

(and wise) than many people give them credit for. Don't make the mistake of assuming that fluffy bunnies, fairy princesses (and their handsome fairy princes), or purple puffy dinosaurs are *de rigueur* for children's books.

Expert Quote

"You have to write the book that wants to be written. And if the book will be too difficult for grown-ups, then you write it for children."

—Madeline L'Engle, children's author

10. If I send my story to a publisher they might steal my ideas.

    Here is another persistent myth that has been around for quite some time. To be quite honest, editors simply do not have the time (or inclination) to steal ideas. By and large, editors are not looking for ideas, but rather how you treat those ideas with your own unique spin on a plotline or distinctive approach to an issue or concern. Please don't waste your time worrying about whether someone will steal your idea. Trust me, it happens so rarely that it is practically nonexistent.

11. I need to protect my work with a copyright before I send it in.

    To boil down the complexities of copyright law into an easy-to-digest format, please know that whenever you write something it is automatically protected by copyright law. You do not need to place a copyright mark (©) on your manuscript, because the moment your work is created in fixed form (a complete manuscript, for example), it is automatically considered to be copyrighted. In fact, most editors consider it a sign of amateurism if a copyright symbol is added to a manuscript. Several editors told me that if they see that symbol on any submission, they reject it right away. Again, please don't put a copyright symbol on any submission.

    Now, for a more complex explanation: in accordance with current statutes, ideas are not protected by copyright laws. An idea is simply that: an idea. It may surprise you to know that there are very few original ideas. You may argue that a story such as *Where the Wild Things Are* by Maurice Sendak was an original idea. However, when you boil down that story to its singular idea (a child and some imaginary monsters), the idea is not so original after all. Just think about all the books you've ever seen that focus on a child's encounters with one or more fictional monsters. There are literally hundreds of those books. It's what Sendak did with that central idea that makes his book such a pivotal one in children's literature.

12. Once I've sold a book, my writing will support me.

A very small percentage of children's authors are able to support themselves with their writing. Most authors have day jobs that provide an income, benefits, insurance, and a pension. The old saw, "Don't give up your day job" has particular relevance for children's authors. Even though I had written about four dozen children's titles just before I officially retired from my full-time position as a college professor, I had no economic reason to give up my regular employment to be a full-time writer. I knew that my passion for crafting children's books would simply provide a small supplement to my regular income; it would never take the place of that income. If you are fortunate to have a partner who can economically support the two of you while you write full-time, please go for it. Otherwise, know that financial security as a full-time children's author is more fantasy than it will be reality.

13. After I publish a children's book, the publisher will spend a lot of time promoting my book.

Publishing a children's book is only half the battle. The other half is in bringing that book to the attention of the buying public in such a way that they will rush to their computer or brick-and-mortar store to purchase a copy. While a publisher is responsible for some of the marketing efforts, it's important to remember that authors are, perhaps, the best marketers for their own books. Maintaining a web site, doing personal appearances in your local bookstores, posting notices on

Facebook and Instagram, distributing special bookmarks and business cards, doing school visits, talking to independent bookstore owners, and a host of other marketing strategies are all part of the job. With more than 6,000 new children's books entering the market every year, the competition is keen for the buyer's dollar. You will be expected to be an active element in the marketing of your own book.

While the marketing aspects of children's books is beyond the scope of this guide, know that a great deal of the success of your book(s) will be on your shoulders. Publishers have hundreds (or thousands) of books to promote; a new author only has one. Self-publicizing and self-promoting your book(s) is an expectation of the publishing process. In many respects, it's like another full time job.

14. Once my first book is published, my other books will be just as successful.

    Maybe yes, maybe no. Each book is usually evaluated on its own merits. Just because you've written one good book doesn't always mean that your next book will rise to the same level. You've certainly read several books by the same author and noted that they aren't all of the same quality. You may have enjoyed one book more than another. The same holds true with children's books. A great first book doesn't guarantee an equally great second book.

Know that these myths will continue to be promulgated by the uninformed, the unknowing, and the unwilling. They are actually defenses or barriers to the realities of writing quality children's literature. Know that they are preventing other writers (those who aren't reading this book) from entering the field. That's not only less completion for you, but more knowledge on the road to your own publishing success.

Expert Quote

"I don't write for children. I write. And somebody says, 'That's for children."

—Maurice Sendak, children's author.

Chapter 3

Occupation: Author

It's time, once again, for a quiz. I think you'll find this one to be quite easy and very straight-forward. Here are your instructions: Please place a check mark in front of one of the following two statements, the one you agree with the most

❑ A. I would like to write lousy manuscripts, get a lot of rejections, publish very few (if any) children's books, and moan and wail about how unfair life is.

❑ B. I would like to write outstanding manuscripts, have editors fall in love with my work, publish truckloads of award-winning books, and have legions of youngsters request my autograph every time I go out.

Now, let's do the same thing with two more statements. Again, put a check mark in the box in front of the one statement that best fits you.

❑ A. At work I want to do a really terrible job, have people hate me, complain about my boss/supervisor incessantly, be constantly on the verge of being fired, and moan and wail about how unfair life is.

❑ B. At work I want to make many positive contributions to my assigned job, build strong friendships and positive lines of communication, become a respected member of the company, receive praise and acclamations for what I do, get regular raises and promotions, and truly enjoy my job.

I'm going to go out on a limb and guess that in both cases, you placed a check mark in the "B" box for each of the two pairs of statements above. Now, I'd like to invite you to go back and re-read each of those two "B" statements and see if you note any similarities. No doubt, you did!

When I meet folks for the first time and they learn I'm a published children's author, I'll often get a question something like this: "Hey, Tony, is there a secret to success? Is there a secret to becoming a published children's author?" I'll always answer something like this: "Yes, there are actually several secrets to success; but there is one that stands head and shoulders above all the others; one that will truly guarantee your achievement in this very competitive field." And that secret is:

Insider Tip

To be a successful children's author, you must treat writing as a job, not as a hobby.

Let's dig into that statement in a little more detail.

For the sake of the next two paragraphs, let's pretend you are a full time elementary classroom teacher (I know, I know, you really wanted to be a long distance truck driver, but please stay with me here for a few moments!). You've been teaching for six years and this year you have a truly eclectic crew of second graders in your charge. Your lessons are full of innovative academic adventures. All day you have your students singing, laughing, learning, studying, and engaged in a plethora of wonderfully creative endeavors. Parents love how much their children are learning in your classroom and the principal is singing your praises to everyone within earshot. You have the best job in the world and your enthusiasm is contagious.

When you began this journey, you quickly learned that the more you put into your job the more you (and your students) got out of it. You read many teacher resource books, attend one or two education conferences a year, subscribe to several educational periodicals, and confer with colleagues through blogs and social media sites. You are well aware that the more you learn, the more you improve and, ultimately, the more your students succeed. You discovered very quickly that your education didn't end when you graduated from college, but that it would be a continuous process throughout your teaching career. What you do now determines, in large measure, the success you will enjoy weeks, months, or years down the road. Taking it easy simply because you've completed your formal education, is always dangerous—both for you and your students. Quality teaching is a continuous journey, never a completed product.

And guess what—the same thing holds true as a children's author! If all you do is write a simple story, send it off to a publisher, and keep your fingers crossed, you may be very disappointed—and very unpublished! You need to treat writing as a job, rather than as a hobby. Doing so will put you ahead of about ninety-five percent of all the other folks who want to become published authors. You'll be doing the daily training that they won't. You'll be more likely to win the gold medal (a published children's book) than a significant percentage of those other writers.

Here's the bottom line: Becoming a children's book author must be an active process; it should never be a passive project. Doing what everyone else does (writing a quick story and sending it out to an endless succession of publishers) will seldom guarantee you a book contract. You need to set yourself apart from the crowd, you need to distinguish yourself as a writer of promise, and you need to demonstrate initiative, drive, and enthusiasm. Anything less and you'll be seen as *one of many* rather than *one of a kind*!

> ### Expert Quote
> "Everything worth doing starts outside your comfort zone."
>
> —Demi Stevens, editor

Eight Occupational Themes

No matter what your occupation may be—blue collar or white collar—there are certain expectations for every worker in that organization. Everyone, from the person who sorts the mail all the way up to the CEO or president of the company, is expected to adhere to certain expectations and guidelines. If you would like to be a successful children's author, there are certain expectations you need to satisfy as well.

Below you will discover a set of eight occupational themes that have appeared in countless business journals and textbooks. Each of these themes has been promulgated as essential in every employee's performance—irrespective of the job assignment. They should also be expectations for your job as a prospective children's author. Success as a writer does not come arbitrarily or haphazardly; it is, quite frequently, the result of embracing certain standards of performance proven to be essential in both good employees as well as good authors. Let's take a look.

1. Show up for work every day.

    You can't get the job done if you don't come to work every day. The same is true for authors. Writing must be a normal, regular, and sustained activity—*every single day*—if you are to grow, develop, and succeed as an author. It must be a regular habit just like brushing your teeth or putting on a pair of shoes every morning. For me, I'm up at six a.m. every day and in my office by 6:45. I know that between seven and eleven is my most creative time of the day—the part of the day when I'm generating ideas, revising manuscripts, and fine-tuning my writing. It's my job and to be any good, I need to put my butt in a chair, turn on my computer, and work every day.

    "But, Tony," you may say, "I have a regular full-time job [you know, the one that pays the bills] and I just can't devote a couple of hours every morning to writing my sure-fire children's book. I wish I could, but I can't."

    OK, fair enough. But, let's look at this conundrum with a different eye. That is, it's not about the amount of time that's important (e.g. several hours), it's the regularity and consistency (You go to work every day, don't you?). Even if you only have fifteen minutes a day, make sure you write for fifteen minutes *every single day*! You may need to get up fifteen minutes (or thirty minutes) earlier in the morning or delay your bedtime by fifteen minutes (or thirty minutes) every evening. The key is not the amount of time, but rather the regularity of time that's important. Make writing a daily habit (just like going to your regular job is a daily habit) and you will be "training" your mind to get into the "writer's zone" consistently and persistently.

2. Learn how to do your job, and do it well.

   A bank doesn't hire an untrained bank manager, a corporation doesn't employ a COO without a business degree, and an NFL team doesn't recruit a quarterback who has never played the game before. All of those positions required some degree of education or training. So, it is with children's writing. You must have the training, education, and schooling necessary to do the job right. That doesn't necessarily mean a formal or college education; but it does mean gaining the necessary background information upon which to build a successful writing career. Few of us can sit down and write "The Great American Novel" without some level of education and preparation. After all, you wouldn't want someone at your local bank handling your mortgage who has never had any formal training or education in dealing with loan applications, would you?

   Where can you get that initial training? Here are a few possibilities:

   • Courses at a local college or community college

   • An evening course at the local high school

   • Tutoring from a local high school English teacher

   • An online course

   • A podcast for new writers

   • A series of YouTube videos

   • An adult education course

3. Always be willing to learn a new skill.

   Just because you have a college degree (for example) doesn't mean that you know everything there is to know about your chosen profession. New discoveries are made, new techniques are developed, and new standards are issued in almost every profession. That's why doctors, funeral directors, teachers, lawyers, electrical contractors, architects, plumbers, and a host of other professions have training seminars, publications, conferences, and in-service programs to keep their members constantly informed of new developments. The same is true of professional writers: there is always something new we can learn throughout our writing careers; there is always some new information that can help us become a more accomplished author—no matter how many manuscripts we've written or how many books we've published. This ongoing education can be accomplished with instructional books (like this one), internet services, magazines and journals put out by professional organizations such as SCBWI (Society of Children's Book Writers and Illustrators), subscription services, webinars, and a host of other resources.

4. Behave professionally.

    Each profession has its own standards for behavior and its own edicts of professionalism. An accountant, for example, is held to certain professional standards that are consistent across the profession. Teachers are held to a code of conduct no matter where they may be working or the subject matter they teach. Biologists, financial consultants, and librarians too, have standards of professionalism that are consistent and constant. Authors are also expected to behave in certain ways. We cannot demand that an editor publish our material; we cannot challenge an editor's decision to reject our work; nor can we demand certain royalties for any published work. There are standards and expectations throughout the industry that ensure its successful operation. After all, a publisher is not in business to make every author happy, they're in business to make a profit.

    One of the best places to get behavioral expectations is at the many professional conferences and conventions sponsored by SCBWI. These are wonderful opportunities to network with other writers—both novice and experienced—and learn about some of the common expectations and responsibilities of all writers. Blogs, podcasts, and webinars also provide you with insight into the "rules" writers are expected to follow (and the consequences if they don't).

5. Learn to take criticism gracefully.

   As an educator, my classroom performance and teaching competencies were evaluated every year. My instructional strengths were noted by my supervisor as well as those areas in which I needed some improvement. Even as a college professor, I was regularly assessed. My department chair or the Dean noted my competencies as well as the traits or behaviors that might need some attention. The same holds true for almost every other profession. There is no such thing as a perfect worker; we can all use some degree of improvement or strengthening. That's part and parcel of every occupation.

   Authors, too, get their share of criticism and assessment. Friends, writing colleagues, and course instructors tell us how to strengthen a character, improve a scene, eliminate needless vocabulary, or resolve a conflict. That input is necessary if we are to create a book that will capture the attention of its selected audience. Input, advice, and judgements about our work are to be expected. Even after authoring more than fifty children's books, I still demand and expect regular assessments of my work. I know that ultimately the result will be a much better publication than it would have been without that input.

6. Always be productive.

   When you are hired for a job, the expectation is not that you will complete a single task and then sail off into retirement heaven. There are a whole host of duties, assignments, responsibilities, and tasks for you to accomplish throughout a workday and throughout your working career. In a sense, the expectation is that you will be a productive worker for the duration of your employment. So it is with writing. A focus on productivity for the long haul is a key for occupational success—irrespective of your profession or job description. One of your tasks in approaching potential editors is to let them know that you are not a "one shot wonder," but rather that you will continue your productivity for a long time. Writing one book and then gracefully retiring is usually not in the cards. Good writers are in it for the long haul—just like good workers.

7. Cultivate good relationships with the people in your organization.

In every profession, the one skill employers look for most often is the ability to get along and work with a diversity of individuals. Fostering a "team approach" to the goals of the organization is one way to ensure the success of that organization. As writers, we deal with many different people—everyone from editors, assistant editors, agents, copyeditors, art directors, to production people. Treating everyone graciously, respectfully, and politely can go a long way to ensuring a long and productive career. Telling an editor she's a "flaming idiot" because she rejected your manuscript will not win you many friends. In fact, it may just send your writing career up the creek without a paddle, down the commode, into the dumpster, or straight to hell (choose your own euphemism).

8. Hold your head high and be confident.

Successful workers are confident workers. Believing in yourself and what you can contribute to an organization or business will engender a positive self-concept as well as a positive spirit. Knowing that there will be challenges or hurdles to face—and that you have the will and fortitude to address those challenges—will make your job all that much more productive. So, too, does the same philosophy hold true for writers. Knowing that there will be obstacles in our way (not enough time), barriers in our path (many rejections), and impediments along the road (where to find ideas)—but that we have the will and strength to overcome them—contributes mightily to our eventual success. Will we write a New York Times bestseller the first time out of the gate? Most likely, no! But, we can persist and persevere towards our goal of successful publication.

Part II

The Facts of Life

Chapter 4

The Biggest Mistake You'll Ever Make!

OK, it's time for another short quiz (I promise it won't be painful). In boxes one and two below you'll see the first paragraph of two separate stories. Each of these was submitted as part of an assignment in a workshop for prospective children's authors. Each paragraph was just the first part of a longer story. After reading each paragraph, I'm going to give you an opportunity to grade each one (Now you get to put on your professor's hat!). Ready? Here goes!

1.

> Tommy liked dogs. He had three dogs at home—Rudy, Mango, and Sarah. Rudy was an Irish Setter, Mango was a German Shephard, and Sarah was a St. Bernard. Tommy loved his dogs and his dogs loved him. Every day he would feed his dogs before he went off to school. Rudy liked dry dog food. Mango liked canned dog food. And, Sarah liked corn flakes.

What grade would you give this essay?

A _____

B _____

C _____

D _____

F _____

2.

> "Hey, guys, I don't know about you, but I'm getting tired living in this swamp," said Freddy Frog. "Yeah, me too," said Stanley Stork, "It's dirty, it smells, and those muskrats on the other side are always throwing their trash around." Debby Dragonfly, who was overhead, told everyone, "You know, Freddy's right. This place is really starting to look like a dump. We have to do something about this, and right away!"

What grade would you give this essay?

A _____

B _____

C _____

D _____

F _____

So, what do you think? Did you give both of these a high grade or a low grade? Or, did one story read better than the other? Well, believe it or not, both these stories get a failing mark. Why? Simply because within six seconds of reading each one it was clear that the authors of both pieces had committed the cardinal sin of children's writing. In fact, this "sin" is so prevalent and so often committed that it dooms more than ninety percent of all children's book manuscripts submitted for possible publication.

Every so often, a friend or a colleague will hand me a children's book manuscript and ask if I would take a look at it and offer an honest review. I'm always delighted to do so. But, over the years I've discovered that almost every one of those potential book projects suffers from a critical and quite frequent mistake. In fact, I've found the same thing occurring in all the writing workshops and courses I offer. To me, this is the most damaging mistake any children's writer can make. Indeed, I can review a manuscript for a mere six seconds and I will instantly know that the author has committed this mistake. When I ask them about it, they will often hang their head and sheepishly admit that, yes, they are guilty of breaking this rule. And, what is that rule:

Insider Tip

If you are going to be a successful children's author, you must read children's books on a regular basis.

For most of my life I was a long-distance runner. In high school, college, four years in the armed services, graduate school, and through most of my teaching career, I continued to run long distances. For me, one of the best parts of the day was when I came home from a long day of teaching. I'd throw on a pair of shorts and a t-shirt, lace up my running shoes, and take off along the rural roads where we lived for a run of seven to nine miles. Occasionally, I'd run up and down rolling hills, along dusty lanes, or around the perimeter of a public golf course. Every so often, I'd lope over to the local high school to do some interval work on the track. About once a month or so, I would enter and run a 10K race. Occasionally I would get a trophy or a medal or some sort of special certificate for my placement in the race. However, it wasn't the awards that were important to me, but rather the opportunity to run faster than I had in a previous race at the same distance.

I had learned early in my running career that the more effort I put into my daily runs, the better I would do in the races I entered throughout the year. Running sixty to seventy miles per week—track workouts, endless hill climbs, and long runs through undulating countryside— were necessary if I was to lower my times or do well in any forthcoming long-distance races. The success I was to have in a competitive race was ultimately based on all the preparations I needed to do in advance of that race. Without those preparations, there was no way I would have a successful race.

Interestingly, many novice writers think that "training" is not a critical part of their goal to become a published author. They think that just because they've raised some children (and told them stories at bedtime), or volunteered at their child's school, or read a book or two to their grandchildren, or spent some time in a day care center, they are ready to write their own book for kids. Unfortunately, just being around kids does not adequately prepare you for writing children's books. You need to soak yourself in the culture of children's literature (just as I had to soak myself in the culture of long distance running in order to become a competent long distance runner). You need to know the language, the themes, the concepts, the tenor, and the presentation. And, the only way to do that is to read children's books on a regular basis: every day, every week, every month.

If you are not reading children's books, then you are putting yourself at a severe disadvantage in the marketplace. The books you read as a child are not the same kind of books kids read today. The books you loved as an elementary student are quite different from the books children embrace today. For example, do you think your parents or your teachers would have allowed you to read books about a character who runs around in his underwear? Most likely, no! But, who do you think is one of the most popular characters in children's literature today? That's right, it's Captain Underpants. As of 2016, the series had been translated into over twenty languages, with more than seventy million books sold worldwide, including over fifty million in the United States.

When I was growing up in the fifties, I read *Hardy Boys* mysteries (by Franklin W. Dixon). This very popular series was about two clean cut lads from a small town (Bayport) who solved mysteries, drove jalopies, were always polite to their parents, dated nice girls, got good grades in school, and never, ever got into any trouble. Titles in the series (there were a total of sixty-six books) included *The Tower Treasure, The Secret of the Old Mill, While the Clock Ticked, The Mystery of Cabin Island,* and *The Melted Coins,* among others.

As of the publication date of this book, here are some popular titles in children's literature:

- *Captain Underpants and the Sensational Saga of Sir Stinks-A-Lot*
- *Diary of a Wimpy Kid*
- *The Hunger Games*
- *P is for Potty*

- *Dragons Love Tacos*
- *The Book with No Pictures*

Do you notice a difference?

Reading current children's literature—on a regular basis—has enormous benefits for you as a beginning children's author. Here are just a few:

1. Introduces you to a wide range of authorial styles.

   Have you ever been to a tapas restaurant? My wife and I have been to several, and we thoroughly enjoy the opportunity to taste a variety of specialty dishes, combining several to make a full meal. In Spain, for example, tapas can include practically anything: from a chunk of tuna, a cocktail onion, and an olive skewered on a long toothpick, to piping hot chorizo sausage served in a small clay dish, to a gourmet slow-cooked beef cheek served over a sweet potato puree.

   The opportunity to sample many different small meals from another country gives us a sense of the distinctive cuisine from a region of the world we haven't traveled to yet. We get a full picture of the variety and uniqueness of a country's distinctive cooking. The same is true for writers! If you want to get a sense of what good writing is all about, you need to sample many different kinds of writing—both the good and the bad. In so doing, you are getting a full picture of what writers can do (or, sometimes, what they are unable to do) in terms of characters, plots, and settings. The more you sample (tapas and other books) the more you know about style (epicurean and children's books).

Expert Quote

"Reading inspires writing. It always has. Writing is a way to say 'thank you' to the authors who have touched our lives."

—Joe Bunting, author

2. Shows you language patterns that resonate with readers.

> There once lived a man who married twice, and his second wife was the haughtiest and most stuck-up woman in the world. She already had two daughters of her own and her children took after her in every way. Her new husband's first wife had given him a daughter of his own before she died, but she was a lovely and sweet-natured girl, very like her own natural mother, who had been a kind and gentle woman.

Do you recognize the story above? Does the language of the story tell you something about when it may have been written? Is this a story written by a present-day author or one written by an author from many years ago? Is this a story that would grab the attention of modern-day readers or one that might appear in a collection of tales from long, long ago? For the most part, I think you can get a sense of when this story was written and the audience to whom it was directed. If you know your children's literature, you'll recognize the selection above as the opening paragraph in the traditional (not Disney) tale of Cinderella.

When you read the stories and books of other authors, you can get a real sense of the language appropriate for different age groups. Suffice it to say, the language in the original version of Cinderella is not language that kids today would embrace. For example, compare the language above with the opening of my children's book, *A is for Anaconda: A Rainforest Alphabet* (2009):

> Watch out! Look closely and you'll see one of the longest snakes in the world—the powerful anaconda. A full-grown anaconda snake can be very big. The longest recorded anaconda was twenty-eight feet long. That's longer than a car!

Knowing the language of kids is essential to writing books that resonate with kids. This is an important piece of homework.

3. Demonstrates how other authors address the beginning, middle, and ends of stories.

   One of the mistakes new writers often make is to create a "stream of consciousness" story. That is, a seemingly endless series of incidents or events that go from "Point A" to "Point B" with no indication that the story has any formal beginning, middle, or end. These stories also suffer from another classic miscue: there is no conflict and there is no resolution of that conflict. Good children's stories are not about a day in the life of a character, they are about a situation, concern, or issue the character must deal with and the means or solution she devises in order to solve/resolve that issue. The only way you can tell such a story is to have a clear-cut beginning, a decided middle, and a satisfactory ending. Without those, you simply have a string of words and sentences that don't add up to very much.

   Read a variety of other authors to see how they compose their beginnings, craft their middles, and create their endings. The more stories you read, the more your mind will be ordered to generate a story that moves beyond the usual and into the extraordinary.

4. Gives you the opportunity to compare good stories with bad stories.

   A few months ago I needed some new dress shirts. I was in a hurry and decided to stop in to a local store to see what they had. There were several display tables piled with a variety of dress shirts—all on sale. I rummaged through a few stacks of shirts and found two that I liked (Admittedly, the sale price was a major inducement). When I returned home, I washed them (after removing the over one thousand pins that seem to hold men's shirts together), ran them through the dryer, and hung them in the closet. The next day, I put one on and noticed that a button was missing, there was a slight discoloration in the pattern, and the front pocket was slightly crooked. I quickly removed it, put on one of my old shirts, and set off for work.

When I got home, I examined the new shirts a little more closely. I noticed a range of imperfections in all the shirts (probably a reason why they were on sale). I quickly vowed that I would never buy that brand (or visit that store) again. I returned to my regular store and found my usual brand and have been happy with them since.

In order to appreciate the good, you need to experience the bad. I have a much better appreciation for my current brand of shirts than I ever will with the sale brand. But, that appreciation came from the fact that I was able to compare the two in a simple test. You probably have a favorite brand of cereal simply because you've tasted other brands and found them lacking. You may have a favorite brand of car, because other brands you have driven break down easily or have poor service records. So it is with children's books. In order to know what good books do you need to experience the bad ones. The bad books give you a frame of reference necessary to your compositional efforts. The more books you read the more opportunities you will have to experience a wide and diverse range of writing styles. That diversity is essential to your writing success.

5.   Allows you to see how different authors handle similar themes.

- "Henry Brown wasn't sure how old he was. Henry was a slave. And slaves weren't allowed to know their birthdays."
  —Ellen Levine, *Henry's Freedom Box* (2007)

- "Once, your old-timey grandfather lived in a village by a fine flowing river, across a wide, deep ocean, in faraway Africa."
  —Margot Theis Raven, *Circle Unbroken: The Story of a Basket and Its People* (2004)

Take a long look at the two opening sentences above. Each is quite different in terms of language, style, and execution. Yet, both are the opening sentences in stories about slavery—one about a slave boy and his escape to freedom, the other about generations of slaves and the unique baskets (and the stories they told) woven in South Carolina. The themes are similar, but the depiction of the theme is very different in the hands of two different storytellers.

By exposing yourself to a wide variety of storytellers, you can get a sense of how various authors tackle universal themes. How do they voice those themes? What words or images do they include in their stories? How are the sentences crafted or paragraphs shaped? By studying the various ways of presenting a story, you are giving yourself an education available nowhere else. Reading a wide selection of books opens your eyes to the infinite variety of storytelling techniques and the ways in which you might approach a topic or issue.

Expert Quote

"The way I am as a writer comes very much out of what I want as a reader."

—David Foster Wallace, author

"So, Tony, what should I read," you may ask.

Good question! Here's my response: Everything you can. Read old books and new books. Notice how the authors of books published twenty years ago developed their characters (or not) in comparison with authors today. Read books at the top of the best-seller list and those at the bottom. How do the plots differ between the two? What makes one group of books stand out from the competition and another group sink to the very bottom of the barrel? How does a writer's writing style propel a book into the hands of readers, while another's make a book seem like radioactive waste?

Read some literary classics like *Treasure Island, Goodnight Moon, David Copperfield, Mr. Popper's Penguins, Little Women*, and *Aesop's Fables*. What was it about the style of those books that made them so popular when they were first published and less so today? Do some of those titles still resonate with kids today or is the language too heavy and ponderous? Are their characters still ones you'd like to meet or invite into your home?

Make sure you read from every possible genre of children's literature (*see* Chapter 10). Even though you may wish to concentrate on contemporary issues, it would be critical to your overall "education" to read from a wide variety of titles including nonfiction, joke books, teenage romances, science fiction, poetry collections, humor, fantasy, and nature books. The more you can fill your mind with the characters, styles, and language of children's books, the more you can zero in on the essential attributes of your own literary creations.

As you read, are there two or three authors who "float your boat?" Are there some authors who are much more interesting than others? What are the good authors doing with their characters, settings, and plots that make their books so memorable? What are other authors doing (or not) that make their characters easily forgettable? What about the vocabulary certain authors use—is it sparse and minimalist, or is it sharp and well-defined?

How does a popular author like Mo Willems paint his characters in a book like *Don't Let the Pigeon Drive the Bus* (2003)? How does his paucity of language compare with an author like Mildred Taylor as she sets up scenes in *Roll of Thunder, Hear My Cry* (1976)? How does a magnificent author such as Sharon Creech (*Walk Two Moons*, 2011) paint such engaging mind pictures with her precise language that makes you go back again and again to read her stories? What does Avi do that grabs you by the collar in the first paragraph and doesn't release you until the final sentence of the book *The True Confessions of Charlotte Doyle* (1997)? What is it about the styles of those popular authors that makes you want to rush out and purchase every book they wrote?

What's the best way to check out what books and authors are "hot?" Check with the children's librarian at your local public library or with the librarian at your child's school. They will be up-to-date on the latest and greatest literature and will be more than willing to make specific recommendations, not only for your child, but also for you as you engage in this all-important, critical, and on-going research. What this process will do is not only sharpen your own sense of what makes a good book, but clue you in to what resonates (and what doesn't) with young readers.

Expert Quote

"I have advice for people who want to write. I don't care whether they're five or five hundred. . . . you need to read. You can't be a writer if you're not a reader. It's the great writers who teach us how to write."

—Madeleine L'Engle, children's author

As you read all those children's books, here are a few questions you may want to consider. You might, as I often do, decide to record the responses to these questions in a notebook. Then, as I begin the initial drafts of a manuscript, I have some guidelines as to how I might design it.

- What did I enjoy most (or least) about this book?

- How did the author introduce and describe the main character?

- What would kids like most (or least) about this book?

- What did the author do to establish the setting for this book?

- How did the author deal with conflict/resolution?

- How did the author help me create mental images about what was happening in the story?

- How did the author demonstrate her/his respect for me as a reader?

- Why would I want to read (or not) another book by this author?

- How does my writing compare (or not) with this author's writing?

- What did the author do that kept me turning the pages?

Here's the absolute key to success as a children's author: If you want to write children's books, you have to read children's books! One without the other is like baking a lemon meringue pie without using sugar, vacationing in Maui without going to the beach, or preparing a romantic dinner for one. They're only half-done! Read, and keep reading, lots of children's books and you will notice a decided improvement in your own abilities to craft stories—memorable stories—for a new generation of readers.

Expert Quote

"I am always chilled and astonished by the would-be writers who ask me for advice and admit, quite blithely, that they 'don't have time to read.' This is like a guy starting up Mount Everest saying that he didn't have time to buy any rope or pitons."

—Stephen King, author

Chapter 5

Other Common Errors, Blunders, and Boo-Boos

This book was written with one goal in mind: to provide you with the most practical information available to help you write and publish a children's book. In order to do that, I surveyed all the literature on writing for kids, interviewed agents, editors and fellow writers both near and far, communicated with librarians and book reviewers in nearly three dozen states and several provinces, and tapped into the collective wisdom of many authors who have successfully negotiated authorship and obtained publishing contracts. This book has been built on the success of others who have gone before you as well as the "inside secrets" of those who review and evaluate children's books. What you have in these pages is a distillation of some of the best experience and best thinking on writing children's books to be found anywhere.

Not only did I want to provide you with the most practical information on how to get your manuscript published, I also wanted to let you know about some of the mistakes novice writers typically make—mistakes that often doomed their chances or derailed their odds for publication. These are the mistakes that pop up often enough that they deserve their own chapter. While the rest of this book is on the "positives" of successful authorship; I'm afraid this chapter will need to be on the "negatives." That's simply because these events happen so frequently and appear in so many manuscripts, that they seem to be persistent—a virus that far too often sneaks its way into an otherwise terrific story and "contaminates" any chance you have of getting published.

But, there's one important thing about this list. As you look over these typical and common "boo-boos," you will note that they all have one thing in common—they can all be controlled by you! Each of these mistakes is under your control, your supervision, your influence. You can choose to ignore all or some of these, or you can choose to do your "homework" and prevent any one of these from sneaking its way into your manuscript. You have the power to address each and every item on this list. People before you have made these mistakes (and are probably continuing to make these mistakes). Let their mistakes be your guidance for a most successful writing experience.

1. Anthropomorphism.

    Please don't make the classic mistake of including talking animals in your story. Dogs don't talk, cats don't converse, mice don't discuss, cows don't interface, chickens don't gossip, giraffes don't chat, and yaks don't yak (Well, maybe yaks yak; after all, how else would they have gotten that silly name?). If you give any animals in your story human characteristics, then you will be guaranteeing the sudden and swift rejection of your manuscript. You could argue that classic books such as *Charlotte's Web* has talking animals and has done quite well for itself. But, keep in mind that that book was written in 1952. Editors today have seen far too many talking animal stories that substitute bad dialogue for an effective plot. If you have animals in your story, make sure they remain animals. Don't put them in pirate ships, wedding dresses, murder mysteries, or heated arguments. It won't work!

2. Illustrations

    You've seen this one before, but it is committed so frequently that it needs repeating. One of the most frequently-asked questions posed by beginning writers goes something like this, "Do I have to submit illustrations with my manuscript?" or "Can I have my third cousin, who is an extremely talented tattoo artist in San Francisco, do the illustrations and then send them in with my manuscript?" Since questions about illustrations are asked so frequently and are persistent queries by lots of beginning writers, I'm going to provide the answer as follows:

Insider Tip

DO NOT SUBMIT ILLUSTRATIONS WITH YOUR BOOK MANUSCRIPT!

Many novice writers assume that because they are submitting a manuscript for a picture book, they should also include the necessary illustrations for that book. So, they have their very talented daughter, or neighbor, or grandmother, or dear friend from college draw a set of accompanying illustrations to include with the story. The truth of the matter is that publishers do not want authors to include any illustrations when submitting their work. A writer should concentrate her or his efforts at crafting a well-told story; a professional artist—always selected by the publisher—will be the one responsible for creating the illustrations should the manuscript be accepted for publication. In fact, as I often tell prospective authors, you're actually doubling your chances for rejection by including illustrations. That's because the editor may like the manuscript and hate the illustrations or she may hate the manuscript and love the illustrations. In both cases, the package will be rejected.

As a rule of thumb, publishers always select the illustrators for picture books. Their job is to match the best illustrator and her/his style with a specific book. They know lots of illustrators (personally or through their portfolios) and are experts in matching words and pictures. They are the ones who hire the illustrators, and they know much more about that matching process than any single author. Just because someone can draw doesn't make them an appropriate artist for a children's book. In most cases, the illustrations submitted with a manuscript are amateurish, two-dimensional, unfinished, and unimaginative.

Here's the best advice I can offer you: leave the illustrations to a professional artist (selected by the publisher) versed in children's picture books. Save yourself time, worry, and anguish and focus all your talents in creating a dynamic book manuscript. If your book is accepted, someone else will take over the responsibility of illustrating it—that's not your job!

3. Stories of inanimate objects

    If you've ever watched a Disney film you will have seen all sorts of inanimate objects dancing across the screen. Everything from brooms, teapots and coffee cups, to silverware and king-sized beds skip and jump and dance and run. Those are great for animated films, but not so great for children's books. They will, most certainly, mark you as an amateur as well as someone who is not up to date with the topics and themes that resonate with children. If you include a smiling, dancing teapot in your story, I can assure you that your story will quickly find its way into an editor's (seldom) smiling and (never) dancing wastebasket.

4. Telling Instead of Showing.

    Please take a look at these two character descriptions:

    *   "Terry always got angry, often at the littlest things, and then said things he later regretted."

    *   " 'You're nothing but a sick old man with a brain full of mush and a belly full of beer,' Terry screamed at his father."

    The first sentence is an example of "telling"—that is, using words to describe something for the reader, rather than giving the reader an opportunity to create an image of a character (for example) in her/his own mind. The second sentence shows the readers a characteristic action by the character and gives the reader an opportunity to paint a portrait of the character in her/his own mind. Good children's books are carefully crafted to show the reader characters or scenes, allowing the reader to draw her/his own conclusions. Telling stories do all that work for the reader—seldom allowing the reader to get personally involved in the dynamics of the story. It's much easier writing a telling story than it is a showing story; but it is considerably less effective and certainly less enjoyable for a prospective reader.

5. Dialogue That Doesn't Sound Real.

   "Gosh, pals, that's real swell of you to help my
   dear mother."

   "Hey, you jerks did all right helping out my old lady."

   The language and dialogue you used as a child is not the
   language and dialogue kids (or even the characters in kids'
   books) use today. Spend a lot of time around kids, listen
   to what they say, how they talk, different ways in which
   they converse. Write down dialogue you especially enjoy,
   words that stand out, and conversations that naturally and
   normally take place between youngsters (other than your
   children or grandchildren). Visit schools, playgrounds, public
   libraries, and public places and make a point to eavesdrop
   in on conversations. Watch kids' programs on TV and read
   magazines geared for certain age groups (e.g. *Ranger Rick,
   National Geographic Kids, Highlights for Children, Jack and
   Jill, Cricket, Spider*).

6. Creating Ideal Characters

   Are you perfect? No! Am I perfect? Definitely not! Are
   any of your friends, relatives, or colleagues perfect?
   Categorically no! We live in a world of imperfections and
   it is those imperfections that create characters. No book
   character—either those in adult books or those in children's
   books—is perfect. We remember characters because of their
   imperfectness, not because they do or say everything perfectly.
   That would be dull and boring. The same holds true for your
   characters. Make them slightly less than perfect. Make them
   crazy. Make them strange. Make them weird. Or make them
   all of the above.

   - An eighty-two-year-old arthritic grandmother
     who skateboards.

   - A basketball player with a facial abnormality.

   - A rich girl who steals from the hardware store.

   - Three gangly brothers who attend ballet school.

   - A kid from "the wrong side of the tracks" who
     writes poetry.

- An angry girl (who hates everyone) and her brother with cerebral palsy.

Memorable (and readable) characters are imperfect just like you and me!

7. Rhyming stories

Here's a very short quiz. Look at the two stanzas (A & B) below and decide which one is better than the other.

A.

> The desert sun
> Is very hot;
> It can burn
> an awful lot.

B.

> Sonoran night,
> Dancing light,
> Shadows playing—
> Full moon bright.

Many beginning writers think that because there are so many children's books out there that use a rhyming pattern, then editors must really want more rhyming books. In fact, quite the opposite is true. For most novice writers, submitting a manuscript in rhyme is often the "kiss of death" and will frequently result in having your story rejected almost instantaneously. The fact that you have a bunch of words that rhyme doesn't mean you have a story. Too often, beginning writers spend their time putting several rhyming verses together, but little time in crafting a story.

Once again, take a look at the two verses above. Yes, verse "A" rhymes, but the rhyming is forced and there's no story. There's no indication that the three basic elements of story— beginning, middle, end— are going to surface in this writing. You'll also note that the rhyming is clumsy and unimaginative. And, truth be told, it only took me only about two minutes to come up with that stanza, and it shows.

Verse "B," on the other hand, has the beginnings of a story. The rhyming is crisp and vivid images are created in the mind of the reader (or listener). In short, this stanza seeks to create dynamic mind pictures. Also, the vocabulary is sophisticated and precise. Interestingly, this particular stanza (all nine words) took almost two months to perfect and is the opening stanza in my children's book *Desert Night, Desert Day* (2011). I worked for more than a year crafting the fifteen stanzas in this rhyming book about nocturnal and diurnal animals in the Sonoran desert. Is it easy writing a rhyming book? It is not!

My advice: if you're starting out, don't do rhyming books. You will, more than likely, increase your chances for rejection.

8. Lack of Conflict.

Memorable children's books have conflict—a problem or a challenge the main character has to solve or overcome. Here are a few examples:

- In *Bridge to Terabithia* (by Katherine Paterson, 2012), Jess has to come to grips with a terrible tragedy that happens to his best friend. Only then does he finally understand the strength and courage his friend has given him.

- In *The Great Kapok Tree* (by Lynne Cherry, 2000), A man in the Amazon rain forest has to make a critical decision after all the forest animals whisper in his ear, begging him not to destroy their home.

- In *If You Give a Mouse a Cookie* (by Laura Numeroff, 1991), The reader must face the challenge of offering a rodent a tasty treat—and all the consequences that follow from that simple act.

If you just offer a "day in the life" story (boy gets up, boy goes to school, boy comes home, boy eats dinner, boy goes to bed, boy goes to sleep), you'll seldom attract the attention of a child; much less an editor. Provide your main character with a conundrum, challenge, or personal obstacle to overcome and your manuscript will, most certainly, rise to the top.

9. A heavy-handed moral.

I'm going to ask you to set this book aside for a few moments and take a trip to your local public library and check out two books by children's author Jacqueline Woodson: *The Other*

Side (2001) and *Each Kindness* (2012). To say that I am in love with these books would be a gross understatement, for Woodson has crafted two stories with quiet, subtle, and gentle messages that don't hit readers over the head, but rather softly reminds them of some important lessons in life. Her wordsmithing is precise, accurate, and engaging; she gets her message across as deftly as a skilled surgeon or world-class ballerina. These are tales as much for adults as they are for children.

Too often, novice writers think that young readers need to be taught a lesson or two. Unfortunately, their manuscripts are heavy with admonitions and diatribes—commands about proper behavior or good manners. Too many of those manuscripts sound like Aesop's Fables: short stories (usually with animal characters) with a clearly spelled out moral at the end. Please don't go there. Sure, kids need to learn some important things in life, but they don't need a moralistic story in order to learn those lessons. Too many of those stories tell kids what to do, instead of showing them what to do as Jacqueline Woodson does so eloquently in her books.

In short, don't write moralistic tales for kids—write stories.

Expert Quote

"No one likes being preached to, and kids, who are preached to enough already, really don't like it."

—Margaret Meacham, author

10. Overuse of Adjectives; Underuse of Verbs

Want to put more power into your sentences? Then, eliminate most of your adjectives and concentrate on your verbs. Believe it or not, there is more power in a carefully chosen verb than there is in all the adjectives in the English language. Here's an example of a sentence overloaded with adjectives: "He was a strong, muscular, handsome, dashing, well-groomed, and outstanding young man." You see, the problem with this sentence is that we know so very little about this individual other than what the author has told us (telling vs. showing). The author has relied on a string of adjectives to describe this person, but has not taken the time to show us the real person he is.

On the other hand, a carefully chosen verb can add considerable power to a sentence: one that helps the reader gain a clear mental image of what is going on or what is happening. For example, take the following sentence: "She walked down the street to give Candice a lesson she would never forget." "Walked" is a weak verb—it's ordinary in the same way that "talk," "say," "run," or "move" are weak. But substitute a potent verb in that sentence, and it carries a much more powerful message. For example, "She stormed down the street, ready to give Candice a lesson she would never forget." See the difference? You'll also note that there is no adjective in the first part of that sentence, yet through the use of a certain verb we know quite a bit about that very angry person.

11. Adults Who Save the Day.

Another of my favorite children's books is *The Tenth Good Thing About Barney* by Judith Viorst. This is the story about a young boy whose cat, Barney, dies. He is asked to think of ten good things to say about Barney at the funeral, but can only think of nine. Later, while working outside with his father he thinks of the tenth good thing and begins to understand. Even though this book was written in 1971, it still stands up for one very good reason. The challenge facing the young boy was not solved by an adult, but by the boy himself.

Too many stories create a challenge or problem for the main character and then have someone (presumably older and wiser) step in to "save the day." This sends a very powerful (and wrong) message to kids: that they can't solve their own problems and it's up to adults (with all their knowledge and experience) to make things right and to solve any challenges. If a child is facing a conflict or challenge, give her or him the opportunity to discover its solution. When adults always do that, you are robbing the reader of a significant life lesson. In a good children's book, adults should be peripheral characters, not the "go to" problem-solvers.

12. No Clear Main Character.

Every good story has a clear and distinct character around which the story revolves. Take a look at the following story characters and see how many of them you remember:

- Amelia in *Amelia Bedelia*
- Stanley Yelnats in *Holes*
- Jonas in *The Giver*
- Sam in *Green Eggs and Ham*
- Lilly in *Lilly's Purple Plastic Purse*
- Milo in *The Phantom Tollbooth*
- Alexander T. Wolf in *The True Story of the Three Little Pigs*2

You may remember those characters simply because the stories in which they appeared focused solely on them. True, there were other (secondary) characters, but the stories evolved through the eyes or actions of a central character. Those characters are critical figures in the plot of the story. So too, were they well-developed and well-described. Your story will benefit if you concentrate on a well-defined character—one involved in most of the action.

13. Multiple Points of View.

Grammatically speaking, there are three points of view in any story:

- First Person—The story is told by the main character ("I" or "Me" predominates). "My day began when I wrote a letter to my brother in Colorado. It ended with murder."

---

2. Incidentally, these titles are those that frequently appear on lists of "The 100 Best Children's Books Ever Written." One of the chief reasons why these books consistently get high reviews is because of their well-defined characters.

- Second Person—The story is directed at the reader ("You" predominates). "When starting out, you should grip the paddle in both hands and alternate your strokes from side to side."

- Third Person—The story is told by an omniscient narrator ("She" or "He" predominates). "Marcus stared at the tombstone for several minutes before he realized he was not alone."

Decide on a singular point of view and stick with it for the duration of the story. Don't flip/flop between two points of view—you'll confuse the reader.

14. Stereotypes

- Girls are always pretty, shy, or talkative.

- Boys are always boisterous, loud, or non-academic.

- Native Americans in the 1800s always lived in teepees.

- Immigrants to the United States are always poor and destitute.

- Grandparents are always old, slow-moving, or have fuzzy cats sitting on their laps.

- Teachers are always middle-aged, drive old cars, or yell a lot.

- Italians eat a lot of pasta.

- Police officers are always mean and angry.

Stereotypes? You bet! Get rid of them.

15. Stories with dream endings

> And then Carrie woke up and discovered that her great tragedy had all been a dream. She skipped downstairs and had a most delicious breakfast of strawberry pancakes and chocolate milk.

Please, oh please, don't end your story in a similar manner. That's cheating your reader—something you never want to do in a children's book. Dream sequences work for murder mysteries and detective novels—never for children's books.

16. A single setting

    Children, just like adults, enjoy stories that have multiple settings (not too many, though). Your story shouldn't take place in a single setting, but should encompass a few different settings just as a child's daily routine takes place in multiple settings, too.

17. Long time periods

    Stories that take place over many years, decades, or centuries often lose the reader somewhere along the line. Keep your book tightly focused on a narrow time frame and you'll keep the reader's interest focused as well.

18. Coincidences

    The dictionary defines this word as, "a striking occurrence of two or more events at one time apparently by mere chance." The resolution of a conflict must occur through the work or efforts of the main character, not because something happens by mere chance. For example, "Thomas couldn't figure out the puzzle; then he saw the solution on a box of cereal and saved the entire village from total annihilation."

19. Stories that haven't been proofread

    It may surprise you to learn that many manuscripts are rejected not because of how the story was written, but because the submission had not been adequately proofread. Here are the classic errors that show up time and time again:

    - Misspelled words
    - Lack of adequate punctuation (commas, periods, question marks, exclamation points)
    - Poor grammar
    - Un-capitalized words
    - Multiple fonts
    - Misuse of apostrophes
    - Sentence fragments

- Misplaced and dangling modifiers

- Unclear pronoun reference

All writers make mistakes when they write, including me. I know that when I begin a new story I'll include all sorts of errors in my writing. That's simply because my first task is to get the central theme or general idea of a story out of my head and down on a piece of paper (or on a computer screen). So I'm less concerned with the mechanics of writing and more concerned about the creative process. Inevitably, I'll slip in some misspelled words, a few dangling modifiers, and a couple of unpunctuated sentences. I'm OK with that. But, then I know that the real challenge of good writing awaits me— the proofreading stage (*see* Chapter 12). That's when I comb through each phrase, each clause, or each sentence looking for errors, mistakes, and gross omissions. I know they're there, and I know they need to be corrected.

20. Submitting a Manuscript Before it's Ready.

Every book I've ever written has gone through multiple drafts and so should yours (*see* Chapter 12). My children's books often take dozens of drafts before I feel they are ready to send out into the world. Even when I think a book is finished, I'll file it away in my desk and let it "percolate" for a few weeks. Then, I'll pull it out for another read. Inevitably, I'll see some things that need to be changed, some necessary modifications, or some new sentences that should be added. I've discovered that good writing isn't an attempt to get a book written in the shortest amount of time, but rather an effort to produce the best book possible, no matter how much time that takes. Take the time, it will be worth it.

So, now you know the biggest blunders that those other writers often include in their manuscripts: the blunders that will be absent for your manuscripts. Now, it's time to return to the "positives" of authorship, the factors that make up a good—no, a great—book!

Are you ready?

Chapter 6

What is a Good Book?

I'm going to begin this chapter by giving you a homework assignment. I'd like you to visit your local public library and locate three or four new children's books (those published within the past three years). Ask the children's librarian for her or his recommendations on the "hot" titles. Check them out, take them home, and sit down and enjoy. As you read, make a few notes on the elements of those books that clearly stand out. How is the main character developed? How is the plot ordered: is it one that hooks you early in the story and doesn't let go? Are the details precise and convincing? Are the scenes painted with brilliant colors? What was it about those titles that made you want to go back and (perhaps) read them again? Make a brief list below:

1. _____

2. _____

3. _____

4. _____

5. _____

6. _____

7. _____

Undoubtedly, you will discover a set of elements common to several books. For example, strong characters, clearly defined plots, memorable dialogue, and precise vocabulary. These are books that are remembered simply because they are well-written. And, what is a well-written book? Here's how four authors define that term:

If a book is truly well written, the words between the covers are arranged in almost magical patterns that stir deep emotional responses in readers. The words do far more than relate the events of the story. The words make the book by defining character, moving the plot along, identifying the setting, isolating the theme, creating the tone, identifying the point of view, developing the mood, establishing the pace, making the story believable, and reporting information accurately.[3]

So, what really makes up a good children's book? Below you will discover those elements of children's literature that clearly distinguish good books from those that are run-of-the-mill. You'll note features and characteristics that define what children expect and what adults demand in a well-written book. I would suggest you consider this list as a recipe for your own writing. As you do your "essential homework" (reading lots of children's books [*see* Chapter 4]) you will clearly see that all of these ideals are fully included in good children's books. Consider these topics as literary markers for your own writing efforts.

Fiction Books

A Powerful Lead/Hook

A good book starts off with a strong "hook." In the advertising world a "hook" is a phrase or sentence written in such a way that readers are immediately drawn into perusing the rest of an advertisement (and, hopefully, purchasing the product). The "hook" serves to grab the reader's attention—an introduction that is so amazingly interesting, incredibly mysterious, or delightfully thought-provoking that readers just have to keep reading. These first sentences are an inducement to learn more or discover what comes next in the narrative[4].

Often, we are "hooked" into reading a book by its first line(s). It is those first few words that entice us into reading the rest of the story. Here are some terrific first lines in children's literature.

a) "When May died, Ob came back to the trailer, got out of his good suit and into his regular clothes, then went and sat in the Chevy for the rest of the night."
 —Cynthia Rylant, *Missing May* (1992)

---

3. Tunnell, Michael, James Jacobs, Terrell Young, and Gregory Bryan. *Children's Literature, Briefly* (6th Ed.) (Boston, MA: Pearson, 2016), pgs 24-25.
4. Go back and reread the first sentence that begins the Introduction to this book ("the hook for the book"). If done correctly, it should have been a successful inducement for you to read the entire Introduction.

b) "Not every thirteen-year-old girl is accused of murder, brought to trial, and found guilty."
— Avi, *The True Confessions of Charlotte Doyle* (1990)

c) "Henry Brown wasn't sure how old he was."
— Ellen Levine, *Henry's Freedom Box* (2007)

d) "On the eve of your birth word of your coming passed from animal to animal."
— Debra Frasier, *On The Day You Were Born* (1991)

e) "My cat Barney died last Friday."
— Judith Viorst, *The Tenth Good Thing About Barney* (1971)

f) "Where's Papa going with that ax?"
— E.B. White, *Charlotte's Web* (1952)

g) "On Thursday, when Imogene woke up, she found she had grown antlers."
— David Small, *Imogene's Antlers* (1988)

h) "The Herdmans were absolutely the worst kids in the history of the World."
— Barbara Robinson, *The Best Christmas Pageant Ever* (2005)

i) "My dad and I live in an airport."
— Eve Bunting, *Fly Away Home* (1993)

Each of these openings is specifically designed to grab your attention and lure you into a story. If done correctly, a good lead also signals a compelling story to follow.

Exacting Vocabulary

The right words, in the right place, at the right time—this is what all writers strive for—a constant linguistic challenge that propels a manuscript, any manuscript, through multiple drafts and multiple decisions. Too many writers are prone to telling about an action or a character, when showing would give readers an opportunity to become part of the story. For example, I could easily describe my friend Jack as follows: "He is always happy, bringing joy wherever he goes." That's a telling statement. In other words, I'm taking the responsibility of *telling* you about my friend Jack.

On the other hand, though the use of very precise vocabulary I can give you the opportunity to actively learn about Jack by *showing* you something about his personality—with very exacting words—that invites you to make a mental deduction and that invites you to discover something on your own. For example, I could say: "In less than twenty seconds, the room was awash in smiles, giggles, and outright laughter, and he had only uttered seven words." With those words, I didn't *tell* you about Jack; instead I *showed* you something about Jack and gave you the opportunity to deduce his personality.

Precise vocabulary is invitational; it summons the reader to make a mental investment in the story. In so doing, the reader's engagement is both promoted and respected. This can only be accomplished when the words selected are as accurate and precise as they can be. For example, in Kevin Henkes book *Chrysanthemum* (1991), the main character—Chrysanthemum—loves her name. She loves the way it sounds, the ways it looks on a letter, the way it looks on a birthday cake, and the way it looks when written with a crayon. In fact, she thought her name was absolutely perfect. Then she went to school for the first time and her classmates started making fun of her extremely long name. Finally, one of her classmates comments that she is named after a flower. The next line is simply, *"Chrysanthemum wilted."* Look at all the emotions those two words convey. It would have been quite easy for the author to say something like, "After hearing that, Chrysanthemum was very sad and depressed." But, instead, he thoughtfully used a very precise word: "wilted." Those six letters tell you everything you need to know about the character's feelings, reaction, and state of mind. The fact that the word "wilted" is used so often to describe flowers (such as chrysanthemums) made its import even more significant. It was absolutely the right word in the right place.

E. L. Konigsburg is a master of the right word, and, as a result, her novels for young adults are both compelling as well as fascinating. They quickly grab the attention of her readers because she knows their language and she knows how to use that language to make a point or define a scene. Her words are as precise as a surgeon's scalpel beginning an incision. In her book *The View From Saturday* (1996) she describes the Academic Bowl which pits a unique team of sixth graders against the best academicians (mostly eight graders) from another school. The official supervisor for the competition was none other than the commissioner of education for the state of New York. Konigsburg describes him as follows:

> He smiled benevolently over the audience as he reached inside his inner breast pocket and withdrew a pair of reading glasses. (Konigsburg, 1996, p. 2)

Notice the word "benevolently" which is not a typical sixth grade word. Yet in five syllables she has completely captured the look and the demeanor of the commissioner. You don't need an illustration of this person to see what he looks like. That picture is already in your mind. Notice the use of the word "inner"—a precise word that effectively describes a very specific piece of clothing. Who wears that kind of attire? You already have that picture in your mind. And, the work "reading" describes the glasses he uses. So, the picture of this individual is now complete because you now know something about the age and character of this individual. With just three very precise words, you have a total and complete picture of a person without the need for any corresponding illustration.

Here's another example of precision language, this time from the book *The Amazing Bone* by William Steig (1976). Notice in the following example how some very exacting words clearly illustrate a scene from the book. This particular scene is accompanied by an illustration (also by Steig), but it also stands on its own as a coordinated series of accurate and specific words that invite the reader to craft a mental image that is both complete and satisfying:

> She saw the street cleaners sweeping the streets and she looked in at the bakery on Parsnip Lane and saw the bakers taking hot loaves of pumpernickel out of the oven and powdering crullers with sugar dust. (Steig, 1976, p. 4)

Notice how very specific words such as "pumpernickel" (instead of "bread"), "crullers" (instead of "rolls"), and "dust" (instead of nothing) clearly define specific aspects of that sentence such that you can actually see those items vividly colored in your mind. The precise language made the entire sentence an invitational one—one that welcomed you and invited you to see exactly what the major character saw. Once again, the right words in the right place.

The Rhythm of Language

Good writing has a melody. It has a cadence and a pacing that sounds rich and warm. It is musical and it is lyrical—an arrangement of words and sentences that compel, engage, and excite. It is something to be read aloud to a group of eager youngsters because its power is in the rhythm of the language. It is like a classical melody (Beethoven Piano Sonata No. 14, *"Moonlight"*) or modern-day guitar riff (B.B. King's *"The Thrill is Gone"*) that sounds wonderful the first time you hear it and every time after that. It is a story to be savored like a song that must be played. It is music!

Here are a few examples of the rhythm of language:

> Mirror, mirror on the wall. Who is fairest of us all? (Grimm Brothers, 1972, p.2)

> Goodnight stars. Goodnight air. Goodnight noises everywhere. (Brown, 1947, p. 1)

> Brown Bear, Brown Bear, What do you see? I see a red bird looking at me. (Martin, 1996, p. 1)

You probably recognize the stories above—all classics of children's literature. While the rhythm of the language is attached to the rhyming words, that doesn't always have to be the case. It surfaces quite often in prose, too. One of the masters of rhythmic language is Jacqueline Woodson (whom we met earlier), whose picture books engage children through the use of precise and engaging words that evoke both rich images and emotional responses. As an example, let's take a look at the last line in her book *Each Kindness* (2012):

> I watched the water ripple as the sun set through the maples and the chance of a kindness with Maya became more and more forever gone. (Woodson, 2012, p. 32)

Here's another example from Woodson's award-winning book *The Other Side* (2001):

> That summer the fence that stretched through our town seemed bigger.

> We lived in a yellow house on one side of it.

> White people lived on the other.

And Mama said, "Don't climb over that fence when you play."

She said it wasn't safe. (Woodson, 2001, p. 1)

Getting the rhythm of language has often been compared to the classic conundrum of "trying to nail Jell-O to a wall." It almost seems impossible and is quite frequently frustrating. It is something that constantly challenges all writers, and something that consumes much of our linguistic energy. For most authors, the use of varied sentence lengths is one way to address this issue. Differing sentence lengths adds variety to a text. They also make the words and sentences pleasing to the ear; we enjoy hearing them read out loud. A combination of short sentences in concert with long sentences creates an authorial melody most satisfying to hear—and, of course, to read.

Expert Quote

"If I emotionally invest myself in a manuscript, then I know I've got to publish it."

—Caitlyn Dlouhy, children's book editor

Simile and Metaphor

Similes and metaphors, when used judiciously, can add power and impact to your writing. By definition, a simile is a figure of speech that compares one thing with another. For example, "He is as crazy as a fox," or "She is wise like an owl." Similes allow you, as a writer, to compare one item (that may not be entirely familiar to a reader) with another item (that may be more familiar to a reader or may be more likely a part of that reader's background knowledge). Here are some well-known similes:

- As happy as a clam
- As light as a feather
- As blind as a bat
- As cold as ice
- As hot as hell
- As tall as a skyscraper
- As tough as nails

Here are some similes that frequently pop up in both articles and books (which means they are too often overused):

- They fought like cats and dogs.
- This house is as clean as a whistle.
- He is as strong as an ox.
- That is as easy as shooting fish in a barrel.
- That guy is as nutty as a fruitcake.
- Don't just sit there like a bump on a log.
- Well, that went over like a lead balloon.
- They are as different as apples and oranges.

Following are similes from various children's books. You will note how they add power and clarity to the writing in addition to expanding readers' background knowledge:

- "Bothered as a bull." (*My Heart is Like a Zoo*, Hall, 2013)
- "Somewhere behind us, a train whistle blew long and low like a sad, sad song" (*Owl Moon*, Yolen, 1987)
- "Amber lived on a mountain so high, it poked through the clouds like a needle stuck in down." (*Amber on the Mountain*, Johnston, 1998)
- ". . .who had a voice just like a giant." (*Wilfred Gordon McDonald Partridge*, Fox, 1989)

Metaphors are another figure of speech that are used to make a comparison between two things that aren't alike, but do have something in common. I find them to be much more powerful, particularly in children's writing, than similes because the comparison is more direct and specific. They don't imply a similarity, but rather state a direct relationship. When used with exacting vocabulary (see above) they can add "punch" to a description of a character or setting that evokes emotional responses and clear insights.

Here are some examples of well-known metaphors:

- It's raining cats and dogs
- She is the apple of my eye.
- I'm really feeling blue.
- He was on a roller coaster of emotions
- She had a bubbly personality that affected all around her.
- You are my sunshine.

- Time is money

Metaphors put power into your language. They add impact and they add strength to your writing. Of course, they should not be used indiscriminately, but rather judiciously. A ripple, rather than a tsunami, of metaphors (see how I used a metaphor there) is preferred. Too many metaphors creates too much confusion. The reader's mind would be flooded with an avalanche of comparisons.

Here's how three children's authors have used metaphors in their books:

- "Mae sat there frowning, a great potato of a woman." (*Tuck Everlasting*, Babbitt, 1975, p. 10)
- "The house was colder than a frog's tail." (*Tex*, Hinton, 1979, p. 26)
- "While Mama, like a magician, turns Mrs. Koo's dark hair the color of sunset" (*Mama, I'll Give You the World*, Schotter, 2006, p. 5)

Metaphors have the power to open readers' eyes to common items and actions with an all-new perspective. They make the ordinary extraordinary and the common uncommon. They add a special layer of spice to your writing that sustains interest and challenges perceptions.

Dialogue

Imagine yourself standing in a long line at the grocery store or at the bank. While you're waiting for the line to move you hear a guy just behind you. He starts complaining (loudly) about the president ("What a big fat so-and-so!"), he complains about his taxes ("Why should I have to always pay the highest taxes in town."), he complains about the weather ("One long freezing day after another. I'm so tired of it!"), and he complains about standing in line ("Come on people, let's get this thing moving along."). After listening to all his complaints for five to six minutes you say to yourself, "Boy, this guy sure is a jerk!" (and some other things which I'm not allowed to print in a G-rated book).

Without even turning around and seeing what he looked like you were able to make a personality assessment. How did you do it? Simply by listening to what he was saying. In other words, you were able to determine a lot about this guy from his dialogue. And, the same is true with book characters. We learn about the personality of story characters, not by how they are described, but rather by what they say. Just like that person you met for the first time at the last social event (you know, the woman who just couldn't stop talking about herself.), you were able to assess her persona simply by listening to her words. In short, speech reveals character.

You want to reveal your story characters in the same way. You don't have to attach a surfeit of adjectives to them, just let them talk and offer your readers an opportunity to deduce character from what each individual says. For example, in *Ira Sleeps Over* (1972), young Ira gets invited to his friend's house for his very first sleepover. But, he has a concern: Should he bring his teddy bear? His older sister challenges him with the following:

> "But, you never slept without your teddy bear before. How will you feel sleeping without your teddy bear for the very first time? Hmmmmmmmm?" (Waber, 1972, p. 7)

Just in that brief exchange, we get a sense of what kind of person the sister is. We also get the sense that she will, most likely, be a constant thorn in Ira's side. With just twenty-four words!

The River (2012) tells the story of Brian Robeson who, two years previously, was stranded alone in the wilderness for fifty-four days with nothing but a small hatchet (*Hatchet*, 2006). He survived and now the government wants him to do it again so that others can learn the survival techniques that kept him alive. In the opening pages of the story, he is approached by a government psychologist and two wilderness instructors and asked to do it all over again. His first response is, "It's a joke, right?" With just four words, the author, Gary Paulsen, allows you to peek inside Brian's head for a moment and get an idea of what type of person he is. No long explanations, no extended descriptions, no fancy adjectives, just four simple words, and we get a sense of what kind of person Brian Robeson is.

In the book *Crossover* (2014), we meet Josh Bell, a basketball phenomenon. He and his twin brother, trained by their father, are athletic superstars. They can do anything and everything and have both the cockiness and talent to run others off the court. The author, Kwame

Alexander, quickly establishes Josh's character on the second page of the story with the following dialogue:

> Josh Bell is my name. But Filthy McNasty is my claim to fame. Folks call me that 'cause my game's acclaimed, so downright dirty, it'll put you to shame. My hair is long, my height's tall. See, I'm the next Kevin Durant, LeBron, and Chris Paul. (Alexander, 2014, p. 4)

In this case, we get a rich portrait of the main character by what he says, not by how he might have been described by the author. We know a lot about Josh from the hip-hop language he shares and the energy with which he infuses each word. His dialogue sets him up as a fascinating, sizzling, and iconic character—not one traditionally found in young adult novels.

Special Insights

The other morning I decided to have some hot oatmeal for breakfast. I put a cup of water in a pot and brought it to a full boil on the stove. I then sprinkled in a half-cup of oatmeal and stirred it every so often as it was cooking. After a few minutes, I removed the pot from the stove and spooned the hot oatmeal into a bowl. I sprinkled a little sugar over the top, added a dab of butter, and then stirred it once again. Then, I had the idea to spice up my breakfast just a little by adding a small handful of dried cranberries to the oatmeal. It was absolutely delicious!

Now, I didn't have to add the dried cranberries, my oatmeal would have tasted just fine without them. But the cranberries added a slightly different flavor, a slightly different taste to an otherwise very tasty breakfast. The cranberries were something special, something unexpected, something that made my breakfast memorable enough that nearly a week after eating it I'm now writing about it in this chapter.

Good writers sprinkle some unexpected literary delights throughout their manuscript as well. These aren't necessarily required for the character, setting, or plot, but they add just a little more spice, making the reading just a little special. They are an added bonus—a treat for both the eyes and the ears. These are the surprises that differentiate a good story from a great story. They make a story richer by their inclusion and our experience of that story a little more memorable.

In the opening paragraphs in *Shiloh*, the eleven-year-old narrator, Marty Preston, describes a big Sunday dinner where the featured meat is fried rabbit. Marty is worried about biting down on some buckshot since the rabbit had been shot by his father. His father tries to calm his fears when he says, "'I looked that rabbit over good, Marty, and you won't find any buckshot in that thigh,' Dad says, buttering his bread. 'I shot him in the neck.'" (*Shiloh*, Naylor, 1991, p. 11). The author could have easily stopped after the word "bread," but added just a little more detail for Marty to consider. It's that little bit of spice that lets you know that this will be a story with some insights and incidents not many people have experienced. As a result, it becomes a one-of-a-kind story.

In *Holes*, Stanley Yelnats, is describing Camp Green Lake, which is a camp for bad boys. During their incarceration, each of the boys is required to dig an endless series of holes in the bottom of a dried lake bed. Day after day they must dig holes in the hot sun under the watchful gaze of the guards and the camp warden. Stanley describes a lone hammock stretched between two trees along the edge of the lake, then he notes: "The campers are forbidden to lie in the hammock. It belongs to the Warden. The Warden owns the shade." (*Holes*, Sachar, 2000, p. 3) With the addition of that last line, the author is letting the reader know that there will be some humor and levity throughout this story. He's also letting the readers know that this will be a battle between the forces of good and evil with many adventures along the way. It's a little tidbit of information that sets a very large stage for the action to come.

In *The Bridge to Terabithia*, the narrator is describing a classroom scene. The teacher, Mrs. Myers, is attending to several administrative duties including the distribution of textbooks for a forthcoming lesson. Here's how the author, Katherine Patterson, sets up the scene: "Mrs. Myers handed out books almost as though she were President of the United States, dragging the distribution process out in senseless signings and ceremonies" (*Bridge to Terabithia*, Patterson, 1977, p. 22). An unexpected detail—"as though she were President of the United States"—adds an unexpected detail to Mrs. Myers personality. It makes her characterization richer and more imaginable. It gives her an unexpected dimension—an added feature that makes her more complete.

One of the classic paragraphs to ever open a book can be found in *The Best Christmas Pageant Ever* by Barbara Robinson (1972). Notice how the author adds several unexpected details to a simple description of a family of kids. You know more about these kids in two sentences than in a whole chapter of individual descriptions. Words such as "dirty," "cigar," "cussed," and "lied," are not vocabulary you would expect to find in a young adult novel. Robinson captures our attention in a mere fifty-three words and doesn't let go until the very end of the book. It is her choice of unexpected details (we've never seen these words or phrases in any other book before) that makes this book a classic. Begin reading this book to a class of third graders and they won't let you out of the room until you've finished the entire story. Yup, they'll even skip recess!

> The Herdmans were absolutely the worst kids in the history of the world. They lied and stole and smoked cigars (even the girls) and talked dirty and hit little kids and cussed their teachers and took the name of the Lord in vain and set fire to Fred Shoemaker's old broken-down toolhouse. (Robinson, 1972, p. 1).

Now, those are what I call unexpected details! Wouldn't you agree?

Nonfiction Books

"Wow! Factor"

I'm a firm believer in the idea that no single nonfiction book will ever have all the answers for a single topic. In fact, I think that the best nonfiction books are those that help readers generate their own self-initiated queries—questions they will want to pursue through the reading of additional books. This concept is also embodied in what I call the "Wow! Factor." The "Wow! Factor" is a collection of book elements that cause readers to exclaim, "Wow, I didn't know that!" or "Wow, that's really cool!" However, when students read a book they should be sufficiently stimulated ("Wow, this is really neat stuff!") to check out other resources on the same or related topics. Authors who can incite additional discoveries by readers are helping to promote inquiry and investigation in a variety of ways.

For example, several years ago I was watching a Discovery Channel program that profiled cannibalistic animals. I was mesmerized by the information shared during the program and found myself saying, "Wow, I didn't know that" several times during the broadcast. I realized that, once again, I was a student. I was learning something I knew nothing about. "Wow," I thought, "I want to learn more." I felt that the best way for me to learn about this topic would be to research this subject and try to put that information into a form that could be understood by youngsters.

I was excited about the topic, but I needed some way to share my enthusiasm with young readers—a way to get them equally excited. As a professional storyteller, I knew that weaving the information into meaningful stories would have the greatest impact on readers. I decided to focus on the life stories of several selected species: praying mantids, guppies, Tyrannosaurus Rex, sand tiger sharks, gerbils, and chimpanzees. It was the life stories that offered a relevant context for all the facts.

However, when I wrote *Cannibal Animals: Animals That Eat Their Own Kind* (1999), I had to be careful that my enthusiasm and excitement didn't become one of sensationalism. I knew I would have to walk a very fine line between the presentation of factual information in an exciting and stimulating format and a fall into journalistic sensationalism. I wanted to present cannibalism as a naturally occurring fact of life (more than 1,500 species of animals engage in cannibalism) while imbuing this behavior with a sense of authenticity that avoided sensationalism.

I decided to take a "You Are There" approach, giving readers an omniscient view of each animal's life cycle. This gave me the opportunity to "connect" with readers through stories that were both amazing and complete.

> You could say that the "diet" of a tiger salamander is like the diet of a typical teenager: anything and everything! Young tiger salamanders have huge appetites and will eat almost anything they can get into their mouths—ants, worms, snails, mice, or other small animals. If it moves, it's food for a tiger salamander. (Fredericks, 1999, p. 26)

Children who read "Wow! Factor" books are those who gain a true appreciation for the discoveries made (and those yet to be made) throughout the world. When combined with the elements of good storytelling, those facts become personal and intensely meaningful. Children begin to sense that learning is a passionate affair—one that puts all the senses on full alert—and one shared by the author as well as the reader.

Fascinating Facts

It's one thing to have a child pick up a book and begin to read it; quite another thing to have a child stick with the book all the way to the end. The inclusion of fascinating facts sprinkled throughout the story piques children's natural curiosity and provides them with insights that might not be available in more formal and staid information sources such as an encyclopedia or internet article. The liberal use of little-known and mesmerizing details help keep a reader glued to the pages, learning new stuff and continually searching for the next tidbit of data. Fascinating facts keep interest levels high and motivation constantly stimulated.

In writing the book *Slugs* (2000), I wanted my audience (kindergarten to second grade) to understand some of the basic facts about these often misunderstood animals. By the same token, I wanted to offer readers some unusual bits of information not often found in science textbooks or specialized internet sites. Every so often I would include one or more fascinating details to spice up the story, as follows:

> Some species of slugs use mucus to get down from trees. These slugs can climb trees thirty feet or higher. This is taller than most houses. When the slugs want to come down, they make a thick string of mucus. They use the mucus like a rope to come down from the tree. (Fredericks, 2000, p. 26-27)

As another example, J. Lynett Gillette's *Dinosaur Ghosts: the Mystery of Coelophysis* (1997) focuses on a cache of hundreds of *Coelophysis* (SEEL-oh-FIE-sis) dinosaurs (about the size of a dog) that apparently perished together at a place known as Ghost Ranch in New Mexico (just north of Santa Fe). The discovery of numerous necks, tails, arms, and legs of these Triassic creatures in 1947 baffled scientists. "Why were all these dinosaurs buried in one place?" was a question that perplexed and stumped the scientists.

Gillette goes into several explanations proffered for the demise of these critters. She offers some scientific reasoning and then challenges that reasoning with basic facts from the site. But, she also offers several little-known facts in order to keep her readers "up to speed" on all the science involved in this unique paleontological mystery.

> Scientists Walter and Luis Alvarez of the University of California have suggested a reason why dinosaurs became extinct around sixty-five million years ago. The Alvarezes said that maybe a huge asteroid falling out of orbit from outer space struck the Earth. The collision would have sent great clouds of dust into the air that blocked sunlight and cooled the Earth. A cooler Earth couldn't support the same kinds of plants and animals. Many species that needed warm temperatures would die. (Gillette, 1997, p. 21)

These fascinating facts are like adding a dash of spice or a dollop of flavoring to a favorite recipe. The recipe is good, but it can be made just a little more interesting (and a little more tasty) with the addition of a unique spice or seasoning. *Dig, Wait, Listen* (2001), for example, describes the desert spadefoot toad's unusual underground living conditions: "the young and adult toads dig back underground to wait until the next heavy rain. It can be a long wait indeed—as long as eleven months—until they hear the rain again." (Sayre, p. 30). Another example can be found in *Dave the Potter: Artist, Poet, Slave* where we are introduced to a slave in the mid-1800s who teaches himself how to make pottery: "With a flat wooden paddle large enough to row across the Atlantic, Dave mixed clay with water drawn from Big Horse Creek, until wet and stiff and heavy." (Hill, 2010, p. 11).

Salt your nonfiction manuscript with several fascinating and little-known facts and you can keep readers coming back for more. You can also show them some of the interesting things that can often be found in nonfiction books.

Interesting Comparisons

Children's books often present information that is outside the realm of their comprehension. Often, that information is not a normal part of children's background knowledge about a particular topic. For example, as adults, we understand the concept of a "million." We've dealt with that number many times in our lives, we know what it means when someone says that so-and-so is a millionaire, and we have seen that word or number in print in the newspapers and magazines we read.

For young children, however, the word "million" doesn't hold much meaning because it's not a word that comes up frequently in their math lessons, nor is it a word that surfaces in most of the books they read. If "million" is to be used effectively in a book, youngsters have to have something against which it can be compared. In other words, they have to balance the new word with something with which they are already familiar. David Schwartz did a marvelous job of this in his book *How Much Is a Million?* (1985). He used a number of comparisons in order to give readers some insight into what the words million, billion, and trillion mean. He did this by outlining how long it would count to each one by saying each number completely and going nonstop. To count to a million would take twenty-three days, to a billion would take ninety-five years, and to count to a trillion would take more than 200,000 years.

When I wrote *Elephants for Kids* (1999), I wanted to give readers a sense of how large these animals were. Big numbers don't convey much information if youngsters can't understand how those numbers relate to something with which they are more familiar— something in their background of experiences. So, I decided to use some familiar comparisons to help readers understand the size of these creatures.

> The African elephant, which lives in central and southern Africa, is the world's largest land animal. A bull elephant can weight up to 15,000 pounds. That's about as heavy as a school bus. Cows are smaller.

> A full-grown African elephant may stand thirteen feet high at the shoulder. That's taller than a basketball hoop. (Fredericks, 1999, p. 8)

In drafting my book *Weird Walkers* (1996), I wanted readers to discover some of the most unusual walkers on the planet. These included a fish that walks *out* of the water, a lizard that walks *on* the surface of water, and even a tree that "walks" *through* the water. But, in order to make these biological specimens meaningful for children, I sought to compare how these forms of locomotion were similar to, or different from, the ways in which children typically walk (or locomote).

In describing millipedes, I drew some comparisons between the legs of these critters and the legs of children.

How would you walk if you had eight legs? How about eighty legs? How about 200 legs? How would you coordinate all those legs so that you would be able to move forward and not trip over a dozen or more of your own legs? (Fredericks, 1996, p. 8)

Comparisons gives readers a frame of reference—an opportunity to learn about something new by matching it with something familiar.

Unusual Viewpoints

Just like the facts you want to sprinkle across your manuscript, consider taking a different viewpoint or creative stance in presenting your information. The viewpoint you take can spark interest in a topic that often, on the surface, looks dull and boring. One of the best proponents of this creative approach is Lois Ehlert, who is known for taking common items and transforming them into dynamic new objects. Her books are some of the most creative available for young readers—opening their eyes to the world around them and stimulating their curiosity about how familiar items can be transformed into something new.

A perfect example is one of my all-time favorite books for very young children: *Leaf Man* (Ehlert, 2005). "With a body made of fallen leaves and acorns for eyes, Leaf Man takes off from a backyard and flutters away on the breeze, traveling past animals, over fields of fall vegetables, above waterways, and across prairie meadows. From ducks to pumpkins, and from cabbages to fish, all the objects described are fashioned out of life-size leaves of various shapes, sizes, and hues. After this visual feast, young nature lovers are sure to look with fresh eyes as they walk through the woods, around a city park, or down a country road."

Another delightful example is *Mojave* (Siebert, 1988), a picture book that describes the Mojave Desert in southern California. Siebert rises above the all-too-common encyclopedic descriptions of deserts by taking on the role of the desert itself. That is, this is the story of the desert as it might be told by the desert. Listen to the magic of the language as the desert speaks:

> My summer face is cracked and dry,
> All blotched and flecked with alkali,
> Until the coming of a storm
> When thunderclouds above me form,

And bursting, send their rains to pound
Across my high, unyielding ground
Where walls of water grow, and flow
Towards my valleys far below. (Siebert, 1988, p. 22).

As you might imagine, teachers and librarians love Siebert's books because they are powerful and engaging read-aloud stories.

In *Making the World* (1998), Douglas Wood explores the impact that every living thing makes on the world. The message is that both animals and humans have a direct impact on the world in which they live. On the opening page of the story he declares, "Everywhere you look and everywhere you listen, someone or something is helping to make the world." (Wood, 1998, p. 6). He then goes on to describe selected creatures and the influence they have on a planet in constant flux: "An antelope, running across an empty plain beneath an empty sky; racing with the wind and writing his signature upon the earth, helps to make the world." (Wood, 1998, p. 14).

Accuracy

I would be remiss if I didn't include a note about accuracy in nonfiction literature. There is a basic assumption we have when we read a nonfiction book. That is, that the author has done her or his homework. That is, she or he has researched all the facts, confirmed all the data, and presented the information accurately. As readers, we expect that what we witness on the page is accurate beyond a shadow of a doubt. Additionally, we assume the author has checked with authorities, consulted numerous publications, or done the laborious research to authenticate every single fact. This is especially true with scientific information, as in my book *Tsunami Man: Learning About Killer Waves with Walter Dudley* (2002):

> The difference in height between high tide and low tide in a specific location is known as its tidal range. On open ocean coasts, the tidal range is typically between six and twelve feet. In some river mouths and bays, the tidal range can be much greater. For example, in the Bay of Fundy in Canada, the tidal range is an astonishing fifty-three feet—the greatest tidal range in the world. (Fredericks, 2002, p. 4).

That accuracy is also expected in historical stories—especially nonfiction ones, but also in historical fiction books that weave accurate facts into an imaginary story about a heroine or hero facing a unique conflict and seeking a plausible resolution. An excellent example is Joyce Carol Thomas's book *I Have Heard of a Land*. In this narrative, a single African-American woman claims a piece of land during the Oklahoma Land Rush of the late 1880s. Based on her own family history, Thomas crafts a story that celebrates the bravery of former slaves who wanted nothing more than the opportunity to carve out a new life for themselves. The accuracy of this unique story is revealed in text such as the following:

> I have heard of a land
> Where a woman sleeps in a sod hut dug deep in the heart of the earth
> Her roof is decorated with brush
> A hole in the ground is her stove
> And a horse saddle is her pillow
> She wakes thinking of a three-room cabin." (Thomas, 1998, p. 22).

Expert Quote

"What makes a good story/book? This one's easy. The story you can't get out of your head. The character that you fall in love with every time you re-read the story. Every time. And the fact that you want to re-read the story—and to re-read the lines—the words—again and again. The story that makes you want to carry the book . . . close."

—Lindsay Barrett George, children's author

If you are writing a nonfiction book, it is imperative that you signal the reader, in some way, that your facts are correct and that your information is accurate. Your editor will demand it and your readers will expect it.

Part III

"Where Do You Get All Those Ideas?"

Chapter 7

A Plethora of Writing Prompts

Where do you get ideas? Let's face it: you've pondered that question a thousand times, and so have I!

- What will children enjoy?
- What are parents and teachers looking for?
- What do editors want?
- Where do successful children's authors get all those great ideas —idea after idea after idea?

Let's be honest here: coming up with great ideas is tough. You've got a million other things on your mind, a million other things that take up your time, and a million different reasons as to why writing is such a challenge. You want inspiration and you want ideas—both of which often seem to be in short supply.

That's where this chapter comes in. This chapter will stoke your creative fires, stimulate your creativity, and get you writing stories, books, novels, YA fiction, and a wealth of other possibilities that engage children and open their eyes to the world around them. This chapter is packed with writing prompts—ideas designed to get your mental motors started, set you on the writing road, and move you to your ultimate goal: a published children's book.

But, like a good coach, this chapter will not go out there and play the game for you. That's ultimately up to you. These prompts are a source of inspiration, it's what you decide to do with that inspiration that will determine how well you play in the championship tournament or whether you score the winning touchdown in the literary Super Bowl: publication. The coach is there to support you (just as this chapter is designed to support you), but ultimately it's up to you to put on your gear and run out onto the field.

Some of the prompts may get you writing a single page; others may stimulate you to craft a 200-page YA novel. The key is to open your imagination to all the possibilities—to take a prompt as far as you can—explore all its dimensions, all its possibilities, and see what happens. The ultimate goal is to have fun; it's that fun that will come across in your writing; it's that fun that will excite a young reader and encourage her or him to return to your story again and again. And it's that fun that will keep your creative juices flowing and your fingers dancing across your keyboard.

Will every one of these prompts result in a best-seller? Of course not! But, each one has the potential to get your creative spirit activated to generate a book that kids will want to read, parents will want to buy, and librarians will want to promote. There is no one perfect idea for every writer. You are, however, encouraged to make these ideas yours. Select an idea and see how far it takes you. Does it get you so excited that you wind up writing fifty-two pages of a young adult novel? Great! Does it produce a single paragraph and then just wither and die on the proverbial literary vine? Well, that's OK, too. The intent is to offer you an incredible variety of possibilities—any one of which has the potential to become *your book* for children.

One thing you'll notice is that these prompts are intentionally short. That's because I don't want to get in the way of your writing. If a prompt had too many elements (young girl, dark night, spooky graveyard, frustrated ghost, mysterious headstone, full moon, thin layer of snow, hollow tree, wide-eyed owl, etc., etc.) then that might be a hindrance to your unique and singular creativity. All those extra details and "conditions" would get in the way of *your* story, *your* unique perspective, and *your* unique creativity. Rather, by offering you a snippet of an idea ("Well, I certainly didn't expect to find you here in the graveyard.") you can now take off in a variety of directions depending on your perspectives, outlook, or creative intent. My job to provide you with a literary spark; how you build the fire and eventually fan the flames is your role.

You will note that there are three types of prompts:

1. Some of the prompts are dialogue prompts. You are provided with a quote made by a potential character in a story. It's up to

you to develop the character, the situation the character is in and how the story is resolved. Here's an example:

• "I wish you wouldn't do that. It really bugs me!"

Now you need to decide who is making that statement. Under what circumstances? Who is it directed towards? How old are the characters? Where is this taking place? What is actually being done that "bugs" the person? How will this situation be resolved? Quite obviously, there are several different possibilities here—and, best of all, there are no rules on how the story could play out. Is this a mystery? A humorous book? A biography? A science fiction novel? A school-related book?

It's your story. Make it happen!

2. Some of the prompts are situation prompts. A character (or several characters) is put in a specific situation. Who are they? How did they there? How will they get out of the situation? What will they learn? What will they feel? Here's an example:

• Jessamine didn't know it, but her first day at Mayfield Elementary School was going to be absolutely unforgettable.

In this case a particular character has been identified along with a specific location. What happens with that character in that location is entirely up to you. Will it be a sad event? A happy event? A scary event? A confrontational event? Who will he interact with? A teacher? A classmate? The principal? The cafeteria lady? The bus driver? The class guinea pig? The possibilities, as they say, are many.

3. Another type of prompt is the "what-if" prompt. These are ideas that are generated by posing questions, each of which start with the two words, "What if ...?" For example:

• What if a girl had the power to start fires by just snapping her fingers?

• What if a T. Rex moved in next door to you?

• What if you could have one magic power? What would it be?

- What if the river slowly rose over its banks (during a raging storm) and flooded the town?
- What if pigs could fly?

As you can see, there are all kinds of possible story ideas when you respond to a "what if" question. These are questions that let your imagination fly off in a hundred different directions—imagination that has no boundaries or limits.

How to Use This Chapter

So, how can you use all these prompts? Here are a few ideas to get you started:

1. Pick a prompt a day. One of the "facts of life" about writing is that the more we write, the more we produce. For example, I write every day. Some days I'm writing children's books, other days I'm writing adult non-fiction books (like this one). The reality is that the more writing becomes part of our daily routine, the more we produce and the more opportunities we give ourselves to create salable manuscripts. No long distance runner, for example, wakes up three weeks before the Olympics and say, "Hey, I think I'm going to win the Olympic Marathon." No way! It takes years and years of practice to achieve that level of athleticism. The same is true for writers: the more you practice, the better you get. The better you get, the more you get published. Pick a prompt a day and use it to "jump start" your creativity. Write on!

Insider Tip

In case you're interested, the average American spends about two years of her or his life waiting in line. Think about how many books you could get started during those two years!

2. Here's something I do. I randomly select five to seven prompts and write each one on an index card. I stuff those cards in my pocket (along with a pen). Then, throughout the day, whenever I'm waiting for something (an appointment with my doctor, a nonfat vanilla latte at the local coffee shop, my turn to check out at the hardware store or the local movie theater) I'll pull a random card from my pocket, read it, and write down some thoughts, dialogue, information, scenarios for a potential story. Nothing elaborate or complex, but rather the beginnings of a new story or new book. By the end of the week, I have some pretty amazing story ideas in their initial stages of development.

3. Photocopy the pages in this chapter. Use a pair of scissors to cut up the photocopied pages into small slips: one idea on each of 201 slips of paper. Put all those slips into a jar or large bowl. Each morning, before you head off to work or begin your daily activities, select one of the slips at random (reach in the bowl and pull out one slip—no looking, please!). Memorize the prompt and whenever you have a free moment during the day, write down some thoughts, scenes, characters, or potential plot lines. I often carry a small voice recorder with me and can then record those thoughts while I'm waiting at a red light, walking through a grocery store, or even out for my daily walk through the neighborhood.

This chapter is designed to offer you 201 writing ideas—ideas you can use to create a story or book that will excite young readers. The possibilities are endless and the creativity is boundless! The first part of the creative process is waiting for you on the next page . . . and the next page . . . and the next page. Grab one, embrace it, make it your own, and turn it into a story that will fly off the shelves of your local bookstore and into the hands of youngsters everywhere. Here are the ideas, the rest is up to you!

1. A monster lives under the bed—Grandma's bed—and she doesn't like it one bit. Nine-year-old Jason has a plan to get rid of it once and for all!

2. Crissy's blanket was very special—her great grandmother created it soon after she arrived in the United States.

3. A small rock has gone through many historical events in its 4.5 billion-year-old existence.

4. Miss Jones has been teaching in Appleton for fifty-seven years. This will be her last year and the town plans a special celebration.

5. The poison dart frog has skin so dangerous that native hunters use the poison to coat their hunting arrows.

6. Richard and his younger sister have many adventures (and a few scares) as they travel the Underground Railroad towards freedom in Canada.

7. Parrot fish get their name from the fact that their jaws look just like a parrot's beak.

8. Maybelle sets out for Oregon to start a new life—a life quite different from the one she led in Dallas, Texas.

9. There are many different skin colors throughout the world. There are as many skin colors as there are food colors. Each of us can be compared to a special kind of food. Me, for example, I'm peanut butter.

10. Mr. Saturday has been working in the steel mill all his life. He has never taken a vacation, but his boss demands that he take two weeks off. Where will he go?

11. Listen carefully and you will hear an amazing collection of sounds in the middle of the night.

12. Josiah travels by wagon train to California. The trip is dirty, dusty and dangerous.

13. In the segregated south two children—one white and one black—learn that friendship knows no color.

14. Enrique and his family are migrant workers in California's Imperial Valley. Enrique has never owned a bicycle until one special day when one literally falls into his life.

15. Felecia is an amazing athlete. She wants to play for the middle school football team, but everyone tells her she can't just because she's a girl.

16. Walter begins to pour the cereal into his bowl when something really strange falls out of the box.

17. "You probably don't think much about nine-year-olds, unless, of course, they're wanted for murder."

18. Nobody has ever seen a baby dragon—except for Kenneth!

19. I knew it was a mistake, but three lives were changed as a result.
20. Professor Clark invents something every kid wants.
21. Maria, who was kidnapped when she was a toddler, is eventually returned to her parents—ten years later.
22. A boy and his father go camping and discover that there's more than rabbits and deer in the woods.
23. "She has to be the world's worst teacher."
24. Patrick finds a strange note on his uncle's desk. The writing is most unusual, but he is able to decipher a message about "a plague of dark days."
25. Henry and his friends decide to row across the lake. They discover something more than treasure on the other side.
26. Alice is always late. She's late to school, she's late to her birthday party, and she's late to dinner. But, of course, Alice is a dragon and dragons are never on time.
27. Robert and Tom travel back in time to the Middle Ages. The bubonic plague is sweeping the land and they may die in the past.
28. Kurt tries out for the Pony Express.
29. A substitute teacher takes over the class. Nobody is happy, especially Howard.
30. Eric wants to be a famous explorer more than anything else. Then, he meets the mysterious Dr. Danger.
31. Maggie is ten years old and is the queen of the neighborhood. Then, her parents decide to adopt a sister from China—a sister who is handicapped.
32. Grandpop is ninety-nine years old and in a nursing home. His great grand-daughter comes to visit him one day and learns a very valuable lesson.
33. While walking through the train station, Terrell sees a man dressed entirely in green.
34. Brian opens a special delivery letter and discovers that he has just inherited a castle—a haunted castle.
35. Katie lives near Honolulu, Hawaii. Early one morning she sees something in the sky she has never seen before. The date is December 7, 1941.
36. "Yeah, he's sorta cute . . . for an alien, that is."

37. Paula is a foster child who has no family, no friends and no self-concept. She is taken in by an old lady with arthritis and bad breath.

38. Jake transfers to a school that is "totally weird." There are no teachers, no homework, and no books.

39. "I don't know about you, but I'm not going in there."

40. Ginger and her best friend decide to go for a bicycle ride one Saturday morning. They accidently run into a man in a wheelchair.

41. "You think I'm tough. You should see my mother!"

42. Leah just can't stop eating "Big Whopper" candy bars. One day she eats so many that she . . .

43. A zookeeper goes to the zoo one evening to feed the animals. She discovers that a lion, an elephant, and a giraffe are missing.

44. Robert wanted to go to Disneyland more than anything else in the world. He delivered newspapers, sold lemonade and did part-time jobs for everyone in the neighborhood. Two days before he is scheduled to leave, his mother passes away.

45. "I'm not sure what that noise is. But I don't like it."

46. Pedro plants a small tree outside his casa. The year is 1492.

47. "I'm afraid I have some really bad news to tell you."

48. John dreams of being a paleontologist. He gets to meet one while visiting his uncle in Colorado and it changes his life forever.

49. The sailboat appeared from nowhere and as it approached the shore Marcia could see two figures standing in the bow.

50. The tuba was three times larger than Molly, but still she wanted to play it.

51. Tyrone was autistic. He hid under the kitchen table whenever there were loud sounds in the house.

52. Kelly has some unusual pets: three armadillos.

53. A drop of water begins life in a cumulous cloud. During its "lifetime" it becomes many different things.

54. Butterflies are amazing creatures with incredible colors and fascinating stories.

55. The Gila monster is one of only two poisonous lizards in the world.

56. Becky learns to grow some of the foods her grandmother used to grow—foods like okra and rutabaga.

57. When no one was watching, Andy snuck away with his dog.

58. While out walking one day, Mary comes across what looks like a fossil. It's only when she takes the object to Professor Brown at the university that she discovers what it really is.

59. "I bet you've never seen a lemur before. Well, let me show you a picture and tell you about his life."

60. The Bird-Eating Tarantula is as big as a dinner plate.

61. Iguanas look like miniature dinosaurs. Are they related?

62. The Dansforth Creek rises higher and higher as the rainstorm persists into a third day. The city zoo is in danger of being swept away.

63. Hammerhead sharks are very unlike other sharks. First of all they look really strange.

64. What you don't know about squirrels.

65. The Equator runs through some very interesting countries. Each of these countries has some very interesting animals.

66. The Florida Everglades is where the Robinsons live—in a treehouse.

67. Mr. Marsden is flying home from a business meeting. He is sitting next to a very interesting passenger—a very interesting nine-year-old passenger.

68. The cheetah is the fastest land animal. What is the slowest?

69. A teddy bear is missing a button. He searches all over for a replacement.

70. A meteorite crashes into Hector's back yard.

71. Corey gets a letter from his brother in Japan. For twelve years Corey was certain he was an only child.

72. Two construction workers, sitting on a girder, watch all the people pass below them.

73. "Somebody's got to stop her!"

74. While entering an elevator at a fancy hotel, Mrs. Cummings discovers a small girl with a torn dress and a dirty face.

75. How camels survive in the desert.

76. Two lame dogs and a mangy cat.

77. Alyssa's grandmother tells her the story of how her relatives came over from Africa and settled in South Carolina.

78. Jamal lifts up an old log in the forest and makes some amazing discoveries.
79. Nicole didn't like the house or the new town her family just moved to. She was angry and sad, sad and angry. Then one day while poking around her bedroom, she discovers a hidden panel in the back of her closet.
80. Lauren is given a chance to save the universe. Unfortunately, it involves an elephant.
81. Slowly, Courtni begins to lose her hearing.
82. Tabitha's mother is abusive and her father is a drunk. She just accepts that fact . . . that is, until she meets an old man at the park.
83. A father and daughter walk into a local store. Fifteen minutes later they walk out with an alien.
84. "Of course she didn't do it. She's much too shy."
85. A young boy looks out his bedroom window and sees a pirate digging a hole in the back yard.
86. A boy with ADHD tries out for the school play.
87. A cowboy and his dog go into the general store. There they meet Billy the Kid.
88. A doctor operates on an emergency patient brought to the hospital after a horrific accident. She later learns the patient is her son.
89. "Here, let me show you how to do it. Just hold it right here."
90. Justin was angry with his parents—very, very angry. He would wind up doing something that was not very smart; in fact, it was very dangerous.
91. A small alligator lives just under the porch at the Madison's house.
92. John's father is an alcoholic, but he gives his son something no other father can.
93. "I wish he would just go away. I wish he would leave forever."
94. Randy found something he never expected on the beach.
95. "I wish I could do it all over again. This time I'd really show them."
96. A new babysitter comes to the Monroe's house. Unfortunately, she doesn't like kids.

97. How the hippopotamus found its way to the corner of Western Avenue and State Street was a mystery. How it got away was amazing.A fierce blizzard blew in from the west covering the cabin in a thick blanket of snow.
98. Rachael has a dream about her uncle, a former magician.
99. Ignacio moves across the country—from the wilds of New York City to the wilds of Carbondale, Colorado.
100. It was his last chance—it was his only chance.
101. Laura was slowly going blind. More than anything else she wanted to be a librarian.
102. A wheelchair-bound boy and his family move to Chicago.
103. As soon as the clock struck midnight, Cinderella turned into—can you believe it—a lizard!
104. Mow the grass, mow the grass—oh, how Terry hated to mow the grass!
105. Ants will move up to forty tons of dirt in constructing their underground colonies.
106. They were the coolest shoes in the whole world. But she couldn't afford to buy them.
107. "Are you sure that's not dangerous? It sure looks dangerous to me."
108. California's official state mollusk, the banana slug, eats poison oak.
109. "I know one thing. I'm never doing that again."
110. "Look. If we don't make a decision right now, we're both in trouble—big trouble."
111. He was the cutest baby, except for one thing—his fangs.
112. "Growing up poor wasn't so bad. I just wish Daddy would come home sometime."
113. A frog must close its eyes in order to swallow.
114. Tammy hires a private investigator to discover the truth about the missing teachers.
115. It was the greatest science experiment ever—that is, until three kids actually disappeared.
116. "There's only one way to answer that question."
117. Mrs. Henderson discovers her daughter's diary while cleaning her room. What she reads sends chills up and down her spine.
118. Only "The Shadow" knows.
119. The history of bubble gum.

120. "You can't bring that in here!"
121. It's Thanksgiving and Gregory and his family must spend it at Grandma's house. The trouble is that Grandma happens to be a werewolf.
122. A letter arrives in the mail that changes Theodore's life. It's a letter from his bother—his brother who died eleven years ago.
123. Timmy and Tammy are brother and sister—and they hate each other.
124. Michael holds a funeral for his guinea pig. He learns a lesson he never expected.
125. Sonia arrives in the United States. She doesn't know how to speak English, but on her first day at school she learns something much more valuable.
126. The attic in Frank's house is full of bats.
127. Aaron's family is poor—very poor. They're so poor that Aaron can't afford a birthday present for his best friend.
128. Jack learns a powerful lesson about forgiveness when his dog is hit by a car.
129. Carrie talks in riddles, which drives all her friends crazy.
130. Abby thinks she is the most beautiful girl in the whole school—that is, until a mysterious stranger arrives in town.
131. Rosie has to move in with her grandparents. It looks like dull times ahead.
132. Martin's father teaches him how to make vegetable soup absolutely from scratch.
133. Harold wants to play basketball for the school team more than anything in the world. Only trouble is that Harold is way too short.
134. T. J. is a sheep dog who lives on a ranch in New Mexico.
135. Abigail is a most gifted artist. One day she draws a picture that brings tears to her father's eyes.
136. Margaret adopts a cat—a very ugly cat no one likes.
137. Paul and Raymond make a pact to be best friends forever. Then, Sally Mae moves into town.
138. After a freak storm, Warner is stranded on a small island in the Pacific Ocean.
139. The Dodgers are the worst baseball team in the history of the school. But their coach never stops smiling.
140. A toucan, an old woman, and a summer day.

141. The mail carrier delivers a package with no return address and a strange sound coming from inside.
142. I found this ring on top of my mother's dresser. It has the name of my great grandmother on the inside.
143. Time: Today. Place: San Francisco. Event: An earthquake begins to rumble underground.
144. "You're just a foolish little monkey—always getting into trouble."
145. It was his last dollar. He put it on the counter and said, "If this was *your* last dollar, what would you buy?"
146. Angel had been looking forward to summer camp ever since January when her mother sent in her reservation. The week before camp started, Angel got a new pet.
147. "You've probably never seen a cripple sailing a ship. Well, neither have I."
148. Someone or something was following him. He was sure of it— he was being followed.
149. My best friend is blind.
150. "I can't see the road in front of me. This fog is way too thick."
151. The aliens came to Earth looking for only one thing: Colleen.
152. Charles was very special; he had a photographic memory.
153. What if for one single day you could have one secret power. What would it be?
154. "I didn't know you came here. How did you learn about this place?"
155. How many different objects are colored red in nature. Boyd searches and searches and finds an amazing variety.
156. A mouse is confused simply because there is always something following him: his shadow.
157. It was one of the most incredible experiences of Barry's life—a train trip across the country. What he sees will be remembered forever.
158. "Well, at the very least, we could build an igloo."
159. The giant was shunned by everyone in the town. "Go away, get out of here," they would yell. But, one small boy shows the townspeople the importance of giants.
160. In the town of Deadwood Gulch lives the meanest, dirtiest and most feared outlaw in the whole of Wyoming.

161. Mr. Merrill had a pet rhino. Every day at 5 o'clock he would take it for a walk through the middle of town.
162. Amy's father is losing his job. Amy decides to do something about it and writes a letter to the president of the United States.
163. One of Anna's dolls assumes human characteristics and behaviors.
164. The small bridge across Wandering Creek has been there for more than a century. It has many stories to tell and many tales to share.
165. Cynthia's brother is coming home after being away for fourteen years. Cynthia finally learns the truth about his absence.
166. Patricia finds a lady's purse on the sidewalk one day. Wanting to return it to her, she looks inside for a name and address. It turns out to belong to the witch at the end of the street.
167. Many artists will tell you that sunflowers are some of nature's most perfect plants. Their design and detail are completely unlike any other flower.
168. Telling the truth is difficult—particularly when it gets you in trouble with your favorite relative.
169. The clocks are stopped and sheets are put up over all the mirrors when Abigail's mother passes away. Abigail learns about this ancient custom and why it continues.
170. Theodore likes to spend lots of time in his garden. It's a whole different world from the one he must endure at school where he is bullied because of his disability.
171. Lee gets a telescope for his birthday. He goes out onto the beach and searches the horizon. What he sees is beyond belief.
172. Helene is called "The Upside-Down Girl" because she likes to hang upside-down on the playground at every single opportunity.
173. Hey, who was this writer called William Shakespeare? Why is he so famous after all these years?
174. The church bell has been the centerpiece of the town since the Revolutionary War. But, its history has not always been pleasant.
175. Lewis does not like guns—no way, no how! One birthday he gets a gun from a distant relative and must make a difficult decision.

176. Two homeless boys sit down at a table for lunch. Neither one can decide what to eat because there are so many choices.
177. Babies come in all shapes and sizes—especially the animal babies found at the pond near the edge of town.
178. Barnaby is bald because of the cancer treatments he is receiving. He comes up with some very unusual and very creative explanations for his baldness—all in good humor.
179. Pepper: where does it come from, how was it first used, and why is it so popular?
180. Mrs. Thomas has been the librarian at Stillwell Public Library for more than fifty years. Boy, does she have some stories to tell!
181. It is the eve of The Battle of Gettysburg and Amos Carpenter, a free black man living in Gettysburg, must make a very difficult decision.
182. Winnifer and her family of twelve children roam through the woods looking for food.
183. It was a ring unlike any other ring she had ever seen. Red, blue, green, and yellow: it was a rainbow of pretty colors. But she could never wear it—ever!
184. A time warp develops in the forest behind the small town. Five children are given the opportunity to travel to another time —permanently.
185. Everybody tells Junior he should be a circus clown because he's always so funny. One day he meets a clown for the first time and learns all about the clown business.
186. A major tornado is headed directly for Moore, Oklahoma. Mrs. Roberts's third grade class is unexpectedly trapped in the school.
187. Everything you ever wanted to know about spiders.
188. Brian is off to his first day in Kindergarten. Brian is fine; it's his father who can't handle this special event.
189. "Hey, look, Miss Crafton has a new ring on her finger!"
190. The river that ran by the Weaver's house could some-times be friendly and sometimes angry. This summer it was especially angry.
191. What seagulls see.

192. The farmer's market is a wonderful place to visit. It's where Selena and her grandmother go every Saturday morning. There, they meet old friends and share lots of stories.

193. Louis can't believe his eyes! There, on the beach, is a real-live mermaid.

194. Mia wants to change her name—especially when she discovers that it means "Uncertain, maybe bitter."

195. How many animals have horns? What are horns used for? What are some of the most unusual horns in the animal world?

196. On the plane were two passengers who looked a little strange. No, they looked *very* strange!

197. Mr. Hastings is the coolest principal ever! He knows every student's name, he always wears a smile, and he has the world's greatest collection of jokes.

198. Dorian takes an incredible car trip to Arizona with her equally incredible aunt.

199. "Obviously, you're not very good, are you?"

Chapter 8

How to Generate Even More Ideas

As a published author, I'm often asked: "Where do you get all your ideas?" I'm tempted to say that I have a secret deal with a little elf who visits me once a month (late at night, of course) and offers me a package of "New Ideas" for the discounted price of $19.95. But, I don't! Instead I tell them that there are tons and tons of ideas—most likely right in front of them—available for the taking. It's all about getting into an inventive frame of mind—a way of looking at the world with a vibrant sense of creativity—a way of generating publishable possibilities that will grab the hearts and minds of young readers.

In this chapter, I'll share with you some of the most innovative and dynamic ways to spawn ideas, lots and lots of writing ideas. These strategies have been used by some of the most creative people in the arts, industry, business, education, social work, and medicine. Most important, however, is the fact that they all have immediate and direct application for authors of children's books. Here you will discover an infinite variety of strategies that will produce an infinite variety of ideas. You'll find yourself mentally engaged in fostering ideas of every imaginable shape, size and color. You'll create more ideas than you'll ever use in a lifetime of writing. By the end of this chapter, you will have earned your P.H.D. (Plenty of Hot iDeas)!

Ready, set, generate!

1. The Leonardo Strategy

    It can rightly be argued that one of the greatest geniuses of all time was Leonardo da Vinci. Not only was he an accomplished inventor, but an equally skilled artist. His skill as a creative thinker was his ability to see things from the inside out, rather than the other way around. In short, Leonardo was able to break something down into its component parts (in his mind and before he began a project) and then build it (or draw it) by focusing on each individual element or component. Most of us, on the other hand, tend to look at the "big picture"—we are going to write a book, we are going to paint a portrait, we are going to create a banquet. Leonardo would reduce a situation, challenge or problem to its individual elements or parameters (factors). He would then list variations of each parameter and combine them. By coming up with different combinations of the variations of the parameters, he created new ideas.

This is best illustrated by a fantastic "idea generator" I refer to as "The Leonardo Strategy." It will literally generate thousands of new writing ideas every time you use it. Here's how it works:

1. Identify a general topic you would like to write about.

2. Separate the topic into several parameters or elements (I prefer about four to six). The parameters are the fundamental components of the topic (For example, if the topic is "Oceans" the parameters might be "Names of oceans," "Marine creatures," "Features," and "Events."). You can select the number and the nature of the parameters you wish to use.

3. Using the sample box below, list as many variations for the parameters as you wish (I prefer to list at least six variations for each parameter). The more variations you list initially will result in a greater variety of original writing ideas later on.

4. When you are finished listing variations, make random runs through the parameters and the variations of the parameters. Select at least one item from each column and assemble the combination into an entirely new concept. I like to use a single die and roll it to get a completely random set of combinations (For example, in the box below I rolled the die for the first column and came up with a "1" (Indian). I rolled the die again and got a "6" (squid) for column two; rolled it again and got a "3" (islands) for column three; and finally rolled it for a "2" (waves) for column four.)

Example: **"Oceans"**

	Name	**Marine Creatures**	**Features**	**Events**
1.	Indian	Coral	Trenches	Wind
2.	Atlantic	Whales	Seamounts	Waves
3.	Pacific	Sharks	Islands	Hurricanes
4.	Arctic	Tuna	Vents	Waterspouts
5.	Antarctic	Jellyfish	Tectonic plates	Tides
6.	North Sea	Squid	Plains	Currents

New Idea: The random combination of parameters ("Indian," "Squid," "Islands," and "Waves") inspired an idea for a chapter in a children's book (*Surprising Swimmers*, 1996) I was writing on twelve ocean creatures, each of whom swim in very distinctive and unusual ways. I needed something exciting to share with readers and my Leonardo Strategy lead me to discover information about the Fire Squid of the Indian Ocean. This creature has specialized organs that flash light in different colors—blue, green, white, and red. A school of them swimming just below the surface of the sea looks like an underwater (and very mobile) Christmas tree.

Here is what I find to be most interesting about this strategy: the plethora of possible writing ideas it generates. For example, if you look at the chart above you'll note that there are six alternatives for each of the four parameters. This would generate 1,296 possible different combinations ($6 \times 6 \times 6 \times 6 = 1,296$). Even if only 10% prove useful, that would yield 129 potential new writing ideas

The Leonardo Strategy works equally well in generating ideas for fictional stories and books. Take a look at this example:

Character(s)	Setting(s)	Time	Genre	Event(s)
Freckle-faced girl	Durango, CO	Saturday afternoon	Picture book	Discovers a strange object
An old homeless man	A run-down apartment	During recess	Historical fiction	Moves to a new town
Twin boys	A city playground	Midnight	Fantasy	Slips and falls
A cat with nine lives	A speeding train	As dawn breaks	Realistic fiction	Receives a letter
A boy afraid of the dark	A prison	Just before breakfast	Biography	Goes on a long trip
A sailor and a pelican	A swamp	Last night	Poetry	Loses a tooth

New Idea: After rolling the die five times the following parameters were identified: "A cat with nine lives," "a run-down apartment," "as dawn breaks," "picture book," and "slips and falls." This might inspire an idea for a story about an alley cat that constantly gets into all kinds of death-defying adventures, but always escapes. One day, just before dawn, it is creeping through a run-down apartment when it falls through a hole in the floor. It is trapped between some fallen timbers and begins to howl. An orphan boy walking nearby hears the sounds. He rescues the cat, nurses it back to health, and the two of them become fast friends.

With the options listed in the chart above you could (mathematically) generate 7,776 separate and individual writing ideas. Again, if only 10% of them prove to be useful, that's a staggering 777 new ideas (And, if only 1% prove useful, that's still an amazing 77 brand new ideas!). I think you'll agree that this strategy has the potential to provide you (as it does me) with an inexhaustible collection of writing ideas—enough to last several lifetimes!

2. What If

This is one of the most powerful idea generators I've ever used (We saw how well it works in Chapter 7). It simply requires that you place the two words—what if—in front of questions or situations you might normally pose. The process of "what-iffing" stimulates the brain to think in very divergent and creative ways. It also moves you away from a tendency to look for isolated solutions.

Insider Tip

Create new Leonardo charts every so often and file them away for future use. I try to create at least one new and very random chart every month. I collect all of these charts in a special file folder. When I need one or more new writing ideas, I just reach into the file, pull out one of the charts at random, roll the die and see what comes up. I'm never disappointed.

For much of our lives we are predisposed to look for a single solution to a single problem (e.g. What is 2 + 2?). We have been "brainwashed" to think that for every problem there is one, and only one, way to solve that problem. Unfortunately, that's not always the case. When we consider that there might be a multitude of potential responses to any problem, we break out of the "one-problem, one-answer" syndrome and begin to look for a host of potential solutions (and a host of potential ideas).

For example, I recently asked a group of elementary students to come up with as many possible solutions to the problem 2 + 2 = ? as they could. I did it by asking them this question: What if there was more than one way to record the answer to 2 + 2 = ?. Here are some of the responses they came up with:

- 6-2
- 2^2
- $\sqrt{16}$
- 1+1+1+1
- $(2 \times 1) + (2 \times 1)$
- ½ of 8
- 40% of 10

- the number of corners in a square

As you can see, these kids were not "boxed in" by the artificial requirement of finding a single right answer. Rather, they responded to a question beginning with the two words: "What if . . .?" The results, you must agree, were diverse, creative and quite inventive.

Here are two ways you can make this strategy work for you to generate a wealth of possible writing ideas:

Technique #1:

Make a list of popular stories, tales, legends, folktales or tall tales (e.g. *Little Red Riding Hood, Cinderella, Jack and the Beanstalk, Paul Bunyan*). For each one ask yourself a series of "what if" questions and see what kinds of creative ideas surface. For example, during a recent writing workshop, I asked a group of participants to generate a list of "what if" questions for the story "The Three Little Pigs." Here is a partial list of their questions:

- What if the story was "The Three Little Wolves?"
- What if all three houses had been made of bricks?
- What if the wolf had emphysema?
- What if the story took place in the city?
- What if the wolf kept kosher?
- What if there was an army of wolves?
- What if the wolves were all women?

Variation #1:

Do the same thing with several headlines from various sections of your local newspaper (e.g. What if hurricanes were common on the west coast of the US?).

Variation #2:

Just for fun, do some "what-iffing" with magazine advertisements from a popular magazine (e.g. *People, Sports Illustrated, Time, National Geographic, Good Housekeeping*) (e.g. What if there was a household product that would make a house dirtier?).

Variation #3:

Another variation of "what-iffing" is to use articles plucked from various magazines. Here are some "what-if's" I generated from an article about Ajijito, Mexico (where many American expatriates live) that appeared in an issue of an in-flight magazine:

• What if you lived in Ajijito, Mexico?

• What if you went into a restaurant where English wasn't spoken?

• What if you were taken to a Mexican hospital?

• What if you wanted to learn how to cook Mexican food?

• What if everyone in your school spoke Spanish?

• What if your town celebrated *Cinco de Mayo*?

• What if su escuela no es muy bonita?

As you can see, any one of those "what if" questions could be used as the stimulator for a possible story idea.

Variation #4:

You may want to do some "what-iffing" with a current mystery novel you are reading. What types of "what if" questions could you ask that would generate possibilities for a children's mystery book?

Technique #2:

I like to do some "what-iffing" with potential story elements. I do this by collecting potential features in each of three major elements of children's literature—Characters, Settings, and Themes. As I read children's books in the library or bookstore, I'll write down (in my ever-present writer's notebook) some of the characteristics of major characters, the various settings in which stories are set, and some of the major themes. For example, here is what I collected in one visit to my community library:

Characters	Settings	Themes
Shy girl	Amazon River	Loses a ring
Mother with two kids	Los Angeles	Discovers island
Orphan	Hawaii	Capsizes boat
Plant lover	Desert environment	Lives in a treehouse
Soldier	Winding river	Meets stranger
Explorer	Train	Learns to read
Five brothers	Beach	Sees alligator
Restaurant chef	Garden	Sets sail
Small monster	Haunted house	Finds a diary
Crab	Under a desk	Burps constantly
Lonely boy	Mexico City	Has a dream
Dolphin	Treetop	Breaks an arm
Two sisters	Arctic Circle	Mother dies
Granddaughter	Prison	Digs hole
Saguaro cactus	Playground	Picks strawberries
Fourth grade student	Rain forest	Laughs loudly
Moon	Deep canyon	Lands on Saturn
Cowboy	Prehistoric world	Saves a puppy
Mystery writer	Farm	Talks to ghosts
Doctor	Volcano	Makes a wish
Broken clock	Grocery store	Loses sight
Quilt	Underground cave	Walks in snow
Blind girl	Birthday party	Wins triathlon
Bully	Florida	Finds treasure

After I collected all these elements, I returned home and played a little game of "What if" with myself. I randomly selected one item from each list, placed the words "what if" in front of the three items and turned it all into a "what if" question. For example, here are a few I quickly generated from the chart above:

- What if a soldier was traveling on a train and met a stranger?

- What if a shy girl went to northern California to visit her aunt who lives in a treehouse?

- What if five brothers sailed up the Amazon River and discovered a new uncharted island?

- What if a mother with two kids moved to Hawaii and while on their first trip in a sailboat capsized their boat in a terrible storm?

- What if a restaurant chef in Arizona learned how to read at age fifty?

As you can see, the possibilities are endless. The trick is to keep reading lots of books and keep collecting lots of ideas in your notebook. I like to record the ideas on individual index cards and then mix and match them in various combinations, each combo prefaced with the two critical words: "What if."

This is the strategy I used for a children's book about elephants (*Elephants for Kids*, 1999). From a "Characters" list I had generated, I pulled the word "immigrant." From a "Settings" list I picked the word "Kenya." Finally, the phrase "remembers a lot" surfaced from the "Themes" list. I began to play around with some possible combinations of these three ideas and came up with the following idea: What if a story about elephants was told through the eyes of a recent immigrant from Kenya. In other words, instead of the usual informational book told in the third person, what if the story was told in the first person. As a result, the second paragraph in the book was as follows:

Sometimes my mother tells me that I have a memory like an elephant. I like that, because elephants are my favorite animals.

I went on to introduce the narrator of the story—Kwasi—a ten-year-old boy who recently moved to the United States from Kenya. He relates his family's experiences with elephants in his native country and also what he has learned in school about these magnificent creatures. "What-iffing" allowed me to generate a story idea and a new point of view that I may have otherwise missed.

Expert Quote

"The most successful children's book authors I've worked with keep their childhoods very close to them."

—Aimee Jackson, children's editor

3. Word Chains

Imagine a room full of mousetraps—each one set up and ready to spring. On the top of each mousetrap sits a ping pong ball. Now imagine tossing a tennis ball on top of the mouse trap in the middle of the room. The ping pong ball is sprung and flies over to another trap setting it off. The ping pong ball on that trap flies up and hits another traps. Eventually all the traps are being sprung and the room soon fills with a wild and crazy array of bouncing ping pong balls flying and zooming (pinging and ponging) all over the place. That's a chain reaction.

You can do the same thing in your mind to start a chain reaction of ideas. That is, one word can set off a reaction when it collides with another and another and another. The result is the creation of ideas that may be far different from the original word. Here's how to do it:

1. Randomly select a single word. It can be from a card file of random words you have been collecting over time. You can open a book or newspaper and just point to any word at random. Open the dictionary to, say, page 234 and point to any word. The object is to identify a random word not currently in your head.

2. Write down this key word on the far left side of a sheet of paper.

3. Start making a list of words—one after the other—that pop into your mind in connection with this word. Don't think about it. Just let the words flow spontaneously from your pen. Let one word trigger the other, and so on. Continue until you run out of words.

4. Read over your word chain and look at the last two or three words you wrote. Select one of those words and write down as many things as you can think of using that word.

Recently, I read a story about a ballet dancer. Afterwards, I wrote the word "ballet" on the side of a piece of paper and began a word chain. Here's what I came up with:

Ballet   Dance   Toes   Hurt   Practice   Hours   Costume
Leotards   Tights

I took the last word in my word chain and wrote it under the chain. I then brainstormed for as many related words and phrases as I could. Here's what I got:

> Tights
> Tightrope
> Tight times
> Tightwad
> Tighten a nut
> Tight lid
> Tight (slang—personally close)
> Tightfisted
> Tight-lipped
> Sit tight
> Airtight
> Shut tight
> Watertight
> Skintight

There was something about the phrase "tight times" that appealed to me. I began thinking about various times in American history when people had to live through tight times. That got me thinking about miners in the Old West who lived and worked in remote mining towns (the previous summer I had visited an abandoned mining town in Colorado). The more I thought about mining towns, the more I thought about ghost towns. I began work on a fictitious story (*Ghost Town*) that blended modern day tourists with late eighteenth century miners in the small town of Independence, Colorado (an actual ghost town in western Colorado).

From *ballet* to *ghost town* may seem like an enormous leap in logic, but the word chain strategy can help your brain produce a chain reaction that might not be immediately clear. It will certainly produce a wealth of possible writing topics.

Exercise: From the lists of words below, select one at random. Write it on the left side of a sheet of paper. Now, as rapidly as you can, write a chain of connecting words (try to get at least six to ten words in the chain). When you're done, list as many connections as you can for the last word in your list. Ready? Here goes:

4. Fishbowl

Here's an innovative way to generate tons of ideas. It takes a little bit of work to get it started, but after the initial work, you will find yourself in an avalanche of creative ideas.

Trunk	Slip	Pair	Calendar	Circus
Number	Canyon	Blinker	Card	Box
Clock	Press	Mouse	Party	Truck
Boat	Frost	Said	Tape	Touch
Face	Scarf	Poster	Dictionary	Run
Wallet	Eye	Slide	Single	Pair
Bear	Scare	Lumber	Coaster	Last
Blue	Disk	Leaf	Envelope	Stream
Camel	Sponge	Rack	Book	Fish
Date	Toast	Journal	Drink	Peak
Hill	Paper	Board	Pot	Fly
Swim	Coffee	Net	Drive	Comic
Dam	Berry	File	Bubble	Band
Smell	Sound	Pen	Round	Computer
Camera	Week	Pig	Apple	Flame
Shoe	Ink	Branch	Finger	Cap
Leg	Clear	Window	Frog	Tower

Go to a yard sale or used book sale and get an old dictionary. Work with family members to tear out random pages of the dictionary. Give each member of the family a set of scissors and invite everyone to haphazardly cut out words. Toss the words into a large fishbowl (which you've purchased from your local pet store or aquarium supply dealer).

Later, after the fishbowl is filled with words (you may wish to schedule several "dictionary cutting parties" to fill your fishbowl) draw out several at a time to see if any new strange, unusual or dynamic combinations emerge. You may want to do this as a way to "jump start" your brain each morning or as a method of generating a new idea for a book or magazine article.

This simple technique can produce insights and ideas that might not normally be possible when you sit down at your desk with a blank sheet of paper or a blank computer screen. You should continue to add words to the fishbowl on a regular basis. Before you discard any weekly newsmagazines or other periodicals you subscribe to, take a few minutes to cut out a set number of words (for example, fifteen new words) from each magazine and add them to your fishbowl.

I recently reached into the fishbowl on the corner of my desk and pulled out the following three words (all of which had been cut from random pages in an old dictionary): **important, noise, bantam**. Here's what I began to create with these words:

> A bantam rooster thought he was the best rooster on the entire farm. In fact, he thought he was the best for miles around. He could crow the loudest of any rooster around, thus he must be the most important rooster anywhere. The noise he made, however, soon caught the attention of a wandering fox. The fox, wise in the ways of the world, decided to visit the farm on which the rooster lived. After hearing the rooster, he hatched a plan that would fool the rooster and get him a delicious dinner, too.

This story starter didn't result in a new children's book, and that's O.K. What it did do was energize my brain to look at all sorts of possibilities—in short, to play around with a multitude of options. Besides, I often find this a unique way to keep my brain "limber" and active—ensuring that when I'm ready to create a new children's book that my brain cells are sufficiently "warmed up" for the journey.

5. Random Thoughts

Thumb through one or more old magazines or newspapers and select twenty-two objects or words at random. Here are some possibilities:

- Turn to one page in one magazine and point to twenty-two random words

- Select eleven random pages in a single magazine and select two random words or pictures on each page

- Collect eleven magazines (all with different themes). In each magazine, point to the first word you see on pages five and twenty, or pages eleven and forty-four, or pages twenty-five and ninety-nine.

- Randomly select six words from the front section of a newspaper, five from the sports page, six from the local section, and five from the entertainment section.

Now, make two lists of eleven items each on the left and right side of a sheet of paper. Number each list (beginning with the number two). Roll two dice and mark the word on the left-side list that corresponds to that number. Roll the two dice again and mark the word on the right side that corresponds to that number. See if you can use the two words selected to create a story, plot, theme, setting, character or potential scenario for a book or article. Here's a listing I recently used:

2.	Coffee	2.	Moose
3.	Island	3.	Calendar
4.	Board	4.	Soft
5.	Wind	5.	Lizard
6.	Blue	6.	Dragon
7.	Film	7.	Toothpick
8.	Hurricane	8.	Elementary
9.	Sadly	9.	Lightning
10.	Telephone	10.	Lake
11.	Cowboy	11.	Lug Nut
12.	Crescent	12.	Vacuum

I rolled my pair of dice and came up with the following combinations:

- 9 (sadly) & 6 (dragon): A story about a puny dragon who was abandoned by its parents. It is feeling alone and sad because it will never grow up to be a mean and fierce dragon. However, with the help of a little old lady, it eventually discovers its usefulness.

- 2 (coffee) & 8 (elementary): This book provides elementary students with the story of coffee: where it is grown, how it is grown, coffee producing nations around the world, and how much coffee is consumed each day.

- 3 (island) & 10 (lake): In the middle of a tropical island in the

South Pacific is a small lake in which an ancient treasure lies. Three adventurous souls set out to find the treasure, but get much more than they bargained for.

- 12 (crescent) & 4 (soft): Maria's father is a baker in New Orleans, Louisiana (The Crescent City). He is known far and wide for his outstanding cinnamon rolls, which are soft and filled with a secret ingredient that only he knows. One day Maria discovers what the ingredient is and shares it with her best friend.

- 11 (cowboy) & 2 (moose): Moose grew up in a family of cowboys in Wyoming. He was one of the biggest dogs anyone had ever seen. Everyone thought he was mean and fierce because of his size. But, he wasn't. In fact, he was actually afraid of cows until one day when the barn caught on fire.

You may want to do as I do and create various lists of words on a regular basis. I like to generate at least one new list every month. I keep old ones on file and add to the collection on a regular basis. This simple idea generator has produced an amazing assembly of viable and dynamic ideas.

6. Picture Portfolios

Pictures, photographs and illustrations can be used as wonderful "idea generators" whenever you're stuck for an idea. I like pictures simply because they energize the right side of my brain and get the creative juices flowing. I like to turn on that side of my brain before I work and then move my thinking over to the left side. I often discover I'm much more creative as a result.

One way you can fire up the right side of your brain is through the use of picture portfolios. Here's how I use them.

1. Obtain one of those plastic file boxes (they look like milk crates) from your local office supply store.
2. Put in a series of hanging files. Insert a file folder into each of the hanging files. You may wish to number each file folder or arrange them according to color.
3. Assemble a collection of old magazines (ask for the ones in your doctor's or dentist's office). Thumb through each one and

when you come to an interesting photo, picture, or illustration cut it out and place it into one of the file folders.

4. Do this for several pictures – randomly placing each one into a file folder. There should be no rhyme or reason for placing a picture in any folder. The only restriction is that a single file folder may not have more than ten pictures.

5. Keep working to continually add more pictures to your collection. After you have at least 100 pictures (ten pictures in each of ten folders) you can begin.

6. Select a file folder at random. Reach in and select one of the pictures at random.

7. Write down the topic, theme or possible title of the picture on a sheet of paper.

8. As with the strategy above, write down all the descriptive characteristics of the pictured item, place, scene, or object.

9. Use these characteristics as stimuli for various story ideas.

Example: I recently selected a page from a newsmagazine that was in my picture file. The page was an advertisement for a flashy red sports car manufactured by a well-known auto maker. As I looked at the picture I was able to generate the following words: speed, red, crimson, wheels, fast, fastest, cruise, vacation, coupe, sedan, convertible, sun, top down, wind in hair, speeding, picnic, ocean, beach, sand, dunes, and summer. I began to play around with some of the words and came up with a possible story idea:

> The twins were in Florida to visit their Grandma. Little did they know that as soon as they walked outside the airport in Sanford, they were being watched by a stranger in a bright red convertible. As soon as Sandy and Jason pulled away from the curb in the taxi, the stranger slipped in behind them. He followed them all the way up Route 4 and into Port Orange where Grandma Jean's house was. As soon as they pulled into the driveway, the red convertible slid over to the side of the road and stopped.

The success of this strategy lies in continually adding more and more pictures to your collection. The more pictures you have, the more possibilities you will be able to generate when you select one of those pictures at random at the start of each writing day.

Looking for even more ideas? Stay tuned!

Chapter 9

Ideas—They're All Around You!

After nearly three decades of writing children's books, I have discovered that some of the best ideas for stories are often right in front of me. Meet me on the street and you'll notice that I always carry a small notebook in my shirt pocket. In fact, I am rarely without that notebook, simply because I'm always on the lookout for new book ideas and new story possibilities. Even if I'm in the middle of a current project, I'm still looking for other potential projects down the road. For example, even as I write this sentence, it's 8:26 in the morning and I already have four possible topics for children's books recorded in my notebook. Here's what I have so far:

The Idea	Where it came from
The migration of Monarch butter-flies from Mexico to the US	An illustration of a butterfly on my coffee cup.
Breakfasts around the world	I had a fried egg for breakfast this morning.
Amelia, who loves spiders, creates a most unusual science fair project.	I saw a small spider scurry across the kitchen floor. The cat was apparently too busy to notice.
The lessons we can learn from trees	The leaves are turning on the tree just outside my office window.

You, too, may discover that some of your finest ideas for children's stories are, quite often, right in front of you. Here are a few places you may want to explore:

The daily newspaper (in print or online)

Believe it or not, I find some of my most interesting topics for children's books right in my local newspaper. Everything including headlines, display ads, photographs, Letters to the Editor, and editorials offer a daily serving of potential topics that will often turn into book topics.

For example, in 2004, a tsunami (generated by an undersea earthquake) swept through the Indian Ocean decimating shorelines and killing thousands of people. The headlines in our local newspaper (as well as those in newspapers around the world) shouted the news for several weeks after this devastating event. The human misery (entire families swept away, villages eradicated, homes disappeared) gave me the inspiration I needed to write *The Tsunami Quilt: Grandfather's Story* (2007), a fictional account of an actual tsunami that struck Hawaii on April 1, 1946. Shortly after the book was released, it was presented with The Storytelling World Award (2008)—a testament to the power of a local newspaper to inspire a book.

Yesterday I purchased a copy of one of the two local newspapers published in my town. Here are some of the headlines, ads, and photographs that were featured, as well as some of the potential ideas I hatched for future children's books:

Statement/Phrase	Context	Possible Book Idea
"Company unveils power line plan"	Headline	Nonfiction book on how power is generated (coal, nuclear, solar).
"Anna Mae, Ninety-Eight-Year-Old Yoga Master"	Display ad for a senior residence facility	Fictional story about a gang of senior citizens and how they face up to the town bully.
"Saving for what's next is important"	Display ad for a local bank	Fictional story about how Sybil has been saving her money for a new bicycle, but then she learns her best friend has cancer.
"Put more color into your life"	Photograph of a child in a multi-colored jacket	Fictional story about a child slowly going blind. What is the last thing she wants to see?
"Erector Set in original red box"	Classified ad	Nonfiction book on toys used in ancient societies (Egyptians, Romans).

Junk mail

I often discover many "nuggets" in the junk mail that arrives every day. A postcard about why I need a new set of windows might evolve into a story about how new windows in a young boy's house allows him to see relatives from the past. An envelope with an offer for life insurance may stimulate an idea about an ageless grandfather and how he remembers the names of his nineteen grandchildren. An ad about a sale at a local furniture store might generate an idea about Momma's favorite chair and all the stories she used to tell from that chair over a period of many years. Or, a flyer about the discounts available at the grocery store may create a story about how various foods make it from the garden or field to one's dinner table. What you discover in your mailbox can be a daily reminder of incredible writing opportunities or plot lines.

Talking with your local librarian

Whenever I do school visits, I always make a point to talk with the school librarian. I ask her or him about the topics kids are interested in reading or the subjects for which there may be few books available. I have discovered that school librarians have their fingers on the pulse of what kids read and what they are asking for. Their knowledge of what kids like in concert with their knowledge of what is available is an incredible resource. I have created two separate series of children's books, both of which emanated from conversations I had with school librarians. Contact the librarian at your child's school and develop an ongoing conversation with her/him and you may find yourself with a plethora of potential story lines—any of which could develop into a popular and successful book.

Talking with your child's teacher

If you have children in school, one of your greatest resources will be your child's classroom teacher. Not only will that teacher be up to date on the books and literature kids gravitate towards, but she or he will also be aware of the different authors kids admire the most. In your regular conversations with the teacher, make it a point to inquire about the reading materials and/or authors kids enjoy most. What are kids talking about in class, what book characters do they admire most, what kinds of stories (mystery, humor, nonfiction, etc.) stimulates their interests and consumes their time?

Talking with kids

A very simple way of getting new ideas is to talk with kids. Your kids, kids in the neighborhood, kids in your child's class, or kids you see at the local playground are all potential sources of information for book topics. If it's a nice Saturday, I'll take a book and visit a local park. I'll find a bench near a playground set and settle in to read for an hour or two. But, I'll listen carefully whenever any children swing on the swings, slide down the slides, or climb over the monkey bars. What do they share with each other? What do they say and how do they say it. What vocabulary or colloquialisms do they use? If I'm writing a lot of dialogue in my story, here is a good place to collect the terms, phrases, and sentences kids use most naturally.

Talking with other writers

What are some of the topics, issues, or challenges other writers are facing? Staying in touch with your local writing community can offer you some unique insights and equally unique writing topics. I've discovered that a conversation with a fellow scribe can help me stay current on popular topics, but just as important, can also keep me in the loop on the subjects and themes that others are addressing in their writing and whether some of those ideas might be appropriate for my consideration as well. Not only that, but regular conversations with other writers is both inspirational as well as incredibly supportive.

Exploring online communities

Finding inspiration and support can also be accomplished via several online communities. For example, LinkedIn offers a host of writing groups, support organizations, and instructional forums directed specifically at both novice and experienced writers. I've found that a few minutes perusing one of those groups can help me work through a mental block or a writing challenge with a new sense of creativity and originality. I've also discovered a few new ideas to add to my notebook.

Watching TV

The TV can be a constant source of inspiration and creativity. What shows are "hot" right now? What characters are talked about most around the dinner table? What are some of the most popular shows watched by your children or the friends of your children? What are the topics or subjects you are drawn to? What gets you excited, enthralled, or enchanted? Did you learn something new in a particular TV special that might be a topic for a future nonfiction book? Don't forget the videos you watch on YouTube or Netflix. What strikes your fancy; what keeps you glued to the screen?

Magazines

Pick up any magazine in your house. Open to any page, and I'd be willing to bet that there is a new book idea somewhere on that page. It might be part of an advertisement. It might be a sentence or a phrase somewhere in an article. It might be the caption for a photograph. Or, it might be the name of the magazine itself. Here are the names of some of the magazines my wife and I currently have on the family room coffee table and some potential children's book ideas that might result from the titles alone.

Magazine Title	Possible Book Idea
Time	Penny has an opportunity to travel back in time to any historical event. Which one does she choose?
Good Housekeeping	A book entitled "How to Clean Up Your Room and Impress Your Parents"
Atlantic	The similarities and differences between the Atlantic and Pacific oceans.
Sierra	High in the Sierra Nevada Mountains is a golden trout that has never been caught.
The Artist's Magazine	Benedict meets Vincent van Gogh and begins to see the world a little differently.

Children's magazines

One of the most lucrative areas for children's book ideas is children's magazines. Authors who write the stories and articles for these magazines know what children like to read and know what keeps them interested. Visit your local public library and look up current issues. What's included? You might also wish to ask the school librarian at your local school to save old issues of children's magazine and share them with you. Make these a regular part of your reading regimen and you will discover a cornucopia of topics, issues, characters, and stories sufficient to generate hundreds of new topics each year.

Daily walk

Something as simple as a daily walk can produce many new ideas for your writing. Keep your eyes and ears open and you might be surprised at all the things that would incite a new story. Here are just a few I found on my walk yesterday afternoon:

What I Saw	Possible Book Idea
A tall tree	What are some of the tallest trees in the world and where do they live?
An antique car driving past	Robert discovers an old car in his grandfather's barn. But, it was the letter in the glove compartment that truly amazed him.
A hawk flying overhead	Sports teams with animal names (Falcons, Bears, Tigers, Hawks)
An ambulance siren	Monroe's mother is rushed to the hospital with a heart attack.
A runner along the road	Alicia enters her first marathon and meets a deaf and blind runner.

It makes no difference whether you live in a rural area or an urban environment, you can put on a new set of eyes and ears every day and discover some topics that will keep your fingers dancing across your computer keyboard.

Vacations

One of the things I enjoy doing whenever my wife and I are on vacation is collecting travel brochures, visitor's guides, and other printed literature focusing on the places and sites we visit. I see many ads for restaurants, leisure activities, special events, sporting events, art and museum shows, cultural events, and all sorts of happenings geared for the tourist trade. Quite often, there will be the germ of a book idea tucked into all of those promotional efforts. For example, beside me is the current *Visitor's Guide for Ocean City, Maryland*, where my wife and I recently spent a long weekend with some very good friends. Here are a few items, display ads, articles, and promotions from that guide and the children's book topics that might result:

Item in the Visitor's Guide	Potential Book Topic
Best seafood restaurant in town	Everything you ever wanted to know about clams.
Parasailing adventures	The history of flight from a child's eye view.
Miniature Golf	The Seashore Miniature Golf attraction has a three-legged cat who can do silly tricks.
Condo rentals	What are all the different types of dwellings that humans live in around the world?
A Day in the Life of a Lifeguard	India's aunt decides to become a lifeguard.

During our visit, we took a long walk on the beach one day. Here are some of the things we saw or found along with some book ideas I generated as a result of those findings:

Discovered on the Beach	Book Idea
Seagull feather	How do birds fly?
Empty shell	A hermit crab searches for a new shell (a new home).
Piece of driftwood	How many different shorelines has a single piece of driftwood touched in its oceanic journeys?
Lighthouse	What would it be like to live in a lighthouse?
Old man fishing on the shore	A young girl and her father go fishing at the same beach every year for thirty-two years. Then, one year, he can't make it.

I usually discover that a visit to a new place resets my brain cells and help me create many new ideas simply because I'm seeing some new things for the first time.

Grocery store

Walk through a grocery store and you might be surprised how many potential book ideas jump right off the shelf. Just the other day I walked a clockwise circle just inside the four walls of our local grocery store and jotted down the following ideas:

Grocery Item(s)	Book Possibilities
Apple	An apple's "journey" from a tree in Washington state to an apple pie in Atlanta, Georgia.
Cheese	How is cheese made around the world?
Donuts	Honor's uncle owns the oldest donut shop in Los Angeles.
Shrimp	A hurricane decimates the shrimp industry in southern Louisiana.
Turkey	Alex makes a wish with a turkey drumstick and gets more than he bargained for.

Grocery Item(s)	Book Possibilities
Peanut butter	Franklin and his brother discover an ancient weapon on a peanut plantation in Georgia.
Ice Cream	How to make your own homemade ice cream (in only five minutes)

I have discovered that when my creative well is running dry, a quick visit to the grocery store will often provide me with an incredible variety of new ideas in every aisle. Look at a box of cereal, not as a breakfast item, but more as a stimulant for a children's book (e.g. What are traditional breakfast items eaten by children around the world?) and you might be surprised at all the topics waiting for you every time you venture out on a shopping trip.

I've learned that ideas can pop up at any time: in the doctor's office, in line at the grocery store, at a concert, while walking through the neighborhood park, or while at a movie. My job is to be ready for those ideas whenever they may appear. In essence, I don't just write when I'm at my desk in the morning, I'm prepared to write at almost any time of the day or night. Writers live, breathe, and exist to write. Ideas may surface at any time, any place. It takes discipline to be ready and waiting for them.

Indeed, some of my best writing has come, not necessarily when I'm sitting in front of the computer, but rather when I'm

    A. Eating sushi with a pair of chopsticks;
    B. driving Route 70 across Kansas;
    C. Hiking a mountain trail near Aspen, Colorado; or
    D. Pulling weeds in the garden.

I discipline myself to think "writing" wherever I am. Each of the four examples in the first sentence of this paragraph generated a future children's book:

    A. *Fearsome Fangs* (2002);
    B. *P is for Prairie Dog* (2011);
    C. *Mountain Night, Mountain Day* (2014); and
    D. *On One Flower* (2006).

I was sufficiently disciplined to recognize them as writing opportunities, jotted them down in my notebook, and worked all of them into successful books.

I've discovered that the key to *getting* lots of ideas is to be *ready* for lots of ideas. Ideas are all around you, you just have to be prepared to see them and record them. Wait—hold on a second!! I just glanced at a photograph of the Grand Canyon on the calendar over my desk. That reminds me of the time this past summer when my granddaughter and I zip lined over the Colorado River. Please excuse me, I think I have a story about an adventurous grandfather and his equally adventurous granddaughter.

Part IV

Children's Books and the Writing Process

Chapter 10

Genres and Formats

Walk into your local bookstore and you're likely to see a range of children's books: those with flaps to lift and wheels to spin all the way up to serious young adult novels about a transgender best friend or an alcoholic and abusive mother. To say that there is a wide diversity of books and topics available for children would be to understate the obvious. To say that, as an author, you have an infinite variety of opportunities to share stories with children would be equally obvious. Those opportunities come in two all-encompassing literary groupings: genres and formats.

Genres of Children's Literature

In children's literature, genre identifies books according to content. Most librarians and classroom teachers recognize eight basic genres (or categories) of literature (although there is always some degree of disagreement on the exact number). For our purposes, we will designate the following categories: Picture Books, Modern Fantasy, Traditional Fantasy, Biographies, Historical Fiction, Informational, Poetry, and Realistic Fiction.

It's important to note, however, that the eight genres listed above are not cut and dry. That is, a fantasy book may also be classified as a picture book. A biography can also be an informational book. A book of poetry can also be a picture book and an informational book. What is important is the fact that children's literature has a range of tastes for every reading appetite as much as it has an infinite variety of writing opportunities for prospective authors, such as yourself.

As a children's author, you may decide to concentrate on one specific type (or genre) of children's literature. While many prospective authors initially decide to focus on picture books, it's important to consider other genres as well. Most editors will tell you that they get an extraordinary number of picture book manuscripts and very few historical fiction or biographies. You can significantly enhance your chances for publication by considering genres other than just picture books.

However, before you decide on a specific genre in which to write, it would be very important to visit your local bookstore to obtain several books (by several different authors) in that genre. Also consider visiting your local library to ask about (and check out) recently released titles in a certain genre. What are some of the new historical fiction titles, modern fantasy, or informational books being published? These periodic and regular visits will help you stay abreast of the newest books published throughout the year.

For example, I am a frequent visitor to my local public library. About once a month I stop in to check out new titles and rediscover some familiar classics. The staff knows me by name and they have been extremely helpful in my searches for relevant books in a specific genre. I consider my local library an invaluable resource in my quest to write compelling and engaging books for kids. I sometimes tell the librarians that, "I'm here to scope out my competition," which, although rendered facetiously, has a good measure of truth in it.

Insider Tip

The internet has scores of book lists profiling the best books in each of the eight genres of children's literature. Here are some of the best sites:

- Children's Literature Web Guide: http://people. ucalgary.ca/~dkbrown/lists.html
- Children's Literature: http://childrenslit.com/
- Award Winning Children's Literature: http://www. dawcl.com/
- Carol Hurst's Children's Literature Site: http:// www.carolhurst.com/

For each of the eight genres below, I have provided you with some representative titles. You may wish to obtain these titles (as well as other recommended titles) at your own library or bookstore. Use the resources in the box above to identify additional titles for your review and reflection.

Picture Books

Picture books are defined by their format rather than by their content. I like to think of picture books as a marriage between text and illustrations. Each has to compliment the other; each has to enhance the other. These are books that offer a visual experience; books that can be read aloud by an adult who also shows the accompanying pictures; and books that can often be read independently by kids for their own pleasure.

Picture books may be of any genre, including poetry. They are unique because illustrations and text share the job of telling the story or teaching content. No other type of literature works in quite the same manner. Picture books come in a wide variety of sub-categories, including alphabet books, counting books, concept books (shapes, directions, colors), wordless picture books, beginning reader books, and board books (thick cardboard pages with an abbreviated story).

Some Popular Titles

- *Actual Size* by Steve Jenkins
- *Amelia Bedelia* by Peggy Parish
- *Freight Train* by Donald Crews
- *Ira Sleeps Over* by Bernard Waber
- *Officer Buckle and Gloria by Peggy* Rathman
- *Parts* by Tedd Arnold
- *Song and Dance Man* by Karen Ackerman
- *Strega Nona* by Tomie dePaola
- *Tops and Bottoms* by Janet Stevens

Modern Fantasy

Modern fantasy is distinguished from the other genres by story elements that violate the natural, physical laws of our known world. Another way of characterizing this genre is to say that these books are outside the realm of possibility. One of the basic responsibilities of authors in this genre is to convince the reader to temporarily suspend belief by creating a world that seems to be both logical and plausible. The most popular series of children's books in the world is the Harry Potter series—a classic example of the power of modern fantasy. By the way, as this book was being written, the *Harry Potter* books have sold more than 400 million copies worldwide. They made J.K. Rowling the world's first billion-dollar author.

Modern fantasy embraces six basic motifs: magic, other worlds, good vs. evil, heroism, special character types, and fantastic objects. In these books, readers discover mythical creatures, imaginary worlds, fanciful characters, and magical beings. Science fiction—a subgenre of modern fantasy—differs in that it has elements of scientific fact embedded in the story line.

Some Popular Titles

- *A Stranger Came Ashore* by Mollie Hunter
- *Charlie and the Chocolate Factory* by Roald Dahl
- *East* by Edith Pattou
- *My Father's Dragon* by Ruth Stiles Gannett
- *The Book of Three* by Lloyd Alexander
- *The Goose Girl* by Shannon Hale
- *The True Story of the Three Little Pigs* by John Scieszka
- *The Wings of Merlin* by T.A. Barron
- *Tuck Everlasting* by Natalie Babbitt
- *Watership Down* by Richard Adams

Traditional Literature

Traditional literature includes those stories told around ancient campfires and eventually passed down from generation to generation. They were a primary form of entertainment long before iPods and digital TV's. Born in the oral tradition, they come in many different shapes and sizes and include folktales, tall tales, fables, epics, myths, legends, and religious stories. Many of these tales begin with the four most wondrous words in the English language: "Once upon a time. . . ."

Traditional literature is distinguished by characters with special traits or abilities, simple plots, and traditional themes such as good vs. evil, love conquers all, and honesty is the best policy. Since they are part of our oral tradition, they often change and evolve over time. The original *Cinderella*, for example, has its roots in an ancient Greek tale (circa 7 BC). The first European version of the story was published in 1634. Interestingly, there are versions of this classic tale in almost every culture throughout the world, including (among others) Albania, Bulgaria, Argentina, Denmark, the Philippines, India, Ireland, Norway, Russia, Slovakia, and Thailand. Suffice it to say, traditional literature stands the test of time!

Some Popular Titles

- *Arrow to the Sun* by Gerald McDermott
- *Mufaro's Beautiful Daughters* by John Steptoe
- *One Grain of Rice* by Demi
- *Rapunzel* by Paul Zelinsky
- *Tales of Wonder and Magic* by Berlie Doherty
- *The Enduring Ark* by Gita Wolf
- *The Girl Who Loved Wild Horses* by Paul Goble
- *The Lion and the Mouse* by Jerry Pinkney
- *The Names Upon the Harp* by Marie Heaney
- *Why Mosquitoes Buzz in People's Ears* by Verna Aardema

Biographies

The word *biography* renders its own definition: *bio*, life; *graph*, writing. This specialized variety of nonfiction writing focuses on the lives (or part of the life) of famous or notorious individuals (your friendly author excluded). Good biographies are a deft combination of storytelling and nonfiction. They brings characters to life through a rich array of compelling vocabulary and equally compelling narration.

Typically, biographies are organized by either the careers of the individuals or some other factor responsible for their fame (or infamy). These individuals often served as role models for youngsters as they consider additional goals or occupational roles. The current emphasis on minorities and female figures underscores the immediate need for additional stories of typically under-represented social groups. Authors looking for an underserved genre would do well to consider biographies that offer positive role models for young readers of all genders and ethnic groups. Typically, biographies fall into one of four groupings: picture book biographies, simplified biographies, complete biographies, or partial biographies.

Some Popular Titles

- *A Boy Named FDR* by Kathleen Krull
- *Balloons Over Broadway* by Melissa Melissa Sweet
- *Joan of Arc* by Diane Stanley
- *John Lennon: All I Want is the Truth* by Elizabeth Partridge
- *Lincoln: A Photobiography* by Russell Freedman
- *Michelangelo* by Diane Stanley
- *MLK: Journey of a King* by Tonya Bolden
- *So You Want to be President?* By Judith St. George
- *The Life and Death of Adolf Hitler* by James Cross Giblin
- *When Marion Sang* by Pan Muñoz Ryan
- *Woodsong* by Gary Paulsen

Historical Fiction

Historical fiction must, of course, be set in the past. The main characters generally are fictional, although they often rub shoulders with historically prominent people. Sometimes the story's focus is not on events in history, but rather on a wholly imaginary plot that is accurately set in a particular period and place from the past. These books blend authentic historical facts and settings with some imaginary characters and equally imaginary plots.

Historical fiction brings history to life through the eyes of a major character or through the detailed explanations of an event, period, or situation. By definition, the story is set in a time period not experienced by the author. Interestingly, children tend to remember (and appreciate) history when it is presented in the form of a good story (after all, just look at the last five letters in the word "History."). These books are also memorable because, unlike a textbook, history is seen through the eyes of a young protagonist, rather than through the eyes of a professional historian or academician.

Some Popular Titles

- *A Single Shard* by Linda Sue Park
- *Alphabet of Dreams* by Susan Fletcher
- *Chains* by Laurie Halse Anderson
- *Crispin: At the Edge of the World* by Avi
- *Elijah of Boston* by Christopher Paul Curtis
- *Paperboy* by Vince Vawter
- *Prairie Songs* by Pam Conrad
- *Roll of Thunder, Hear My Cry* by Mildred Taylor
- *Shadow Spinner* by Susan Fletcher
- *So Far From the Bamboo Grove* by Yoko Kawashima Watkins
- *The Slave Dancer* by Paula Fox
- *The Tsunami Quilt: Grandfather's Story* by Anthony D. Fredericks

- *Tiger, Tiger* by Lynne Reid Banks
- *With a Name Like Love* by Tess Hilmo

Informational Books

Informational books (also known as nonfiction) provide young readers with scientific or documented facts. They also offer current and accurate knowledge about something found in our universe. The information in them is verifiable, which is the key word in defining an informational book. Everything in an informational book can be documented in published sources like books or magazines, in original sources such as letters and journals, or from firsthand, observable facts.

Informational books in "the good old days" were nothing more than compendiums of dry facts—encyclopedias of mindless data and uninspiring details. Today, informational books combine the best elements of fiction and nonfiction to share compelling stories or riveting experiences. These are storytelling ventures—dynamic wordsmithing that actively engages youngsters in a topic of interest. This genre is one that weaves story with facts to create books that motivate and inspire.

Some Popular Titles

- *An Extraordinary Life* by Laurence Pringle
- *Candy Bomber* by Michael Tunnell
- *Courage Has No Color* by Tanya Lee Stone
- *Desert Night, Desert Day* by Anthony D. Fredericks
- *Fooled You* by Elaine Pascoe
- *Leonardo's Horse* by Jean Fritz
- *Locomotive* by Brian Floca
- *Mummies Made in Egypt* by Aliki
- *One Night in the Coral Sea* by Sneed Collard
- *Shipwreck at the Bottom of the World* by Jennifer Armstrong
- *The Great Race* by Gary Blackwood
- *The Mysterious Universe* by Ellen Jackson

- *The Snake Scientist* by Sy Montgomery
- *We Are the Ship* by Kadir Nelson

Poetry

Children have a natural affinity for poetry, which is exhibited (before they enter school) by their love for nursery rhymes, jingles, and childhood songs. This type of literature introduces children to the rhythms of language—the ways in which words work together to tell a story—or the fun that can be shared when certain patterns of language are demonstrated to kids. Poetry is an artistic expression of language and the beautiful ways in which that language can be shared.

What children like about poetry relates to their early childhood love for poems that are heavily rhymed and straightforward in meaning. Undoubtedly, you remember several Mother Goose rhymes and nursery rhymes from your childhood. Why did these poems/songs stay in your memory for so long? Simply because they sparked an appreciation for the joyfulness of language. That rhythmic, humorous verse builds a love for poetry in general and can also be used as a bridge to more sophisticated and traditional literature.

Some Popular Titles

- *A House is a House for Me* by Mary Ann Hoberman
- *A Light in the Attic* by Shel Silverstein
- *Dance With Me* by Barbara Juster Esbensen
- *I Heard a Blackbird Sing* by Aileen Fisher
- *Joyful Noise: Poems for Two Voices* by Paul Fleischman
- *Mojave* by Diane Siebert
- *Omnibeasts* by Douglas Florian
- *The New Kid on the Block* by Jack Prelutsky
- *Where the Sidewalk Ends* by Shel Silverstein
- *Yes, We Are Latinos!* by Alma Flor Ada

Realistic Fiction

Realistic fiction (sometimes referred to as "contemporary realistic fiction") tells a story that never happened but *could* have happened. The events and characters of contemporary realistic fiction flow from the author's imagination, just as they do in fantasy. Unlike fantasy, which includes at least one natural law, object, or circumstance not found in this world, everything in contemporary realistic fiction is possible. Many of these stories are based on current events and feature children as the central characters.

Besides picture books, realistic fiction is one of the most popular genres in children's literature. That's simply because realistic fiction is about the lives of those reading it. It talks to them in a language they understand and about events they may have or could have experienced. These books often present real-world problems and conflicts and how a young person solves those issues. The implication is that the reader, too, can take charge and solve her or his own problems. These books are most frequently written as chapter books.

Some Popular Titles

- *Because of Winn-Dixie* by Kate DiCamillo
- *Frindle* by Andrew Clements
- *Hatchet* by Gary Paulsen
- *Holes* by Louis Sachar
- *Maniac Magee* by Jerry Spinelli
- *Shiloh* by Phyllis Reynolds Naylor
- *The Great Gilly Hopkins* by Katherine Paterson
- *The Present Tense of Prinny Murphy* by Jill MacLean
- *Waiting for Normal* by Leslie Conner
- *Where the Red Fern Grows* by Wilson Rawls

Formats of Children's Literature

In the section above we discussed the eight basic genres of children's literature. Here we will take a look at the six formats of children's books;

that is, the various ways in which a book is presented or produced. A book's format is usually based on its intended reading level or designated age level. For example, the first format presented below, board books, is designated for the youngest of children. However, it could encompass any of the aforementioned genres. A board book could be a book of poetry, an informational book, a picture book, or realistic fiction. By the same token, a young adult novel could be a historical fiction tale, a modern fantasy, or a biography.

Suffice it to say, as a prospective author you need to consider the genre in which you will specialize as well as an appropriate mode of presentation (or format). What is the best age level for your book? What format will allow you to address your subject or topic in the best way? If, for example, your book is a biography, for what age is it intended? These are all questions you may need to answer before you set pen to paper or before you begin manipulating the cursor across your computer screen.

Board Books

These books are short, compact, and small. Using heavy cardboard (to reduce wear and tear), these books are intended to be read to young children (birth to age two) by their parents. They are infrequently used in elementary classrooms and are specifically designed for a one-on-one reading experience, typically at home. The word count may range from five to fifty words.

The story is quite simple—often told with isolated words and extremely simple sentences ("The cat saw the mouse."). Colorful illustrations predominate, with words taking a secondary position.

Some Popular Titles

- *Brown Bear, Brown Bear, What Do You See* by Bill Martin, Jr.
- *The Little Mouse, The Red Ripe Strawberry, and The Big Hungry Bear* by Don and Audrey Wood
- *The Escape of Marvin the Ape* by Caralyn Buchner
- *Mrs. Wishy-Washy's Scrubbing Machine* by Joy Cowley
- *Up Dog* by Hazel Hutchens

Picture Books

This category of children's books is the most well-known as well as the most misunderstood. That's often because it is both a genre as well as a format. As a format, these books are typically thirty-two pages long and can include anywhere from 50 to 1,000 words. They encompass all the genres of children's literature and represent some of the best known children's authors: Dr. Seuss, Eric Carle, Maurice Sendak, Bill Martin Jr., and Lois Ehlert (among many others). These are authors who have created classics that have continued to sell for many years.

As mentioned earlier, the illustrations in a picture book are just as important as the words. Both must convey rich visual images in the mind of a young reader. Typically geared for youngsters ages three to eight, these books are standards in family libraries and are also stalwarts of reading programs in elementary classrooms from coast to coast.

As a format, picture books often fall into three very broad categories. Concept Books present a concept such as the alphabet, shapes, numbers, families, or colors. Story Books are the most popular type of picture books. These have a complete story with a beginning, middle, and end. For most stories there will be a central character, a conflict, and a resolution. Novelty books have flaps to lift, windows to open, pop-up figures to find, and textures to touch. While popular with young readers, they are not often found in public or school libraries due to their "destructibility."

Some Popular Titles

- *Amelia Bedelia* by Peggy Parish
- *Under the Moon* by Dyan Sheldon
- *Olivia* by Ian Falconer
- *The Woman Who Married a Bear* by Elizabeth James
- *Knuffle Bunny* by Mo Willems

Early Readers

These books are designed primarily for children who are beginning to read. They may be designated as read-aloud books—books that adults (parents and teachers) read aloud to one or more children—or read-alone books—stories written at a level that encourage independent reading by a child.

Most early readers have between thirty-two and forty-eight pages and use between 500 to 1500 words. They are often "leveled;" that is, the difficulty level is in accordance with established age-appropriate guidelines or educational standards in terms of word usage and recognition. Repetitive phrases and controlled vocabulary are often features of these books. The sentence structure is typically straightforward with a simple plot line.

Early readers often follow a cumulative pattern with a new idea or sentence added to previous ideas or sentences to build a complete story by the end of the book. You may be familiar with stories such as *I Know an Old Lady* and *The Green Grass Grew All Around*—excellent examples of this format. I've used traditional songs and rhymes for several of my early reader books including *Near One Cattail: Turtles, Logs and Leaping Frogs* (2005), a book that uses the cumulative rhyme scheme of *The House That Jack Built*:

> Sunbathing turtles on a moss-covered log
>
> Bask in the warmth of this mug-muggy bog,
>
> Neighbors to frogs with big bulging eyes,
>
> Who whip out their tongues to capture some flies,
>
> Within a rich land, all swampy and green,
>
> Creatures abound in this waterlogged scene. (Fredericks, 2005, pp. 12-14)

Some Popular Titles

- *First Grade Takes a Test* by Miriam Cohen
- *Spark* by Kallie George
- *Uncle Elephant* by Arnold Lobel
- *Henry and Mudge and the Great Grandpas* by Cynthia Rylant
- *Nate the Great and the Hungry Book Club* by Marjorie Sharmot

Chapter Books

Chapter books are designed for children who are independent readers. The vocabulary is still controlled, but the plots may be somewhat more sophisticated and detailed. Most chapter books have between three and six chapters along with a minimum of illustrations. These books often evolve into popular series such as *The Babysitter's Club* and *The Magic Treehouse* series.

The stories designed for chapter books may be either fiction or nonfiction. Each of the chapters may be self-contained or may build upon each other to create a story with a defined beginning, middle, and end. Most often the stories are about contemporary issues or themes directly relevant to the lives of the youngsters reading them. Dialogue is used in these books more so than in picture books or early readers. Chapter books are essentially "first novels" for children ages six to ten.

Some Popular Titles

- *Matilda* by Roald Dahl
- *Because of Winn-Dixie* by Kate DiCamillo
- *Stuart Little* by E.B. White
- *The Adventures of Super Diaper Baby* by Dav Pilkey
- *Flat Staley* by Jeff Brown

Middle Grade Books

Geared for children in grades three, four, and five, these books deal with persistent issues all kids face during this time in their lives. Divorce, family problems, bullying, friendships, school problems, and sibling rivalry are typical issues that fill the pages of these books. There's usually lots of conflict (but always a resolution) and the themes can range from historical fiction to fantasy.

These books take many different approaches to their subject matter— from the downright humorous to the intensely serious. In all cases there is some issue or problem to be solved, and it is always solved by the main character (never an older adult or parent). Those of us who can relate to (or remember) the angst of this age level can often create some of the most memorable stories for this group of readers. Word count for these books ranges from 20,000 to 55,000 words and they are typically organized into longer and more detailed chapters than is the case with chapter books.

Some Popular Titles

- *Freckle Juice* by Judy Blume
- *Frindle* by Andrew Clements
- *How to Eat Fried Worms* by Thomas Rockwell
- *The Cricket in Times Square* by George Seldon
- *Dear Mr. Henshaw* by Beverly Cleary

Young Adult Novels

These books are the most sophisticated of all, often addressing themes or topics that may seem to be more "adult" in nature (e.g. murder, sexual encounters, death, abuse). The language is often stylish and urbane, reflecting the thinking and comprehension of pre-teens.

The word count for young adult novels ranges from 55,000 to 80,000 words. They are always conflict-driven with a well-defined protagonist and a deeply emotional issue to confront and solve. Rarely are illustrations used (with the exception of graphic novels) and the vocabulary is more adult in tone and usage. What some adults may designate as "offensive vocabulary" (swearing, sexual euphemisms, racial slurs) is often part of these stories. Many of these books cross over into the adult market and are frequently purchased, not by their intended audience, but by adults themselves.

Some Popular Titles

- *The Outsiders* by S.E. Hinton
- *The Giver* by Lois Lowrey
- *The Fault in Our Stars* by John Green
- *The Book Thief* by Markus Zusak
- *The Maze Runner* by James Dashner

As you will discover, there are some genres and formats more popular than others. That is to say, many beginning children's authors will concentrate on certain genres and formats more than others. For example, many novice writers will draft picture books simply because that seems to be the most visible and recognizable genre/format when they visit a local bookstore. Truth be told, that is also the genre/format editors see most often; the bulk of the manuscripts they review are in this category.

Other authors, in order to evade the "crowd" of picture book manuscripts on an editor's desk, will concentrate on under-represented genres and formats. These would include picture book biographies (focused on people of color and females), informational (science and nature) early readers, and realistic fiction (contemporary issues such as bullying, sexual orientation, and race relations) middle grade books.

But, be careful here! Don't choose a genre or format simply because it is under-represented. Choose it because it is your passion, your interest, and your desire. You'll write a better story as a result. And a better story will always grab the attention of an editor—much more so than a thinly drafted (and forced) manuscript in one of the less popular categories. My rule of thumb: always write for a passion, not for a category.

Insider Tip

Some authors identify the genre and format of a book before they begin writing. Others (like myself) write the story first without regard to its genre or format, working more on its presentation, than its designation. There is no best way to begin. Over time, and with lots of writing under your belt, you'll determine your own style. Know that there are multiple ways of approaching the writing process— yours will evolve, just as mine has, with the more books read, and the more manuscripts drafted.

Chapter 11

Beginning Your Book: The "How To's"

Writing a good children's book, as you know by now, is not as simple as sitting down at your computer, throwing 800 or so words down on the screen, and sending the whole thing off to a publisher. What constantly amazes me, after nearly four decades of professional writing is that I and every other writer in the universe draw from the same dictionary of words, use all the conventional rules of grammar, and apply all the essential dictates of good literature. And, yet, some writers can take those ingredients and create a literary feast with her/his arrangements, while others create verbal mush. Suffice it to say, writing a book that will grab the imagination and interest of a young reader is much more than stringing some simple words together, it is both an art and science of knowing an audience and how to satisfy their intellectual and/or emotional needs.

As children's authors, we can all grow and develop; we can all improve our writing skills such that youngsters will flock to our books and embrace our characters. That, as you know, does not come about overnight—or in a couple of months. Like a great pianist performing Beethoven's concertos or an actor taking on the role of Hamlet, it comes about through constant practice, commitment, and determination. It also comes about through a workable plan of action—a dedication to a sequence of inviolable steps that move you as a writer from concept or story idea to completed manuscript.

So, how do you ensure that your story is crafted logically and deliberately? With an outline. No matter if you are writing fiction or nonfiction, an outline helps you organize the elements of your story into a workable plan. But (and this is a very big "but"), know that an outline is both flexible and malleable; it's not something set in concrete, but rather an elastic plan of action constantly subject to changes, modifications, and adjustments as the writing process progresses.

Here is a potential "plan of action" for your own outline.

Suggested Strategy

A. Capture an idea. Select your own idea or use one of the prompts or creative options outlined in Chapters 8 – 10. [Fiction & Nonfiction]

B. Draft a theme statement (main idea) as described below. Can you encapsulate your entire story in a ten to fifteen word sentence? [Fiction & Nonfiction]

C. Create a main character. Create a visual image in your mind and then write down all the descriptive words to identify who that character is in terms of personality and temperament. Think about people you know (children and adults) or who you were as a child. What words would you use to describe those individuals? "What are some words or phrases that character would use? What would she/he say? [Fiction]

D. Provide a conflict for your character. What issue or problem will she/he face? This is critical for any fiction story. [Fiction]

E. Decide on how the conflict will be resolved. What will the character do that will solve a puzzle, finalize a decision, or settle a contradiction? This is also critical. [Fiction]

F. Develop a plot for your story. A plot is simply a general sketch of how the story will develop from beginning to end. Don't try to write the entire story at this point; rather, use words, phrases, and random sentences that demonstrate the movement of the plot from a beginning to an end. As an example, here is how I began to draft the plot for my book *The Tsunami Quilt: Grandfather's Story* (2007):

> Grandfather + Kimo are friends → annual trip to Laupāhoehoe → quiet time → "The ocean gives, but it also takes" → Grandfather dies → Kimo asks father about Grandfather's secret → story of April 1, 1946 tsunami → Grandfather and his brother → destruction by third wave → trip to tsunami museum → tsunami quilt → Grandfather's younger brother → trip to monument → father & son together watching surf

Insider Tip

Start your writing process by crafting a one-sentence main idea (theme) of your book before writing anything else. This main idea will help you focus specifically on the basic theme of your book. For practice in writing these statements, you may want to take some of your favorite children's books and write a main idea statement as it may have been initially written by the author. This practice will help you write a similar statement for your book. Here are a few examples of potential theme statements that could have been drafted by selected authors in advance of writing their books:

- *Thunder Cake* (1997) by Patricia Polacco—A grandmother makes a special cake to help her granddaughter overcome a fear of thunder.

- *Officer Buckle and Gloria* (1995) by Peggy Rathman—When Officer Buckles gets a new police dog, his safety lectures become much more interesting.

- *The Wall* (1990) by Eve Bunting—A father and his young son have come to the Vietnam Veterans Memorial to find the name of the grandfather the little boy never knew.

You'll note that, even at this early stage of my writing, a definite conflict and resolution began to surface. The conflict was the secret that grandfather never told anyone and the resolution was the grandson's (Kimo) discovery at the museum that one of the tragic deaths during the 1946 tsunami was his grandfather's younger brother. That conflict/resolution was absolutely critical to this story as it is for any children's book.

A very wise writer (nope, it wasn't me) once said that there are only three basic plots in children's books. No matter what you write or how you write it, you'll undoubtedly use one of these in crafting your tale:

- Survival—This is the instinctive drive of both humans and animals. Examples include: *Julius, the Baby of the World* (1995) by Kevin Henkes and *Jumanji* (1981) by Chris Van Allsburg.

- Love and friendship—As humans, we seek and give love in many different ways. This element also includes the dynamics of friendship between individuals. Examples include: *Frog Goes to Dinner* (2003) by Mercer Mayer and *Strega Nona* (1979) by Tomie dePaola.

- Achievement—We all want to succeed in several different aspects of our lives. It can something as simple as doing a chore or something more complex such as being recognized with a major award. Examples include: *Miss Rumphius* (1985) by Barbara Cooney and *One Grain of Rice: A Mathematical Folktale* (1997) by Demi. [Fiction]

G. At this point in your story development, you want to make sure you have the three basic elements of any good book: a beginning, a middle, and an end. While this may seem obvious to anyone who has ever read an engaging novel or captivating book, it is still a challenge for many writers— particularly writers of children's books. Writing an anecdote, a stream of consciousness tale, or a "slice of life" story doesn't qualify as sufficient for a children's book. Yet, many novice authors commit this cardinal sin. [Fiction & Nonfiction]

Let's take a look, in a little more detail, into these critical elements. To illustrate, I'll use sections of my book *The Tsunami Quilt: Grandfather's Story.*

1. The beginning of any story is where you introduce your main character. The character can be introduced to the reader via narration or dialogue. This is also the time when you want to set up some sort of conflict or problem that the main character will have to solve. In most cases,

your main character will be someone who is similar in age to that of the reader. As a result, you want to be sure the problem is well within her or his capacity to solve. Don't have your nine-year-old main character try to overthrow a cartel of drug lords in a major metropolitan area. It just won't work. Here's an example from *The Tsunami Quilt* where the main character (Kimo) is wondering about his grandfather.

> Grandfather had been a fisherman all his life. He told me stories of the sea and ancient Hawaiian legends. Every weekend, he and the other fishermen would gather to 'talk story' about the ocean. Sometimes I got to listen. The April visit to Laupāhoehoe was the only time I ever saw him so quiet.

2. The middle of your story is where your main character tackles the problem. Here is where you also want to add a series of events that will eventually build to some sort of dramatic moment. Although every writer will have her or his own style of writing, I have often found it advantageous to write the middle of my story last. That gives me the opportunity to set up the problem (beginning) and decide how that problem is eventually going to be resolved (end). Then, I have the story "bracketed" on both ends. The bulk of my writing will then be centered on the middle portions—those parts where significant details are added, the character(s) are engaged in one or more events, and the action is moving at a suitable clip. Here's one of the critical events in the middle of *The Tsunami Quilt*:

> "Is that the reason for the marble monument by the cove?" I asked.

> "Yes. On that monument are etched the names and ages of the children and teachers who lost their lives that day."

> "So that is why Grandfather and I visited Laupāhoehoe each years?"

"Yes, Kimo, but there is something more you must know."

3. The end of your story is where a resolution to the problem or conflict occurs. It is important that this ending be a "satisfactory" one, not something contrived ("Just then Josh found the missing piece, put everything back together, and they all lived happily ever after.") or an abrupt ending simply because you're getting close to your word limit for the book ("The sun was setting so Belinda crawled into bed and went to sleep."). The following paragraph from *The Tsunami Quilt* is the second to the last one in the book. It sets up the final actions of the main character (Kimo).

> The next day was April 1. My grandmother made a beautiful lei of plumeria blossoms and placed it gently around my neck. I rode with my father to Laupāhoehoe. He eased the car down the winding road to the peninsula and we parked in the grass near the small cove. In silence, I walked over to the marble monument and up the stone steps. I removed the lei from around my neck and gently placed it on top of the monument. As I did, I heard my grandfather's voice, "The ocean is both friend and foe. It gives, but it also takes."

H. Now that you have a basic outline, a conflict and resolution, and a beginning, middle, and end for your story, it's time to begin adding the details and dialogue that make a story a story. What are some of the specific actions the main character will participate in? What are some of the things she or he will say that will either describe her/him or move the action along? At this point (remember, you are still working on your first draft), don't try to write the perfect story. All you want to do now is get some thoughts down on paper - the refinement of those thoughts will come during succeeding drafts (*see* Chapter 12). [Fiction]

I. Consider the descriptive words you will use to identify, describe, and highlight the main character. Who is that character and what is her/his personality that will engage the reader? How will the reader identify with this character? Keep in mind that we often learn a lot about a book character through his or her dialogue. What characters say and how they say it gives us, as readers, a great deal of information; often more than a whole bank of adjectives. Here's some dialogue by the Grandfather in *The Tsunami Quilt*. You'll note that I didn't use adjectives to describe him, but rather wanted readers to infer his character by the words he used [Fiction]:

> "When you are older, Kimo, I will tell you the story of this sacred place," Grandfather promised each year. "You'll learn why it is a place of tragedy and a place of remembrance. For now, know that the ocean is both friend and foe. It gives, but it also takes."

J. By this point in your initial draft you will have settled on a point of view. That is, who is telling the story? You'll note in all the examples relative to *The Tsunami Quilt*, that the point of view that evolved was first person (Kimo, the central character, told the story from his perspective). This point of view worked best for me simply because of the poignant aspects of the tale. I wanted readers to sense the emotionality of the events and felt that could best be accomplished if they happened directly to the narrator. Of course, I could have written this book in the third person, but it wouldn't have had the same affective sway. [Fiction]

Your Personal Checklists

Here are two checklists for you to use after you've completed your first draft. Select the one (Fiction or Nonfiction) most appropriate for the story you are writing. Check either "YES" or "NO" after each statement. For those statements for which you have checked a "NO", please consider how you will address that element in your initial draft before moving on to your formal revision process (*see* Chapter 13).

Fiction

	YES	NO
1. I have identified a major character.		
2. I have a conflict in place.		
3. The initial language and vocabulary is appropriate for the designated age.		
4. There is a beginning, middle, and end.		
5. There are several different settings.		
6. I have written the main idea (plot) of the story.		
7. The chronology of the story seems to be logical.		
8. The main character resolves the conflict (rather than adult).		

Non Fiction

	YES	NO
1. All the facts have been carefully researched.		
2. There is a logical sequence of information.		
3. There is a link between readers' background knowledge and the facts.		
4. I have included stories and anecdotes.		
5. As appropriate, there is some human intervention.		
6. The book is written as a story, not an encyclopedic entry.		
7. Appropriate vocabulary has been used.		

You have now completed your initial or first draft of your story. There's still a lot of work to do, which we'll cover in the next chapter, but you now have a basic outline: a framework that ensures that essential story elements are included in a logical pattern.

Insider Tip

Kid's Book Revisions (www.kidsbookrevisions.com), run by celebrated children's editors Eileen Robinson and Harold Underdown, offers an eclectic and all-encompassing list of editorial services. Through their site, you can take workshops and webinars (topics range from picture books to novels), obtain their newsletter, join a Facebook group, access revision resources (books and web pages), and sign up for intensive individual manuscript tutorials. This site is ideal for both children's and YA authors.

For What Age?

A persistent question that always arises during the creation and drafting of a story is, "For what age should I write this book?" It's a valid query. Oftentimes, it's complicated by two other equally perplexing questions: "Should I decide to write for a particular age group and then come up with an idea that fits them? Or should I decide to write a story or article about a particular idea, then choose the age group right for it?"

Actually, the answer is that either response is OK. That is, you could decide, before even writing a single word, that the appropriate age for your story was eight years old (for example). Then, you could write a story that uses eight-year-old vocabulary and an eight-year-old plot, and an eight-year-old character. Or you could go ahead and write your story, get it all down on paper, and then stand back and look it over to determine if (for example) your book about a shy and reluctant girl who raises a dragon by hand is appropriate for eight-year-olds to read. Or, would it be more appropriate for a twelve-year-old reader? In short, there's no single right answer to this eternal question.

That said, I'm going to suggest something a little different; something I've found to be quite successful. To be honest, it is the reason why I put this topic at this particular place in the chapter. That is, let the story determine its own appropriate age range or grade level. How? By going through the various stages of your initial draft (as outlined above) you will be able to get your basic ideas down on paper. Then, it's time to stand back and carefully read what you have. I like to read this first draft aloud in front of a mirror to see what kinds of words I'm using, what kind of plot I have developing on the paper, and how sophisticated (or not) the story is in terms of vocabulary level, intensity, conflict complexity , and character depth.

Since kids prefer to read about characters their own age, how old am I imagining this particular character to be? If I'm writing a first person story as told by a seven-year-old girl, then it is very likely that I have a story geared for seven-year-olds. If I am writing a story with short sentences, brief paragraphs, and less than 500 words, then it is likely that I'm writing a tale geared for Kindergarten and first grade students. And, if I'm crafting a tale about a romantic relationship gone wrong, then it would seem that I have a book that would be most appropriate for middle level readers.

In short, I've found that the story itself (not me) often determines its appropriate age range. For example, when I began crafting the first draft for *The Tsunami Quilt* I had no idea the age level it was destined to be. But, as I completed the first draft I saw that I had a boy (Kimo) who was asking a lot of questions, who was perplexed and confused about part of his family history, and who had strong emotions for his grandfather. Those factors told me that the most likely age for the main character— and thus the audience who would read this book—was approximately eight or nine years old.

The table on the next page offers some ideas about the topics and issues appropriate for specific age ranges. Please use this as a guide, not an unbreakable plan, as to suggested topics for specific ages.

Category	Age Range	Fiction Elements	Non-Fiction Elements
Infancy/Toddler	birth – 3	Families, playtime, toys, rhyming, songs, lullabies	Families, education topics, the five senses, daily routines
Preschool/Kindergarten	3 – 5	Predictable stories, repetitious stories, animal characters, friendships, families, nonsense tales, imagination	Animals, colors, shapes, letters, sounds, counting, self-development
Primary	5 – 7	Sports, friendships, school, familiar characters, fantasy, make-believe, surprise endings, multicultural stories, mystery	Animals, nature, environment, humor
Middle Grades	8 – 11	Friends, sports, danger, mystery, adventure, school situations, dramatic situations, drugs, raging hormones, fantasy, peer group, science fiction, historical fiction	Science, nature, sports figures, biographies, humor
Young Adults	10 and up	Mysteries, romance, science fiction, horror, fantasy, sexual attraction, moral and social issues, historical fiction	Self-concept, science, famous people, natural disasters, mysteries, biographies, history

Here are three recommendations that will help you determine the most appropriate age or grade for the book you want to write:

1. Get to know kids as much as possible. Listen to your own kids, listen to their friends, listen to the conversations they have with each other. Visit a park, a public library, or a local family restaurant. What do kids talk about, how do they interact with

each other, and what kinds of vocabulary do they use? Key in on the differences between the language used by younger kids and that used by older kids. Jot down notes or parts of conversations in a notebook and indicate the approximate age of the kids who spoke those words. Which words or expressions are you most comfortable in using in your book? Those words will determine the best age range for your story.

2. I know I'm going to repeat myself here, but this is important (please see Chapter 4). Read lots of children's books. Read books at various age ranges—books for primary kids as well as books for young adults (and everything in between). Look at how different authors handle the language in those books. Which language do you lean towards? Which phrases or colloquialisms are you most comfortable with? By reading a plethora of children's books you will also be exposing yourself to a wide variety of language and language patterns. One of those patterns will seem "just right" for you and just right for your story.

3. You may turn up your nose at this suggestion; but, consider watching TV programs geared for kids. Programs on Saturday morning, Animal Planet, or on Nickelodeon. What kids of vocabulary do kids at a certain age use? What are some typical words, phrases, or colloquialisms? Take a look at popular videos on You Tube Kids. Make notes on the vocabulary and phrasing used in those productions.

Now, we're ready to get into the real "nitty gritty" of writing—the revision process!

Chapter 12

Revision: The Author's BFF

There were more than 300 youngsters in the auditorium at Tully Elementary School in Tully, New York. I had just finished a slide show sharing my life as an author, some of the books I had written, the kinds of research I did as an author, where I got all my ideas, and some forthcoming projects. It was now time for the Q&A portion of my presentation. Scores of hands shot into the air—everyone wanted to ask "the author man" a question. I initially called on a third grade student who was waving her arm so wildly I was sure it would fall off if she continued any longer.

"How long does it take to write a book?" she inquired.

It's a query I get asked over and over again whenever I do school visits. And, according to other children's authors who also make frequent school visits, it's one of the most common questions asked of every writer. And, the reaction to my response is usually quite predictable.

"It usually takes me anywhere between one and two years to write a book," I respond.

A wave of disbelief sweeps over the audience. Eyeballs expand into saucers and mouths expand into large cavernous openings. They are shocked and amazed. Their minds are thinking, "How can it take so long to write a book that's only thirty-two pages long. Either he's the dumbest writer on the planet (a fact I'll not argue), he has absolutely no idea how the English language works, or he needs to sit in mean old Mr. Hendrickson's class for a few days and he'll really know how to write."

Since this is an expected reaction to my response, I go into some detail as to why the authorship of a book is such a long process. It's called revision. I'll tell kids that when I write a book I usually need from twenty-five to thirty drafts of that book before I have the story down perfectly. I'll change or eliminate words, I'll restructure limp sentences, I'll eliminate weak nouns and unnecessary adjectives, I'll throw out entire paragraphs, and I'll tweak, adjust, and modify words over and over again until I have a manuscript that is worthy of being read by a child. In short, I won't send a book out into the world until I feel it is my absolutely best work.[6] Anything less and I'm just cheating my readers (as well as getting a lot of editors very angry).

When I share my need and reasons for revision during school assemblies, I always look to the back of the room where all the teachers are sitting. A collective smile crosses all their faces and several are silently applauding. For most of those teachers, this is the one element of writing instruction they wrestle with the most. Many students (elementary and secondary) are content to scribe a single draft of a story, turn it in, and declare that it's perfect as it is. "Why should I revise it?" they ask, "I got all the words down on the paper and put them all into complete sentences." Instructing students on the value of revision remains a constant challenge for most teachers.

Expert Quote

"I am not a writer. I am a rewriter."

—James Thurber, author

In June of 2015, my wife and I took a long-anticipated journey to Redwoods State and National Park in northern California. We had planned a week-long sojourn in and amongst these towering and majestic arboreal behemoths. With the Best Western Hotel in Eureka as our base

---

6. Several years ago, I was conducting a Writer's Workshop for a class of fourth graders in Pickerington, OH. One of the students asked me the following question: "Have you ever wanted to revise any of your books after they have been published." It was a great question and I thought about it for a while. I responded as follows: "Yes, all of them!" He was both shocked and surprised, but I continued. "You see, writing is always a process, never a product. That is to say, every piece of writing can be improved—whether it is a first draft or a completely published book. I would imagine that almost every writer with a book on the New York Times Best Seller List would agree that there are portions of their work that could be improved with some additional revisions, just like my books and what you are writing right now." Here's another way of thinking about it: Revising is never about creating a perfect piece of writing, but is always about creating a better piece of writing.

of operations, we set out each morning for a new area of this expansive series of parks to walk the trails, take hundreds of photographs, and admire the vistas. We were amazed by these titans - botanical kings soaring skyward in splendid groves tucked into verdant valleys and along sinuous trails. It soon became evident to me that there was a children's book waiting to be written about these magnificent organisms.

Upon my return home, I began some serious research about redwoods. In my travels through my local library and across the internet, I discovered a most amazing fact: Until the late 1980s, redwoods were thought to be so tall that no animals could possibly live in there high branches. It wasn't until a small group of brave adventurers ascended these towering giants that a previously unexplored world of creatures was discovered. There, more than 200 feet above the ground, were unique habitats for many animals typically found on the forest floor.

Thus was born the idea for *Tall Tall Tree* (2017).

I began writing the first draft in July 2015. Draft after draft followed throughout the fall and winter of 2015 and well into the spring and summer of 2016. Each draft was an improvement on the previous one; each draft better clarified the information, tightened up the vocabulary, and smoothed out the rough spots. During that time, I consulted a thesaurus. I stood in front of the bathroom mirror and read passages aloud to check on the rhythm and cadence of the materials (an action that absolutely intrigued my cat). I crossed off words, re-added them later, and then crossed them out again. I shortened some sentences and made others a little longer. I threw away entire paragraphs and then fished through my wastebasket to find them again. I created multiple folders in Microsoft Word and added and deleted files almost every week. Week after week and month after month, I would add and subtract, add and subtract. Finally, after twenty-four separate drafts, I submitted the manuscript to a publisher.

After several weeks of waiting, the manuscript was accepted for publication. I signed the contract and steeled myself for what I knew would happen next—more editing. Over the course of the next several months, my editor and I went through an additional twenty-seven drafts (if you're counting, that's a total of fifty-one drafts). This is when we made sure every single scientific fact was accurate, every word was absolutely precise, the rhythm of the rhyming text was spot on, and every sentence was engaging. It was also during this time that the artist was creating his illustrations for the book.

Finally, in March 2017, the manuscript was complete; we had a finished product. The book went into its final production stages, was sent overseas to be printed, and was then shipped to the warehouse in preparation for its delivery to bookstores and online distributors. Finally, in September 2017 (twenty-seven months after its original conception) the book was released to the public. Was all of that revision necessary? Allow me to answer that question with a five-star review posted on Amazon.com:

"When I asked my grandson to rate the book, he said without hesitation '100 stars.'"

Yup, all that revision was worth it!

It's been said that writing is all about revising and rewriting. The first words and ideas you put down on the page will not be your best, nor will they necessarily be the final words in your book. They are, quite simply, your first words. I always consider the first draft as a visual representation of what's inside my head: it is the ideas, thoughts, and concepts in my head recorded on paper (or a computer screen). It may be nothing more than a random and haphazard collection of words, sentences, and (rarely) paragraphs. It's without form, messy, and frequently chaotic (When I was an elementary teacher, I would tell my students that this first draft was our "Sloppy Copy."). It is from this jumble of disorganized and messy thoughts that a book will arise.

What makes a book a book is the level and intent of revision you put into it. Putting the words down on paper is just a first step (a critical first step, to be sure). It's what you do with those words that will spawn a book that parents, teachers, and the kids themselves will want to read— hopefully over and over again. To that end, I would like to offer you a plan of action helpful in making this rewriting productive and efficient. This plan has been used by many writers (myself included) to create manuscripts that grab the attention of an editor and propel an idea into a published book. However, you are encouraged to adjust and modify this plan according to your own preferences and/or work habits; do not follow it blindly, rather you should adapt it to the types of books you plan to write and the dictates of your own writing habits.

The plan looks very much like an inverted triangle:

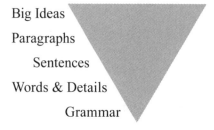

Big Ideas

Paragraphs

Sentences

Words & Details

Grammar

With an inverted triangle, the biggest part is at the top, and the shape gets progressively smaller the further down you go. A revision plan is just the same, the biggest parts are at the top (or beginning) and the smaller parts—the details—are at the bottom (or near the end of the process).

Phase One (Draft One)

This is the "Big Kahuna"—your first draft. This is what I shared in the previous chapter (*see* Chapter 11). Essentially, here is where you get your basic ideas down onto the computer screen or legal pad. Just like what we discussed earlier, your primary objective at this initial stage is to get all the "stuff" about the story out of your head and into your computer. The point is not to write the entire story, but just to create and record some thoughts, concepts, and words.

This is simply the first stage. Don't try to write a complete story—a dazzling story—an amazing story at this juncture. You'll frustrate yourself if you do! Sketch out ideas, throw in some words that may or may not work, decide on a name for your character, get the simple basics of a plot down on paper. Don't worry about perfection, spelling, grammar, vocabulary, punctuation, capitalization or any of the standards "rules" of writing. This is, after all, your "sloppy copy"—the first time you've put your thoughts into some kind of sequence. Nothing more, nothing less!

Phase Two (Drafts Two to Five)

In my next draft (number 2) I try to bring some order to what I've created in the first draft. I turn words into sentences and sentences into paragraphs. This is where I try to set up some sort of organization to my project. I'm not worried about grammar, spelling, capitalization, or punctuation (they will come much later), but rather I'm focused on injecting some sense into what I have on paper.

In this stage, I also concentrate on the development of a complete story—a beginning, a middle, and an end. In my first draft, I am concerned with getting the ideas in my head written down. Now, I need to discover some cohesion among those ideas. I know some ideas will survive and others won't. Perfection is not my goal here, identifying what works and what doesn't is.

Something that often surfaces in these early drafts are "Nowhere Ideas;" that is, ideas that seemed to be good when they were rolling around in my head, but turned out to be nothing more than vapid thoughts with little content or substance. Giving a character a super power ("able to leap tall buildings in a single bound") sounded pretty good when it rolled around in my head, but turned out to be very stupid when it was recorded on a computer monitor. During this phase, I need to get rid of a lot of the junk that often surfaces in the initial drafting process.

Which brings up another point. Many writing experts note that during the early stages of writing, most authors bloat their story (most sentences are distended by ten to twenty percent), adding way too much information, over-described characters, inflated plots, and lots of verbal garbage. Often referred to as overwriting, I simply let it happen in these early stages. I'm OK with it because I want to get all those ideas out of my head and recorded. I know that some of the ideas will eventually be discarded, but at this stage, I don't want to put any brakes on the creative process.

Phase Three (Drafts Six to Ten)

By this point in the writing process, I have the semblance of a story. If I'm writing a fictional story there will be a character; a beginning, middle, and end; a conflict, and a resolution. If the book is nonfiction, there will be a sequence to the information provided, an appropriate amount of research suitable for the designated age level will be included, and there will be the usual beginning, middle, and end.

Insider Tip

Check out www.wattpad.com, an online writing and reading platform where people post their stories in progress—stories still in the drafting stages. It's a great way to build an audience for your work and get some feedback along the way.

Now is when I read the story out loud. I'll either read it into a mirror or into a voice recorder. I'll listen for the pacing, the rise and fall of action, the sounds of various words, and the rhythm of the sentences. There's no specific pattern I'm looking for; it just has to "sound right." I realize that that is a subjective judgement on my part, but I've taken the time to read a plethora of other children's books prior to the creation of this new story, so good patterns of writing are already embedded in my head. I need to answer the question (to my own satisfaction), "Does this sound right?"

Invariably, there will be many sentences that have no "punch" or action. Others will sound trite and hackneyed. Still others will sound flat and lifeless. Now is the time when these sentences have to be changed. Now vocabulary has to be injected, characters have to be specifically described, and factual information has to have a certain flow to it.

I also need to know that the story makes sense. Does one action logically flow into another? Does the character do things in a predictable manner? Does the resolution of the conflict make absolute sense? Does the plot move along in a smooth and constant pace? For the most part, I'm looking for consistency. If the main character is tall at the beginning of the story, does she keep her stature at the end of the story? If the monster is downright ugly at the beginning, he shouldn't become unnaturally pretty at the end.

Phase Four (Drafts Eleven to Fifteen)

Now is when critical and descriptive vocabulary is inserted. What words have I used in previous drafts that need to be changed, improved, or eliminated? I focus on each and every word to ensure that the right word is in the right place at the right time. This is the stage where I fine tune the language. It makes no difference whether the story is fiction or nonfiction, the vocabulary must be accurate, precise, and very specific. Unlike writing for adults, there is a limited number of words (roughly 1,000 for a picture book; 50,000 for a YA novel) that can be used. Now is when I look at each one of those words to be sure it is the exact right word at that point in the book.

One of my guidebooks at this point in the writing is the *Children's Writer's Word Book* (2nd Ed.) by Alijandra Mogilner and Tayopa Mogilner (2006). This resource provides word lists grouped by grade, a thesaurus of listed words, and reading levels for synonyms. For example, it is here where I learn that "run" is a Kindergarten-level word. If I'm writing a book for fourth and fifth grade readers, I might decide to use a vocabulary word more in their reading level: a word such as "flee," "gallop," or "sprint." By the same token, I may be writing a nonfiction nature book for early readers (K-1) and inadvertently insert the word "pilot" into a description of dolphins. A check of the Mogilner book reveals this word to be more appropriate for fifth grade readers. A more suitable substitute would be the word "guide."

A cautionary note is in order here. Never "write down" to your audience. Is it appropriate to use words above the vocabulary level of your intended audience? A resounding "YES!" There are some words that work simply because they sound right. There are other words that work because they convey a specific feeling or specific tone—no other words work in their place. Here's the point: don't let the intended reading level of your story dictate every word you use in that story. It's more important that you have the right words (rather than just the readable words) in your story. How will you know if a word is the right one? It will sound right because you heard it in some other story you read or because it just *feels right*.

Here's an example from one of my children's books. *Desert Night, Desert Day* (2011) is a nonfiction book profiling diurnal and nocturnal animals that live in the Sonoran Desert. As I was drafting the manuscript for this book, I knew two things: A) The book would be geared for kids in Kindergarten and first grade, and B) the book would be used primarily as a read-aloud story; one read to kids by parents, teachers, and librarians. Here's one of the stanzas from the book:

Leaping, popping,

Seldom stopping.

Tiny rats—

Hip, hop, hopping.

The word "leaping" is designated for a third grade reading level; in other words, above the reading level of the audience for whom this book was intended. But, I wanted to use this particular word for several reasons. It had the right rhythm for this stanza (there are four gerunds [-ing words] among the nine words), the word was actually defined by its association with other related words (popping, hopping), and it had the two syllables I needed to ensure that the first line had four beats. It also opened the door for parents and teachers to use the word as part of a formal or informal vocabulary lesson ("Wow, look, here are two words that mean exactly the same thing: *leaping* and *hopping*! Why do you think the author did that?").

Phase Five (Drafts Sixteen to Twenty)

We're getting into the "nitty gritty" of the manuscript—beginning to fine tune it, looking for precise detail and exact language. Changing small bits and pieces so that everything comes together into a cohesive whole.

I sometimes refer to this stage of the writing process as my "Eagle Eye" stage. I am careful to observe every single detail in the story, making sure to examine each and every element from something as complex as the logical sequence of actions, to something as simple as what word do I need at the end of sentence number twenty-seven?

Here are some of the items you may need to focus on:

- If the story is fiction, does the plot work? Is there a conflict along with an accompanying resolution? Is the beginning, middle, and end of the story obvious? Does the plot move along at a sufficient pace?

- Are there adequate transitions in your story? A transition is a "bridge" that connects one part of your story to another. They provide an orientation to both time and place. For example, if some time has passed you need to tell the reader, "later that afternoon." On the other hand, if the setting has changed, the reader need to know that, too ("Jeremy jumped down from the monkey bars and dashed to the fence.").

- Is the main character well described? Can readers get an image of the character just through the words? Keep in mind that most characters are defined by the dialogue they use. What is the character saying? Is what she/he is saying in agreement with their personality? What do we learn about the personality of the character through her/his words?

- If the book is nonfiction, are the descriptions and explanations told in story form? Is the vocabulary exact and precise? Is there a logical sequence to the description(s)? Does everything make sense?

- Be sure you "show, don't tell." This is the one inviolable rule of good storytelling. Don't fall into the trap of telling your readers everything, show them through the actions of characters. Look at every adjective you've used: are there too many, is each one necessary, or can some of them be eliminated? (NOTE: Most writers tend to use far too many adjectives in their writing.)

- Make sure the tense you select is consistent throughout the story. Since many stories are told in the past tense, make sure all your verbs are also in the past tense. One of the most common mistakes new writers make is to (unintentionally) combine two tenses (for example, past and present) in their manuscript. Here's an example: "Polly ran along the edge of the playground, and now she is beside the softball field."

- Check carefully for an active voice throughout both your fiction and/or nonfiction manuscripts. Passive voice really slows down your story and distances the story from the reader. Always work to ensure an active voice in both dialogue and action. Here's an example:

    Passive: "The ball was thrown by LaTisha to the catcher."

    Active: "LaTisha threw the ball to the catcher."

- This is also a good point to check the variety of sentences you included in your manuscript. Readers, as well as listeners, enjoy a variety of sentence types—everything from simple sentences to compound/complex sentences to long and short sentences. A variety of sentence types keeps the attention of the reader/listener and makes your writing livelier.

Phase Six (Drafts Twenty-one to Twenty-five)

This is where you really get "nit-picky" with your manuscript. It's where you deal with the traditional mechanics of good writing—things like spelling, grammar, capitalization, and punctuation. And, while we're on the topic of spelling, here's a very friendly word of advice: the one pet peeve of every children's editor, the one item that frustrates them most of all, and the one thing that will send your manuscript right into the trash can, is bad spelling. Trust me on this one, there is no excuse for poor spelling, and poor spelling has doomed more would-be writers than any other element of the writing process. ALWAYS double-check, triple-check, quadruple-check, quintuple-check . . . your spelling. Trust me, a misspelled word is the first thing a reader will notice on your manuscript, and the first thing that will send the manuscript into the trash bin. Spell it right.

Here are the mechanics you'll need to check during this phase:

- Is every word spelled correctly? Don't rely on your word processing program's spell checker. Most don't know the difference between "Two," "To," and "Too." But you should. If you're not sure how a word should be spelled, look it up.

- How is your grammar? Are you using correct grammatical conventions? Again, don't over-rely on your word processing program to note the differences between good grammar and poor grammar. If you're not sure, ask a friend, a former English teacher, or check out www.grammarly.com, which is a sophisticated software program that can help you with grammar issues.

- Are you using the correct punctuation? Are there enough commas or too many commas? Does every sentence end with a period, question mark, or exclamation mark? Are apostrophes in the right places (and do you know the difference between possessives and contractions)? Did you use ellipses (three periods indicating a pause)? Are quotation marks used for every line of dialogue?

- Be sure to check your capitalization. Does every sentence begin with a capital letter? Are proper nouns, such as names (John Henry), holidays (Thanksgiving), and specific places (St. Louis, MO), capitalized?

Here's something you may have noticed. All of the mechanics of writing were saved for the end of the writing process. The reason for that is quite simple. At the start of writing, we want to concentrate on the big picture (the top of the inverted pyramid). We want to focus on the creative energy necessary to generate a dynamic story *and* the time necessary to record that story on paper or a computer screen. If we were to concentrate on items such as spelling, punctuation, and capitalization early in the writing process, they would have a tendency to curb our creative energy and focus our attention on little things at a time when we need to concentrate on larger issues such as plot, characterization, and setting. Save the mechanics (spelling, grammar, capitalization, punctuation) for the end; you'll discover a considerably improved manuscript as a result.

Insider Tip

If you're looking for some references to consult on the mechanics of writing, you can't go wrong with these:

- *Words into Type* by Markorie E. Skillin, et al (1974)
- *The Chicago Manual of Style* (2017)
- *The Elements of Style* by William Strunk Jr. and E.B. White (2016)
- *Garner's Modern English Usage* by Bryan Garner (2016)
- *McGraw-Hill's Proofreading Handbook* by Laura Anderson (2006)
- *Copyediting and Proofreading for Dummies* by Suzanne Gilad (2007)

Phase Seven (Drafts Twenty-six to . . .)

We're almost there. This is the time when I leave my desk and find another location in the house (e.g. basement, garage, front porch, guest bathroom) to carefully read my manuscript. I enjoy the new location simply because it puts my mind into a new frame of thinking. Once again, I can look at my story with some different eyes and certainly a different perspective.

This is when you want to read the manuscript out loud and quietly; when you want to read it fast and read it slow; read it while sitting down and while standing up; read it inside and read it outside. Put yourself in as many different situations and settings as you possibly can. Look at your story from a variety of angles and a variety of perspectives. Do you have the same level of excitement now that you're at the end of the writing process that you had when that story first germinated inside your head? Is it still full of action, adventure, insight, meaning, and emotion now that it's been fully fleshed-out and recorded?

Or, have you discovered that the story you intended was not the story you wrote? That's OK. Like me, you may discover that what you wound up with was not what you initially envisioned. You may find that your final manuscript doesn't have the rhythm and pace necessary to engage kids (or impress an editor). Maybe you need to put that story inside a file folder and carefully slide it into your file cabinet to "mellow" or "percolate" for a few more weeks or months.

You may want to share your story with friends and relatives for their critical reactions. But, be careful, those folks will often tell you what you want to hear, rather than what you need to hear. Because they are your relatives or friends, they will say things like, "Wow, Uncle Pete, this is the greatest story since that Harry Potter guy entered Hogwarts Academy and made bushels of money for his author." Instead, what you may need to hear is something like, "You know, Uncle Pete, the plot is a little trite and the character seems to be thinly drawn. Perhaps it needs just a little bit more work. But, I'm still in the will, aren't I?"

Insider Tip

Fee-Based Editing Services

If you are interested in professional editing services, you may wish to contact the companies listed below. Each of these reputable firms will assign your manuscript to a professional—one who has extensive experience in reading and publishing children's books. As you might imagine, fees vary among these companies, so before you send off your manuscript, you would be wise to do your research and select the services (and attendant costs) that best meet your needs.

- **Children's Book Editors and Illustrators** (www.childrensbookeditors.com): Editors skilled in children's books also understand the basic elements of good fiction—character, conflict, plot, theme, setting, and dialogue. A children's book editor can make sure that you have strong verbs, vivid adjectives, and language that lends itself to reading aloud. So, whether you've written a picture book, a chapter book, or a young adult/middle grade novel, they can help you polish all these elements while ensuring a fun, engaging read.

Insider Tip (cont.)

- **Kirkus Reviews (www.kirkusreviews.com/ editing-services):** Kirkus offers three options to accommodate varying timelines, needs, and budgets. They only use editors who have worked on books published by the top publishers in the United States. An editor must prove her or his ability to provide thoughtful, productive feedback; show exceptional attention to detail; and exhibit expert knowledge of grammar and mechanics.

- **ServiceScape (www.servicescape.com/services/ editing/childrens-book):** ServiceScape's children's book editors can help you refine your manuscript so that it is ready for publishing. Their editors will correct grammar, spelling, punctuation, or syntax errors and will also attend to any factual errors, inconsistencies, or contradictions.

Check Them Off

Listed below are two checklists you may find helpful during the processes discussed above. As you go through the editing process, you may want to check off the essential ingredients of a good children's book using either of the charts below. If you discover some "blanks" at the end of your editing, then it may be appropriate to go back into the sequence of steps and determine where an essential component might be addressed.

Fiction

Element	Description	Addressed?
Style and Language	Style is how a writer manipulates language in order to create a story. What words are chosen, how are those words arranged, and how are the various lengths of sentences are all involved?	YES ☐ NO ☐
Character	Is the character believable and identifiable to a young reader? A dancing moose may not be believable; a girl in a wheelchair is.	YES ☐ NO ☐
Dialogue	Does the dialogue sound natural?	YES ☐ NO ☐
Plot	Plot is the plan for the story; it's a conflict and how the conflict is resolved.	YES ☐ NO ☐
Pacing	How quickly or slowly does the story evolve?	YES ☐ NO ☐
Continuity	Does each of your characters behave consistently throughout the story?	YES ☐ NO ☐
Setting	This involves not only where the story takes place, but also when it takes place.	YES ☐ NO ☐
Tension	Tension is key; it's what sustains interest in how a conflict is resolved.	YES ☐ NO ☐
Passiveness	Do you use an active voice (not a passive voice) throughout the text?	YES ☐ NO ☐
Emotional Reality	This is the essential "connection" between the reader and the plot. The story may be fiction, but the emotion must be real.	YES ☐ NO ☐
Mood	This is the "atmosphere" of a story. Is it scary, funny, sad, or emotional in some specific way?	YES ☐ NO ☐
Point of View	This is the position taken by the narrator. Is it told by the main character (first person) or is it told by someone outside the story (third person)?	YES ☐ NO ☐
Theme	This is the story's central idea or main idea. It is typically a one-sentence summary of the entire plot.	YES ☐ NO ☐

Nonfiction

Element	Description	Addressed?
Style and Language	Just as with fictional stories, the words chosen and how they are used to convey information are critically important.	YES ☐ NO ☐
Compelling Details	Are the facts interesting and engaging or does the document read like an encyclopedic entry?	YES ☐ NO ☐
Sequencing	Does the sequence of information make sense? Is the date in a comprehensible order (simple to complex, for example)?	YES ☐ NO ☐
Fascinating Comparisons	How does the information relate to the child's previous experiences? Making those relationships is essential in quality nonfiction.	YES ☐ NO ☐
Run-on	Are there run-on sentences or sentences that are overly long?	YES ☐ NO ☐
Unusual Viewpoints	This is often what reaches out and grabs readers' attention. Is the book about something I've never considered before?	YES ☐ NO ☐
Redundancy	Is there evidence of redundant information or language?	YES ☐ NO ☐
Variety	Do you use a variety of vocabulary, terms, and phrases?	YES ☐ NO ☐
Language	Have you eliminated clichés, "purple prose," inflated vocabulary, or "puffy" words?	YES ☐ NO ☐
Personalized Content	Does the book offer a new or different perspective on a topic?	YES ☐ NO ☐
Accuracy	How accurate are the facts and figures presented throughout the book. Has each fact been verified?	YES ☐ NO ☐
Point of View	This is the position taken by the narrator. Is it told by the main character (first person) or is it told by someone outside the story (third person)?	YES ☐ NO ☐
Theme	This is the story's central idea or main idea. It is typically a one-sentence summary of the entire plot.	YES ☐ NO ☐

Final Point

While the plan above has seven phases and suggests more than twenty-five drafts, please don't accept this writing outline as your personal gospel. It is an outline that has worked well for me and many other children's authors. You, on the other hand, may have a different philosophy or different style of working. You may find elements of this plan to be redundant or unnecessary. That's OK. The more important issue is that, as a writer, you need a working plan—a personal writing strategy that will engage you and keep you moving forward. That plan will help ensure that the revising of your manuscript is both systematic and dynamic. It will equally ensure that your writing is part of an evolutionary process that will help you continue to grow and develop as a successful children's author.

Expert Quote

"Revision is what helps you actually recapture some semblance of that first, dazzling vision, which you then lost when you tried to get it down on paper."

—Jane Yolen, children's author

Chapter 13

How to Format Your Manuscript

Just for a moment, let's assume you are in charge of the Human Resources Department at a large company. One of your major responsibilities is to hire people to work in your corporation. Not only do you have to post positions as they become available, you also have to read through stacks of résumés and applications to select the most qualified individuals to interview. Then, you have to schedule all those interviews, draft appropriate questions, talk with several prospective candidates, and finally select the one individual who best meets the requirements of the position. Because you work for a large company, there are many positions to fill and much of your time is devoted to this seemingly non-stop responsibility.

Now, let's assume it's a Monday morning. You've just arrived for work and sitting outside your office is an applicant waiting for his 9 o'clock interview. He has applied for a job with a $150,000 starting salary and is one of several people scheduled for interviews this morning. You immediately notice how he is dressed:

> He is wearing a faded and frayed purple hoodie with an illustration of a skull and crossbones on the front. He is also sporting a pair of jeans that haven't been inside a washing machine since the Reagan administration. There are patches on the left leg and a long tear across the right knee. Yellow paint adorns the left side and the cuffs are adorned with silver bells. He wears an old pair of muddy tennis shoes with both laces untied. His hair is uncombed, his fingernails are dirty, he hasn't shaved in days, and it is clearly evident he hasn't been near a bar of soap in two weeks or more (Whew!). It's also apparent he ate something with lots of garlic for breakfast.

After the interview, it's time to go through a stack of applications sitting on the corner of your desk. These applications are for another high salary position in the company and there are easily more than 100 envelopes awaiting your attention. You begin opening each one and quickly read the contents, assigning each one to either a "YES" pile or a "NO" pile. One application catches your eye and you stop to peruse it for a few moments:

- It is written in pencil.
- It is scribbled on pink paper.
- The paper has the scent of Chanel No. 5.
- A note from the applicant's six-year-old daughter is attached: "Please hire my Mommy, she's really nice."
- A coupon for a free hamburger at a local fast food restaurant is included.
- The application begins, "Since two of my boyfriends went to jail I really need a job."
- There is a coffee stain in the upper right corner.
- The paper is wrinkled.

So, which of the two applicants do you hire? Did either one impress you? Or, did both of the applicants essentially "shoot themselves in the foot" with their unprofessional appearance and unprofessional attitude?

Guess what? Many writers make the same kinds of mistakes!

In fact, editors tell me that hardly a day goes by that they don't receive manuscripts that are clearly unprofessional or that truly don't follow the rules. In a matter of seconds, those submissions are assigned to the "NO" pile, tossed into the trash can, or sent a pre-printed rejection letter ("Sorry, but we find your submission to be unacceptable. . . .").

This chapter is designed to prevent that from happening. Read this and you can assured that the story you sweated over for the past fifteen months will get the attention it deserves from a prospective editor or editorial assistant. It won't guarantee acceptance or publication of that manuscript, but you will distinguish yourself as someone who knows "how to follow the rules." In short, the presentation of your work will be according to accepted standards—not according to how your Aunt Barbara or your brother-in-law (you know, the one who always crashes on your living room sofa) thinks it should look.

General Manuscript Format

As you are writing a book, your manuscript will look quite different from what I am about to describe (mine certainly do). Your primary task during the constant editing and perpetual revising of your story (Chapters 11 and 12) is to get the right words in the right order in the right way. The format is of less concern than is the structure, plot, and design of your story. You want to create a final story that will grab the attention of children (and a certain editor)—a story they will want to read again and again.

When that story is complete, it's time to think about how it should be formatted (how it looks on the page). The following conventions ensure that your story gets the (positive) attention it deserves. Dismiss these or ignore them altogether and you can guarantee your manuscript a very quick trip to the trash can. Yes, these guidelines are set in stone: break them at your peril.

1. Your manuscript must be printed on 8½" x 11" white paper using black ink. Do not make the mistake of using colored paper, legal paper (8½" x 14"), or colored ink (e.g. red and blue ink for a book about the American flag).

2. Absolutely no handwritten documents, please.

3. Use twelve-point Times New Roman or twelve-point Arial font. Whatever font you select make it consistent throughout the entire manuscript. One of the classic mistakes many new authors make is to type their manuscript using thirty-seven font styles to demonstrate their stylistic creativity or artistic inventiveness. Please don't!

4. Double space your manuscript. When I'm drafting a manuscript, I often single space it to examine how the various ideas come together. However, what it's ready to submit I automatically double space it. The only time you will use single space is detailed in number six below.

5. The preferred margin settings for a manuscript have always been 1" on top and bottom; and 1" side-to-side. However, if

you are using a word processing program such as Microsoft Word, the default margin settings are perfectly acceptable.

6. In the upper left corner of your title page, type your legal name (not a pseudonym), street address, city, state, and zip code. Also add your email address and phone number. This makes it easy for an editor to contact you if she/he is interested in your manuscript. In the upper right hand corner of the title page, type the approximate number of words (your word processing program will calculate this for you automatically). All material in the upper corners of the cover page should be typed single space.

   Skip down to the halfway point on this cover page and type the title of your story. This title should be centered on the page. It is acceptable to use a somewhat larger font for your title (I prefer 20-point Arial Black). Then skip down lines spaces and type "by" (twelve-point Times New Roman). Skip down an additional three lines and type your name or pseudonym (18-point Times New Roman). Note: This is the ONLY time you should ever use different fonts. Please see the following page for an example of a properly formatted cover sheet.

7. Use the 'Headers" tab on your word processing program to type an identifier in the top left hand corner of each successive page of your manuscript (from page two to the end of the manuscript). Say, for example, that your story was entitled "Ben's Big Breakfast" and your name was Chris P. Bacon. Your header might read as follows: *Ben's Big Breakfast/Bacon*. If your story was titled "The Mambo King" and your name was Dan Saul Knight, then the header in the top left corner of each page (starting with page two all the way to the final page) could be: *Mambo King/Knight*.

Manuscript Cover Sheet Format

Brooke Trout   924 words
9277 River Road
Highsierra, CA 94068
rrhoads@xxx,.net
(567) 555-5555

A River to Remember

by

Brooke Trout

8. On page two drop down about one-third of the way and type the title of your book (sixteen-point Arial Black). Skip two lines and type "by" (twelve-point Times New Roman; skip two more lines and type your name (fourteen-point Times New Roman).

9. Skip down two more lines and begin typing your story. Your page two should look like the example below.

Manuscript 2nd Sheet Format

River/Trout   2

A River to Remember

by

Brooke Trout

This is what your manuscript should look like. Include a cover sheet (previous page) that has all your contact information (name, address, email, phone number) in the upper left-hand corner (single-spaced). Then, in the upper right-hand corner type the approximate number of words. All word processing software will automatically count your words.

Skip down about ten to twelve lines and type the title and author's name, both in large type.

The actual first page of your manuscript is page two (this page). Put a header (book title and author's last name) in the upper left-hand corner of this page and on each successive page.

Each page should be numbered consecutively. Allow for a one-inch margin all around your manuscript (this is the default in MS Word). Double-space your manuscript and type on only one side of the paper. Your manuscript should have a ragged right edge (like the previous page) rather than a "justified" (straight, vertical, and imaginary) line on the right edge (like this page).

10. Page three and all the pages to follow will have a header in the upper left hand corner. Make sure all pages, from page two to the end of the book, are numbered (Microsoft Word, for example, does this automatically for you). The manuscript will look like the example below.

Manuscript 3rd Sheet Format

River/Trout   3

The next page of your manuscript should look like this. Be sure to maintain a one-inch margin all around. Insert the header and page number (MS Word will do this automatically for you on each page).

Do not include any illustrations with your manuscript. Nor should you pencil in suggested illustrations on your manuscript. Also, do not make any marks, corrections, or other handwritten insertions on the manuscript. If you make a mistake, correct it in your word processing program, and re-print the entire manuscript (everything submitted must be typed).

###

Picture Book Format

A picture book manuscript will follow all the conventions as described above. Make sure the entire manuscript is typed double-spaced (no matter how long or short it may be). Do not make the mistake of typing your story with page breaks. That is, don't segment your manuscript into the thirty-two pages of a typical picture book, typing one or two sentences on each page. Simply type the story from beginning to end. If your manuscript is accepted, it will be up to the editor or copyeditor to decide where those page breaks will occur. It is not necessary for you to do that in advance. If you do, you will only increase your chances for rejection.

Insider Tip

As I've mentioned in other places in this book, please don't submit any illustrations or drawings as parts of your manuscript. This is an absolute NO-NO! Don't add them to each of the pages of your manuscript and don't submit them as a separate document along with your manuscript. Don't include any drawings, illustrations, or doodles. Never! Ever!

Chapter Book and YA Format

A chapter book or YA novel, like a picture book, will follow all the directions above. The only modification will be for you to start each chapter on a new page. Center your chapter title about one-third of the way down the page, drop down two spaces, and then type the chapter.

No matter where a chapter may end (at the top of a page, the middle, or near the bottom of a page), you should always begin the next chapter on a brand new page.

A chapter book or YA novel manuscript, just like a picture book manuscript, will have a header in the upper left hand corner of each page as well as a page number in the upper right hand corner (again, your word processing program will do these automatically for you). Take a look at the example of a manuscript on the next page.

Sample Chapter Book Page

Fly Away Home/Byrd   32

The formatting of a chapter book is quite similar to the format used for a picture book. Each page includes a header as well as a page number. The manuscript is typed double spaced with sufficient margins all around. The major difference is that you will begin each new chapter on a brand new page.

So, let's pretend this is the end of Chapter 4. It ends right here on page 32.

Fly Away Home/Byrd   33

Chapter 5
Skeleton Cave

Now, we begin the next chapter of the book. The chapter number and chapter title have been centered about one-third of the way down the page. Then, you would insert a double space and begin typing Chapter 5. This format is repeated throughout the manuscript for each successive chapter.

At the end of the final chapter in the book, place the "end of manuscript" symbol as illustrated below:

###

How Many Pages?

Writers often ask how long a manuscript should be. Unfortunately, there's no fixed answer to that question other than the standard, "It all depends." I have submitted picture book manuscripts as short as three pages and as long as twenty-seven pages—all designed for a traditional thirty-two-page published picture book.

Suffice it to say, there is no minimum and no maximum. It will depend on the type of story you write and the audience for whom it is intended.

What follows is a chart indicating some page ranges for different types of books. Please do not follow this chart blindly: it only offers some parameters, not absolutes. Please know that the length of a manuscript is not the deciding factor in whether or not it is accepted for publication. The quality of that manuscript is the ultimate decider.

How you format your book is just as important as how you write your book. If you want your manuscript to get professional attention, then you must make sure you present that manuscript professionally. Look like you've done this for years, like you are well-versed in all the rules and dictates of what it is to be an accomplished author, and you will get your manuscript the positive attention it deserves.

Genre	Age Range	Number of Typed Pages	Sample Books
Board Books	birth – 3 years	1 – 5	*One More Bunny; Ella Sarah Gets Dressed; Black & White; Fix-it Duck*
Picture Books	3 – 8	3 – 25	*The Very Hungry Caterpillar; Chicka Chicka Boom Boom; In the Small Small Pond*
Easy-to-Read Books	5 – 8	10 – 30	*First Grade Takes a Test; Frog and Toad Are Friends; The Cat in the Hat; Spark*
Chapter Books	7 – 10	30 – 60	*Captain Underpants; Dead Guys Talk; Soup; Princess for a Week*
Middle Grade Books	8 – 12	75 – 250	*Roll of Thunder, Hear My Cry; Holes; Walk Two Moons*
Young Adult Novels	12 and Up	200 – 350	*The Fault in Our Stars; A Summer to Die; Hope Was Here; Snakehead*

Part V

Into the Fray

Chapter 14

Finding the Right Publisher

Marcia had long wished to be a published children's author. It had been a dream of hers ever since childhood. So, shortly after graduation from college, and just as she was beginning her new job in an accounting firm in Phoenix, Arizona, she began to draft a story entitled *The Dragon's Alphabet*. Using each letter of the alphabet, she crafted a rhyming tale of all the things that would keep a dragon happy and satisfied—especially a dragon named Howard. She worked for about a year on the manuscript, revising it in her spare time (which wasn't much with the new job) until she felt her story was ready to send to some publishers.

Marcia was well aware of the competitive nature of children's book publishing and had heard all sorts of "horror stories" about how difficult it was to break in, particularly for a first-time author. So, she decided to increase her chances for acceptance by sending her manuscript to every publisher she could find. After a visit to her local public library, she had a list of sixty-eight different children's publishers. And she thought, "What the hell, I'll send my book out to every one of them. The more I send it to, the more likely I will be to have one of them accept it for publication." And, so, one Saturday morning she printed out sixty-eight copies of *The Dragon's Alphabet*, slipped them into sixty-eight separate envelopes, and mailed them off to sixty-eight individual publishers.

After six months, she had thirty-six rejection letters and thirty-two "no responses." What went wrong?

Kristina was a paralegal in a large law firm in Minneapolis, Minnesota. She, too, had always wanted to publish a children's book. She also knew the field was difficult to break in to, with each publisher getting thousands of unsolicited manuscripts every year. But, she believed in her story—a heart-wrenching young adult novel about a homeless teenager and the personal battles she must endure each day just to survive. Her story, *Death is a Stalker*, had gone through many revisions over the course of the past year-and-a-half; in fact, she was still changing a verb here and an adjective there even after twenty-three different drafts.

Instead of sending out her manuscript to every children's publisher, Kristina decided to target her story to a few very specific houses. She had recently read a book on writing children's books and the author (a published author himself) had made a point about the importance of targeting manuscripts for specific publishers. He had pointed out that just because a publisher publishes children's books, doesn't mean that they publish all kinds of children's books. The author of that book was careful to point out that some publishers don't do alphabet books, some don't do rhyming stories, and some don't do fictional stories. The author of that book pointed out that many publishers specialize in one or two specific niches of the children's book market. Some only do nonfiction books, some only do YA novels, and some only do thirty-two-page picture books.

So, Kristina did some extra homework. She ordered lots of publisher's catalogs, made lots of visits to her local public library and nearby bookstores, and spent a lot of time on the internet to discover which specific houses published the kind of book (YA novels with graphic themes) she had written. It was extra work, above and beyond the actual writing of the book, but the author of *Writing Children's Books* assured her that it would be time well spent.

In the end, Kristina had a list of five specifically targeted publishers who had published books similar to hers. Two of the publishers were small (less than twenty books per year) and the other three typically published more than twenty-five books each year. She printed out five copies of her manuscript, stuffed each one into an envelope, included a personalized cover letter for each, and mailed them off.

Six weeks later, she received two e-mails from two separate editors, each one expressing an interest in publishing her book. She silently thanked the author of *Writing Children's Books* and now faced her newest challenge: Which publisher would she choose?

No doubt, you've heard stories about how difficult it is to get a children's book published—especially for first-time authors. There's a certain amount of truth in that statement. You may have also heard that there's a lot of luck involved in getting a book accepted and published - you have to be in the right place at the right time with the right editor in order to get anything accepted. It often seems as though you've got a better chance at winning the Mega Millions Lottery or sweeping the competition at the next edition of *America's Got Talent.*

But, the truth is, your chances have less to do with luck than they do with research. As mentioned elsewhere in this book, there are more than 800 publishers of children's books in the United States alone, but they all don't publish the same thing. Not everyone publishes YA novels. Not everyone publishes rhyming books. Not everyone publishes alphabet books. Not everyone publishes fiction or fantasy. To be a successfully published author you need to know which publishers produce the type of books you write—and which publishers don't!

For example, if my Toyota car needs a specialized part, I go to the local Toyota dealership because I know they will carry that part. I don't waste my time driving around to the Ford dealership, or the Chevrolet dealership, or the Volkswagen dealership. They may be closer and they may carry some similar looking parts, but not the specific Toyota part that will help me repair my car. By targeting my search to one type of supplier, I can be assured of getting my car fixed right.

One of the publishers I've worked with in the past (seven published books so far) only publishes thirty-two-page nature picture books. They do not publish alphabet books—never have, never will. So, a few years ago, when I drafted an alphabet book about the plants and animals that live on North American prairies (*P is for Prairie Dog: A Prairie Alphabet*, 2011), I knew I would not be sending it to my nature publisher. No matter how successful my nature books have been, I knew, beyond any shadow of a doubt, that they would never publish my alphabet book. It would have been a waste of their time and my time to submit the manuscript to them. It was submitted (and accepted by) a publisher who specializes in alphabet books. In other words, it was targeted to a very specific publisher.

One of the great lamentations of editors is that much of the material they typically receive is not suited for their house. In other words, far too many manuscripts are submitted to a publisher who just doesn't publish that type of work. By doing so, you virtually guarantee yourself a constant flow of rejection letters (or no response at all).

The key is to target your submissions, not send them off to every publisher you know or to every publisher you'd like to distribute your work. It's vitally important you know what each publisher publishes. Study their guidelines (available directly from their editorial offices or on-line), read the latest copy of Writer's Market, or search the web for each publisher's specific submission rules. Request a copy of every publisher's catalog and read it from cover to cover several times. Know exactly what each publisher publishes. Go to your local bookstore or public library and check out several recent books published by a specific publisher. What genre(s) do they specialize in publishing? What is their market niche? What is the background or experience of some of their authors? Do they specialize in series books or stand-alone books?

Here are some terrific tools that will help you with this most necessary assignment:

1. SCBWI

    The Society of Children's Book Writers and Illustrators (<u>www.scbwi.org</u>) has some wonderful resources to help you pinpoint specific houses who publish the kinds of books you write. One of the most valuable books you can obtain is *The Book: The Essential Guide to Publishing for Children* (issued annually). Not only does this guide have essential information on how to craft powerful stories, it also has two critical lists every author should consult. The "SCBWI Market Survey of Publishers of Books for Young Readers" is a great place to begin your research on relevant publishers. Also included is the "SCBWI Edited By" list profiling specific editor's tastes and the types of manuscripts they look for.

2. *Children's Writer's & Illustrators Market* (annual)

    This is the "Bible" of the industry and an essential resource that every children's author (or potential author) should have on her/his desk. This book has articles on the "ins and outs" of writing children's books, interviews with accomplished authors, advice from editors and agents, and listings of every children's publisher and the specific requirements of each of those houses. To say that this resource is indispensable would be a gross understatement. It is one of the best thirty dollars you will ever spend on a book.

3. Children's Book Council

   This nonprofit organization (www.cbcbooks.org) maintains a list of publishers who are committed to publishing books for young people. Check out their website frequently to get updates on those publishers who would be most responsive to your story.

4. *Literary Marketplace*

   This is a fantastic resource that not only lists current children's publishers, but also has an up-to-date listing of literary agents. It is revised annually and can be obtained at the reference desk of most public libraries across the country. If you'd like to get your own personal copy (and you have plenty of money to burn), you can purchase this paperback for a mere $429.50 online.

5. *Publisher's Weekly*

   Here's another resource (www.publishersweekly.com) available at most metropolitan libraries. You can also find it in many large brick-and-mortar bookstores. Each year in February and July, this periodical has ads, interviews, reviews, and general information regarding the trends and issues in children's books.

6. Writer's Guidelines

   Many publishers list their writer's guidelines (or Submission Guidelines) on their web page. These guidelines offer specific instructions on the types of books a publishing house produces and the specific requirements of a formal submission (hard copy vs. electronic submission, cover letter, font, biography, etc.). This is a resource you should put at the top of your research agenda and one you should consult regularly (specific requirements sometimes change). Most guidelines can be downloaded and printed or simply read on screen.

7. Catalogs

I find it advantageous to get as many publishers catalogs as possible. This gives me the opportunity to see all the books released by specific publishers. I like having the hard copy of the catalog in front of me. I can see all the books at one time and get a sense of the overall philosophy of the publisher(s). I can quickly get a sense of the kinds of books they publish as well as those they don't publish.

Of course, you can always look at the publisher's catalog online. The advantage of this approach is that you can access many different publishers in a short amount of time. The disadvantage (at least for me) is that you don't have the opportunity to lay competing catalogs side by side to compare house differences. Decide for yourself the approach that works best for you. Whatever you decide, know that a review of several different publisher catalogs will give you some critical information about each one's specific editorial requirements.

8. The Books Themselves

I spend a lot of time in bookstores and libraries. There, I can sit down and read lots of children's books and get a sense of what each publisher produces. I'll sometimes go so far as to get a stack of books and sort them by various publishers. As I read the books by one publisher, I'll jot down some notes about their style, subject matter, philosophy, or editorial preferences. I'll try to write notes on at least three different publishers looking for commonalities and similarities.

These book reviews also give me an opportunity to see how one of my current manuscripts in progress might fit with a particular publisher. If I'm writing a story about a child who survives a personal tragedy, I want to look at some books that also deal with a similar theme. Is there a publisher who seems to have several books published about children of color who do something extraordinary in the community? Is that a publisher to whom I want to send my manuscript when it is complete? This research has, in the past, turned up publishers I was previously unaware of, but which turned out to be ideal for a future submission.

Writing a children's book is much more than simply typing some thoughts into your word processing program. As you have read, it also involves a considerable amount of homework if you are to be a successful author. The "homework" you do both before and after writing a children's book will often determine whether that book is accepted and ultimately published by a reputable house. Indeed, you can save yourself lots of time, aggravation, and postage by specifically targeting each manuscript to a very select group of publishing houses. Think of it this way: if you were writing two emails at the same time, one to your lover and one to your father, you would be especially diligent to address each one very carefully. In fact, you would probably double and triple-check to be sure the email to your lover did not get sent to your father and vice versa.

Publishers receive an overwhelming number of submissions every year. In my conversations with editors, I've been told that upwards of ninety percent of the submissions they receive are inappropriate for their house. That's right—fully ninety percent of all the manuscripts sent (snail mail and electronic mail) for review should not have been submitted in the first place. To get an idea of the burden that places on the folks who have to read those inappropriate submissions, I have randomly selected a few publishers of children's books and showcased the approximate number of manuscripts they receive each year. If you are inclined to do the math, calculate 90% of the number of manuscripts a publisher receives annually and you'll get an idea of the scope of this issue.

To make the numbers below more concrete, let's take a look at Dawn Publications. Of the approximately 2,500 children's book manuscripts they receive each year, about 2,250 are NOT in line with the types of books they traditionally publish. In short, only about 250 manuscripts are! Here's another way of looking at those numbers: only ten percent of the manuscripts they receive are suitable for review.

Have I just given you some extra homework beyond that necessary for your manuscript? An emphatic "YES!" But you need to take the same care in submitting your manuscript as you do in writing it. Your rejection rate will be significantly reduced and your acceptance rate will be significantly enhanced simply by targeting your submissions to the right publishers.

Publisher	Manuscripts received each year	Average response time	Children's books published each year
Arbordale Publishing	1,000	Up to one year	12
Chronicle Books	30,000	Up to six months	100-110
Dawn Publications	2,500	Up to two months	4-6
Kar-Ben Publishing	800	Up to twelve weeks	20
Lee & Low Books	1,200	Up to six months	12-14
Pants on Fire Press	36,300	Up to three months	10-15
Ripple Grove Press	3,000	Up to five months	3-6

Insider Tip

In your research, you'll discover that many of the large publishers have separate imprints— smaller divisions within the larger company with their own staffs, separate missions, and editorial styles. You will have greater success if you send your manuscript to someone within a specific imprint, rather than to "Dear Editors" at the large conglomerate. You'll be able to distinguish these imprints by visiting various publisher's websites. Each site will list the various imprints with information about the specific types of books each one publishes.

Chapter 15

How to Submit Your Manuscript
(and impress an editor)

We're going to start this chapter with an exercise. Not to worry, it isn't difficult and it will only take a few moments to complete. You'll need a pen or pencil, and you will be writing in this book (yes, you have my permission to do so). When you have an appropriate writing instrument, please begin the exercise in the box below. Ready? Go.

An Author's Exercise

DIRECTIONS: There are ten statements printed below. Please read every item carefully before beginning this exercise. This exercise is not timed and you may take as long as you need in order to finish. When you are done, please put your pen or pencil down and turn to the next page in this book for a discussion of the exercise.

1. Write the word "book" in the upper left-hand corner of this box.

2. What is the state capital of California? _____

3. Completely fill in the square at the end of this sentence ☐.

4. Who was the 16th president of the US?_____

5. Make an X somewhere on the right side of this page.

6. How many feet are in a mile? _____

7. Place a circle around the number 5 above.

8. What is the 3rd planet from the sun? _____

9. Draw a small triangle in the space after this statement.

10. Now that you have finished reading everything carefully, only do step 1.

Well, how did you do? Were you one of those people who carefully read the directions for this exercise (please see the second sentence in the directions) and simply wrote the word "book" in the upper left-hand corner of the box? Or, perhaps you were one of the many people who carefully and systematically responded to the first nine statements of the exercise and then realized, when you read the last statement, that you had made a big boo-boo. Interestingly, when this exercise is given to college students, most of them will fall into the latter category. In other words, whether we are college freshmen or adults, we don't always follow directions.

And, as you know, not following directions can get us into trouble.

This is particularly true when we are trying to break through in the very competitive world of children's book publishing. Not following the specific directions for submitting your manuscript to a particular publisher will ensure you an almost instant rejection. And, how serious is this? So serious that it is cited as one of the major reasons why editors reject so many manuscripts.

Manuscript Submissions

Here's something very important to remember: Every publisher has their own specific set of manuscript submission guidelines (e.g. rules) they expect prospective authors to follow. The guidelines of a particular publisher are designed to make their evaluation of manuscripts systematic and efficient. They have been tried and tested and have proven to be most appropriate for that particular house.

Let's take a look. Here are the directions for submitting a children's book manuscript to Candyland Books[7]:

General Guidelines

- Candyland Books prefers to receive children's book submissions on paper. No compact discs, flash drives, etc., will be reviewed.

- No materials submitted will be returned.

---

7. All publisher names in this chapter are fictitious names for actual publishers.

> - If we are interested in your submission, you can expect to hear from us within six months after we receive your submission. Candyland Books will not respond to an unsolicited submission unless interested in publishing it.
>
> - If your proposal is a simultaneous submission, please indicate this in your cover letter.
>
> - Please include your email address with your submission.

Now, if you would like to ensure that your manuscript—the one you have toiled over for the past fourteen months—is instantly and unceremoniously rejected by the good folks at Candyland Books, then you are encouraged to do one (or more) of the following:

- Submit it in as a Word attachment to an email.
- Neglect to include your email address
- Post your submission on Facebook and tell the editor that she can find it there.
- Include your manuscript as the body of a very long email—say 83KB or so.
- Submit your manuscript on a thumb drive sent via FedEx.
- Call the editorial office and offer to read your book to the receptionist.

In case you were thinking I just made up the bulleted list above, I can assure you that editors have received many submissions sent just as described—not just at Candyland Books—but at many other publishers as well.

Almost every children's book publisher has a set of Submission Guidelines they want potential authors to follow (something we shared in the previous chapter). It is important that, as a prospective author, you follow those guidelines explicitly. Some houses prefer electronic submissions; others prefer hard copies. Some will want submissions in a particular format; others in a format quite different. It is important to know (and explicitly follow) the specific directions as required by each individual publisher.

There are three ways you can obtain the submission guidelines from a publisher:

1. Write directly to the editorial offices of the publisher requesting its submission guidelines. Make sure you obtain the correct (and current) address, since many large publishers often have multiple offices in different cities. When requesting those guidelines, be sure to include a self-addressed, stamped envelope (SASE) with the correct postage attached.

Insider Tip

If you live in the US and are contacting a Canadian publisher, don't use US stamps on your SASE. Instead, use International Reply Coupons (available at your local post office).

2. Consult the latest edition of *Children's Writer's & Illustrator's Market* which is published each year by Writers Digest Books. You can obtain a copy at your local bookstore, public library, or via an online bookstore.

3. The best and most efficient way to get the necessary guidelines for a particular publisher is to visit the publisher's web site. Here you will discover the most current and most accurate information as promulgated directly from a specific publishing house.

Please keep in mind that every publisher will have their own unique set of submission guidelines. If you are planning to submit your manuscript to ten separate publishers, each of those publishers may have a completely different set of directions to follow. Please take the time to submit your work according to the guidelines as promulgated by a specific publisher. Don't make the mistake of assuming that just because two of the publishers (for example) require electronic submissions, that all of them wouldn't mind if you submitted your work as part of an email. To do so would surely increase your chances for rejection.

Let's take a look at the submission guidelines for two other publishers:

Larry's Books

How to Submit a Manuscript

- All submissions should be sent to the Larry's Books imprint.

- Picture book manuscripts should be no longer than 1500 words for fiction and 4000 words for nonfiction. Early readers may be between 100 and 2500 words, depending on reading level. Chapter books are between 4,000 and 13,000 words, again depending on reading level.

- Please send the complete manuscript. Do not include illustrations unless you are a professional illustrator. Do not send original or irreplaceable materials.

- Manuscripts should be typed doubled-spaced and accompanied by a cover letter that includes a brief biography of the author, including your publishing history and the inspiration that led to the story. The letter should also state if the manuscript is a simultaneous or an exclusive submission.

The good folks at Larry's Books offer some specific guidelines on the length (or word count) for any submissions. Please consider these to be rigid and inviolable guidelines, rather than casual suggestions. If you submit a 4,529 word manuscript for a fiction book, you will be guaranteed an instant rejection. By the same token, if you include a portfolio of ninety-six oil paintings you will also be assured of a quick and sudden rejection. You can probably guess what will happen if everything you submit to Larry's Books is single-spaced.

Now, let's take a look at another publisher—Penny's Press.

Penny's Press

Manuscript Submission Guidelines

What to include in your submission:

- Copy of the full manuscript
- Cover letter
- Author's pertinent biographical information (social media handles, website, contact information, past publishing credentials, education, etc.)
- Self-addressed stamped #10 (letter-sized) envelope for a response. If no self-addressed stamped envelope is included, you will not hear from us.
- If you would like your materials returned, please send an appropriately sized envelope with adequate postage and note in your cover letter that you would like your manuscript to be returned. If there is not sufficient postage, the manuscript cannot be returned and will be recycled. Penny's Publishers is not responsible for the return or condition of submissions.
- All manuscripts must be sent by US Mail. Penny's Publishers will not review any manuscript submissions via social media, fax, email, CD, or other digital method.

You will quickly notice that the guidelines for this publisher are quite different from those of the previous publisher (Larry's Books). If you would like your manuscript to receive serious consideration from this publishing house, you need to follow their instructions to the letter. For example, you don't want to submit your manuscript electronically or on a CD. To do either would ensure a quick rejection. At the same time, you will note that this publisher (unlike the previous one) asks for a brief biography. As part of that biographical outline, you also need to include information regarding the social media you use, your education, and any other published work. Suffice it to say, the requirements here vary considerably from those in the previous example. You may be sending the same exact story to each; but the guidelines for those submissions is quite different.

Basically, there are two ways to submit your manuscript for review: as a hard copy or as an electronic copy. Let's take a look at the specifics of each one as delineated by two completely different publishers.

Hard Copy Submissions

ABCD Press

Submission Requirements

Manuscript Submission Process

- All manuscripts should be submitted via regular mail to Ms. Page Turner, ABCD Press, 1234 Literature Lane, Bookville, IN 54321.

- We only accept submissions by regular mail. Submissions received via email, FedEx, UPS, or other delivery services will be discarded without being read.

- Please number each page in the right hand corner. Put the manuscript title and your last name (e.g. "Dance of the Whale—Smith") in the upper left hand corner of each page.

- The manuscript text must be typed in Times New Roman twelve-point font throughout.

- In your cover letter please include a biography of 300 to 400 words. Tell us what other works, if any, you have published. Let us know about any applicable awards you have won.

- In your cover letter include a paragraph explaining why you wrote the manuscript; tell us about any competition (author/illustrator, publisher, year published, sales data if available, etc.). If there are competitive books, please explain why your book is different and why you believe it should sell better.

- How do you envision the marketing of the book? (three to four sentences)

- Only one submission per envelope. Be sure to include a stamped, self-addressed envelope so that we may respond.

- Do not include any illustration suggestions. That would be the illustrator's job.

What You Should Do:

1. Mail your submission directly to the person listed in the guidelines.

2. Make sure your envelope has sufficient postage.

3. Include a single manuscript, a one-page cover letter, and a SASE in the envelope.

4. Use only Times New Roman font for everything you type.

5. Include a cover letter with a brief biography, anything else you have written, why you wrote this book, and the competition.

6. Exclude any sample illustrations or suggestions for illustrations.

What You Should Not Do:

1. Mail a manuscript and send an electronic copy just to be sure the editor got your story.

2. Stuff the envelope with four or five different manuscripts so that the editor can savor your diverse authorial talents, as well as all the subjects you can write about.

3. Forget to include a SASE (Jeez—those publishing people are so rich they can certainly afford to spring for one lousy stamp for my envelope, and a secretary to address an envelope).

4. Send the manuscript via an overnight service because your manuscript is truly the next million dollar bestseller and you want the editor to read it before she has to waste her time reading all that trashy stuff taking up space on her desk.

5. Type your manuscript using twenty-seven different fonts ("Boy, that lucky editor will get to see just how creative and innovative I am. This is one manuscript she will truly remember for a long, long time!").

6. Include a sixteen-page marketing plan including all the morning news programs and afternoon talk shows you'll be willing to visit.

7. Invite your cousin Norma to draw those cute little animals she did at your nephew's birthday party and enclose those with your manuscript.

WXYZ Publishing

SUBMISSION GUIDELINES

We are seeking fiction and nonfiction manuscripts for picture books for children ages three to nine. Word count: up to 1000 words.

For All Submissions:

- All submissions must be sent electronically to submissions@wxyzpub.com.

- The subject line should read: "PICTURE BOOK: (story title) by (author name)." Emails that do not use the subject line formatting will not be read.

- Include a cover letter in the body of your email. The cover letter should include: A) a brief description of the story, B) a short bio mentioning previous publications or other background information relevant to your story, C) the titles for up to three comparative books published in the past five years. These should be books that have a similar audience to your book and that you feel will compare with your book in the marketplace. Explain how your manuscript is different from these books.

- Include your personal contact information with phone number.

- Attach your manuscript as a WORD document (preferred) or PDF. File sizes cannot be larger than 4MB.

Due to the great number of submissions we receive, we cannot respond to individual submissions unless we have further interest. You may assume that after six months we are not interested in publishing your work. You may send your work to other publishers at the same time. We do not require exclusive submissions.

What You Should Do:

1. Write a cover letter and make it the body of an email.

2. Attach your manuscript as a WORD document to the email.

3. Make sure your attachment is smaller than 4MB (if it is approximately 1,000 words, there will be no problem with this limit).

4. Make sure you include all your contact information (address, phone number [cell or home], email address) as part of your cover letter.

5. Include a short biography (no more than four to five sentences) as part of your cover letter.

6. List some books similar to your manuscript and how they compare. No boasting here; just the facts.

What You Should Not Do:

1. Print out your manuscript, stuff it in an envelope, and mail it to the editor.

2. List fifty-seven other books similar to yours and why yours is the best children's book on the subject since the invention of bread.

3. Submit photographs of yourself from birth to the present day—particularly those of you reading the manuscript to your twenty-three grandchildren and eleven great-grandchildren (plus assorted neighbors and other relatives).

4. Forget to include any contact information assuming that the editor is so smart that she will be able to figure out how to get hold of you with that multi-million dollar contract.

5. Send the editor additional letters telling her about the terrific manuscript that now resides in her slush pile.

The Cover Letter

When you meet someone for the first time there's usually a handshake and the exchange of a few pleasantries. The conversation is cordial, typically informal, and respectful. After a few minutes you may get into some deeper issues (say, if you're being interviewed for a job) or you may move on to talk with other people (say, if you're at a social occasion). You can often get a sense of the individual(s) you met in those first few minutes of your initial contact. In short, you have a fairly good idea of their personality, attitude, and demeanor.

A cover letter does the same thing. It is an essential part of your manuscript package and just like a social introduction, it presents a quick snapshot of who you are. Your cover letter adds personality to your manuscript. It is not a standalone document, rather it is intended to present a positive first impression to someone who doesn't know you. That first impression will be the incentive an editor wants and needs to read the accompanying manuscript.

Cover letters (whether sent as hard copies or part of the body of an electronic submission) are typically scanned very quickly. The editor wants to make sure that the manuscript is a fit for the publisher's editorial needs and that the author has the credentials to write a publishable book. As a result, cover letters need to be brief and focused.

Here are some tips that will make your cover letter stand out:

1. Good cover letters are not mass produced. Each cover letter you send out must be unique, singular, and targeted to a specific publisher. Do not (and I repeat) **do not** make the fatal mistake of writing a generic cover letter. It will be spotted in an instant and it (and the accompanying manuscript) will surely take a speedy journey directly into the nearest trash can.

2. **NEVER** (notice the capital letters and bold type) send a cover letter that is more than one page (single-spaced) in length. Simply put, editors don't have the time to read expansive and extensive cover letters. Think about that social introduction mentioned at the start of this section. How would you feel if you had to listen to someone's résumé for ten or fifteen minutes nonstop while shaking his hand? That's the same

feeling an editor would having reading a four or five page cover letter.

3. A good cover letter consists of four brief paragraphs. They include the following:

First Paragraph—Present the title of your book, its specified age group, and its genre.

Second Paragraph—In a few specific sentences tell the reader about the basic plot of your story. You may also want to address how this story fits in with the publisher's philosophy or editorial needs.

Third Paragraph—Describe your qualifications for writing this story. If you have published anything related to the topic, say so. If you are unpublished, what work experiences, training, or special conditions do you have that make you qualified to write this tale. Make a connection between your education, training, or interests and this manuscript.

Insider Tip

In your cover letter, DO NOT indicate that this is the first story you've ever written (if, indeed, it is). That raises a "red flag" in the mind of any reader. Focus instead on the circumstances that distinguish you as a qualified author.

Fourth Paragraph—Thank the editor for taking the time to read your submission. If you are submitting a hard copy, you would also ask for a reply via a SASE (self-addressed stamped envelope) that you have also included. Don't ask the reader to return the entire manuscript, that's just more work for her. A brief note will be more than sufficient. If you are submitting your work electronically, ask that a return reply be sent via email.

Let's take a look at a sample cover letter to see how those four essential paragraphs work together.

Sample Cover Letter A

Hazel Nutt
948 Orchard Road
Filbert, PA 17666

October 26, 20XX

Frankie N. Johnny
Muskrat Press
6338 Terrace Blvd.
Los Angeles, CA 95567

Dear Ms. Johnny:

I am pleased to enclose Seven Steps to Freedom, a picture book for early elementary students, for your consideration. This book is geared for six- to eight-year-old readers who enjoy a family mystery combined with historical fiction.

Seven Steps to Freedom is the fictionalized account of Jeremiah, a plantation slave in 1852 South Carolina. During renovations on his master's house, he unearths a jug with his grandfather's initials etched into it. Thus begins a quest to discover his roots and decipher a family secret that's been buried for nearly a century.

I am a volunteer at our local library where I share books with children every Friday morning. In addition, I am a docent for the local historical society and have assisted a history professor (Dr. Adam Reynolds) in his research on early African-American artifacts discovered at a nearby plantation. I am a voracious reader of historical fiction and have penned several historical articles for the local newspaper.

I have enclosed a SASE for your reply (it is not necessary to return these materials). Thank you in advance for your consideration of this submission. I look forward to hearing from you.

Sincerely,

Hazel Nutt

4. Spelling and Grammar. In my conversations with various editors it became very clear that spelling and grammatical errors were the primary criterion that eliminated many manuscripts from any potential consideration. One editor went so far as to tell me, "Spell my name incorrectly and I won't even read the rest of the letter—and I certainly won't read your manuscript!" Check, double check, and triple check your spelling and grammar, they do make a difference.

5. Make sure you send your manuscript (either via the postal system or electronically) to a specific editor. Don't address your cover letter to "Dear Editors." That shows you haven't done your homework. The Writer's Guidelines on each publisher's website will often list the name of the editor to whom submissions should be sent (Some will, however, indicate that submissions should be sent to "Editorial Assistant" or simply "Submissions."). You will have considerably more success if you send your manuscript to a real live actual person, rather than to "Dear Sir" or "Dear Madam."

6. Rewrite for each publisher. Do not make the classic mistake of writing a generic cover letter—one that can be mass produced and sent to every publisher in the universe. You'll only be shooting yourself in the foot. Mass produced letters can be spotted a mile away. Besides, don't you like getting personalized letters rather than "Dear Occupant" missives? So do editors.

Common Boo-Boo's

In my conversations with editors, I gathered data on the most common mistakes writers make in their cover letter(s). Please consider the observations of these editors as serious "food for thought" in the construction of your own cover letter(s). Know that other writers will be making these mistakes and that you can stand above the competition by systematically excluding any and all of these errors from your cover letter(s).

1. Spelling. Use the Spell Check feature on your word processing program, but don't over-rely on it. Invite several people to read your cover letter to see if everything is spelled correctly.

2. Grammar. Again, invite friends to read your letter and note any grammatical errors.

3. Tentative Phrases. Eliminate any phrases that signal a lack of confidence in your writing. These include, "I think . . . ," "I believe . . . ," or "I feel. . . ."

4. Wrong Name/Wrong Title. Check (and double check) the name typed on your cover letter. Make sure it is the correct individual to whom the letter should be sent.

5. Stating What You Want. Focus on how your story will satisfy the editor's needs rather than your own needs.

   NO: "I think you should publish this story because I spent a lot of my very valuable time writing it."

   YES: "*Josephine's Journey* incorporates six elementary social studies standards and is ideally suited for your 'Historical Trails' imprint."

6. "Cookie-cutter Letter". In an effort to save time with multiple submissions, many writers make a serious and fatal mistake. They will try and craft an all-purpose cover letter that can be sent along with every manuscript they submit.

7. Not Doing Your Homework. Here's a tip that will put you "heads and shoulders" above your competitors. Research the publisher's web site and be sure to reference an item from that site in your letter.

8. Bland Adjectives. Your book isn't "a very nice story," it's "a compelling narrative." Your story isn't "different," it's "distinctly unique." Your story isn't "something kids will want to read," it's "an adventure story across time and space."

9. Too Long. Repeat after me: "One page. Four paragraphs. The end." Thank you.

10. Forgetting to Address a Specific Person. Take the time to write a unique and personal letter to each editor/publisher. Trying to save time by writing a generic cover letter will, most definitely, mess up your chances of having your manuscript read.

11. Writing in the negative. Phrases such as "I didn't . . . ," "I won't . . . ," and "I can't . . . " often frame you as a person who lacks skills, talents, and desires. They cast you in a negative light.

12. Boasting: Over Confidence. "You are about to read the next *Harry Potter*—a book that will sell millions of copies and make us both very rich!" An overabundance of confidence or a boastful attitude will surely turn off any editor reading your letter. Be confident, not arrogant! There's a big difference between the two terms and that difference will reveal itself in the tone you establish in your cover letter.

13. Listing References. There is no need to tell a reader that your former high school English teacher (Miss Tayke) thinks your story is A+ material or that your aunt Gertrude (who once wrote an essay for her local newspaper) says your book is "much better than that Horry Pewter guy." Eliminate all references to references.

Sample Cover Letter B

Barb E. Dahl
3002 Vogue Ave.
Beverly Hills, CA 95320

April 6, 20XX

Ginger Rayl
Carbonation Press
999 Bubbly Place
Soda Springs, GA 39527

Dear Ms. Rayl:

I am delighted to submit *The Tragedy of Humpty Dumpty* for your consideration. This compelling picture book is written for readers ages four to seven, especially those who enjoy comedic characters and fantasy.

In *The Tragedy of Humpty Dumpty*, a rotund character whose athletic skills are far past their prime boasts that he can surmount a massive structure around his town. His proclamation quickly spreads as nobody has ever scaled the great height in the 200-year history of the town. Our hero will be the first! On the big day, he grunts and groans his way to the top. However, once there, something quite unexpected happens and he suffers a fate almost too terrible to describe. This enchanting tale, packed with humor, makes this book an ideal addition to the "Tales From Near and Far" imprint of Carbonation Press.

I am a second grade teacher at Whistling Pines Elementary School and have made fairy tales and fantasy an integral part of my classroom reading program for many years. In addition, I am a volunteer reader at our local library and have contributed several stories to regional children's magazines.

Enclosed please find a SASE. It is not necessary to return the materials enclosed—you are welcome to dispose of them in an environmentally friendly manner. Thank you in advance for your consideration.

Sincerely,

Barb E. Dahl

A well-written cover letter can create a very favorable "first impression" for the manuscript to follow. Please be as diligent and dedicated to this document as you are to your overall manuscript. It is a "professional handshake"—one with the potential to open the door to a very interesting and rewarding relationship.

Other Considerations

Simultaneous Submissions

Often known as either "Simultaneous Submissions" or "Multiple Submissions," this is when you send copies of the same manuscript to several different publishers at the same time. Although frowned on in the past, this is now considered standard practice by both authors and editors. This reduces the time factor considerably; that is, sending one manuscript out, waiting three months for a decision, then sending it out to another publisher, waiting another three months for a decision, and so on and so on. Instead, you can submit multiple copies of your story to multiple publishers. My personal suggestion is to send between four to six manuscripts out at the same time.

In the past, it was also considered good form to inform editors that the submission in their hands was one of several simultaneous submissions. Today, the practice of multiple submission is so well accepted, that it is no longer necessary to indicate that in your cover letters. Editors have come to expect that any manuscript they receive will have also been sent to other publishers at the same time.

Do not make the mistake of enclosing several different stories in the same envelope. Nor should you attach a variety of manuscripts to the email you send to an editor. Editors appreciate it when they only have to review one manuscript at a time. If you send several different ones, they may read only one, find it not to their liking, and assume the others are of equal quality, rejecting them without even reading them. So, the rule is: One envelope, one manuscript; one email, one attachment.

How Long Do I Wait?

Once you've sent your manuscript, now begins the most difficult part of the writing process: the waiting game. Now you have to wait for a reply and sometimes it seems as though that time period takes forever!

Many publishers will indicate (in their "Writer's Guidelines") the length of time they need to make a decision on whether to accept or reject a specific submission. That time may range anywhere from one month to a year. If the decision time is not stated in the guidelines, you should give the publisher three months before writing—respectfully inquiring about the status of your manuscript.

If you have not received any word about your submission in the stated decision time (or in approximately three months if no time is indicated), then it is perfectly acceptable to write and inquire. If you submitted your manuscript via the mail, then you should mail a short letter to the same editor you sent the manuscript (be sure to include a SASE). On the other hand, if your story was sent electronically, then it is perfectly acceptable to inquire via an email.

Your letter or email must be respectful and polite. Making lots of demands or charging the editor acts of gross stupidity will do you no favors. It is likely your submission got "lost" in the slush pile, may have been inadvertently overlooked, or may have been set aside for further review. Telling the editor that she probably came from a Neanderthal gene pool or that second grade dropouts shouldn't be publishing children's books will not garner you any favors. Always be polite! Always be professional!

NO

Ella Vader
9386 Rising Way
Updown, OK 72948

September 21, 20XX

Lewis N. Clark
Explorer Press
55 Trail
Omaha, NE 68102

Dear Stupid Stupid Editor Person:

You promised me you'd have a decision on my submission *Chipmunks Don't Dance Very Well* in three months and you haven't done diddly squat. Listen, I've got lots of important stuff to do and don't need you to yank me around. I'm really tired with you hotshot editors who think you can just dangle fame and fortune in front of us and then play your silly waiting games. You have got to be the most exasperating person I've ever dealt with. Come on, get a life! Tell me yes or tell me no. And make it quick.

Frustratingly,

Ella Vader

Here's the best thing you can do while waiting for a reply from an editor: write another book. Once a manuscript has been sent to an editor, I quickly record it in my submissions file, and get to work on my next book. I keep myself busy with one or two new projects and check on the status of various manuscripts about once a month. That way, I'm making the best use of my time.

Oh, by the way, **never call** an editor to check on the status of your manuscript! Did you note that the words "never call" were bolded? There's a good reason for that. Editors simply don't have the time for phone calls from prospective authors. Calling an editor to inquire about the status of your work is considered bad manners and bad form. Don't do it.

YES

Marsha Mellow
6587 Candy Lane
Sweetness, OH 23927

April 28, 20XX

Stanley Cupp
Hockey Press
867 Puck Place
Goalee, AK 99987

Dear Mr. Cupp:

I am writing in reference to my manuscript, Tyrone's Favorite Brother, which I sent to you on January 24. Have you had an opportunity to review it? I would sincerely appreciate it if you could let me know at your earliest opportunity. For your convenience, I have enclosed an additional SASE.

Thank you in advance for your consideration. I look forward to hearing from you.

Sincerely,

Marsha Mellow

Following the guidelines of each identified publisher will enhance your chances for success. They won't guarantee that your manuscript will be accepted for publication; but they will guarantee that that manuscript won't be rejected because the author just couldn't follow directions.

Chapter 16

Do You Need an Agent?: Yes! No!

There's an old saw that goes something like this: "You can't get published without an agent; and you can't get an agent unless you're published." It's truly a Catch-22 situation. Fortunately, there are some very effective ways to deal with this issue, which we will address in this chapter.

What agents do

Several publishers won't accept manuscripts unless they are submitted by an agent. A literary agent is like a "clearing house;" they know what a good book manuscript looks (and feels) like and will only submit the best ones to various publishers. As a result, a publisher knows that a manuscript has been appropriately vetted when submitted by a literary agent. Those that don't rise to the level of "Excellent" aren't submitted. This saves considerable time on the part of a typically overworked editor. She can then focus primarily on agent-submitted manuscripts knowing they have passed a critical first test.

Agents also know each editor's tastes—what she or he wants, the books that fit into their editorial philosophy, and, of course, the books that will sell. One of the chief responsibilities of a good agent is to be in touch with, and in tune with, selected editors throughout the industry. By knowing what each editor really wants, an agent can then target each one with only those ideas that would get their undivided attention. If a specific editor has an affinity for fantasy novels, a good agent will know that and not submit picture book manuscripts or coming-of-age stories.

Agents also provide authors with important feedback on their manuscripts. Editors, with all their various and sundry responsibilities, don't have the time (or inclination) to respond to each and every manuscript. Agents, as valuable intermediaries, can offer a writer some critical feedback on a story that may not be quite ready for submission. Suggestions for improvement, grammatical corrections, and editorial changes can all be proposed by an agent so that when those changes are made, the manuscript becomes one that is ready for immediate review by an editor. In fact, one of the chief benefits of the agent/author relationship is that the agent gets to know the style and personality of a writer and can specifically help that writer craft a final manuscript that will stand up to scrutiny by an editor. A good agent will only submit the best manuscripts, and by having a solid relationship with a specific author, she can make sure that her/his manuscripts meet the editorial demands of a specific editor.

Agents also serve authors in several other ways beyond manuscript review. They ensure that royalty statements are correct and up-to-date, they will negotiate foreign, film, and merchandising rights, and (of course) they will collect the money due you and ensure it is disbursed in a timely manner.

It's important to remember that there is one thing an agent cannot do—she or he cannot sell an unsellable manuscript. That places a large responsibility on the shoulders of an author to create a book manuscript that is engaging and marketable. If you (or I) write a really lousy manuscript, no amount of pressure, influence, or cajoling by an agent will get an editor to accept that document. As much as I might like to think that my agent has a t-shirt with a big red "S" on it and a flaming red cape attached to the back, she cannot (and will not) be able to convince a prospective editor that my current manuscript is worthy of publication unless I have done a good job writing it. In short, she can't sell junk.

Expert Quote

"Ideally, it comes down to good storytelling."

—Brooks Sherman, children's book agent

Finding an Agent

When I first began writing children's books, I knew that I was in it for the "long haul"—that is, I wanted to write many books and devote many years to this profession. I knew that eventually I would like to have an agent on my side to make that possible. But, I also knew another reality: I couldn't get an agent just because I had decided to write children's books, I had to prove myself. No agent in the world is going to take on a brand new writer just because that writer wants to write. By the same token, no employer is going to hire someone for a specific job in their company just because that person want to work there. That person has to prove herself or himself with some related work experiences, training and education, good references, a positive attitude, and other employment factors that underscore that individual's worthiness for the company. Securing the services of an agent is quite similar to applying for a new job. You have to prove yourself worthy of being "hired" by the agent. You have to convince a potential agent that you have the "chops" to be a dedicated and successful author.

The other important consideration is that there are some agents more appropriate for your writing career than others. If you are like many people, you probably didn't select your spouse as the first person you dated. You, most likely, went out on dates with many different people; you got to know different personalities, different philosophies, and different outlooks on life. The dating process gave you an opportunity to "narrow the field," finding the one right person with whom you wanted to spend the rest of your life.

In many ways, finding an agent is similar to finding your life's mate (of course there are no diamond rings, house mortgages, or diaper changing involved with an agent). You need to do your research, sifting through all the possibilities to discover the right one; the one with whom you have a high degree of compatibility and the one who will best advance your career as a children's author.

There are several resources available as you begin your search for an agent. Here is a list of some of the most useful:

- *Children's Writer's and Illustrator's Market* (annual) has listing of agents, along with their contact information, guidelines, and specific needs of each agency.

- The Society of Children's Book Writers and Illustrators (SCBWI) has a list of agents available free of charge to all its members.

- AgentQuery.com offers one of the largest, searchable databases of literary agents on the web—a collection of reputable and established agents from a variety of agencies.

- *Literary Marketplace* (annual) has an up-to-date listing of agents for both children's and adult authors.

- Agents Directory in *The Book: The Essential Guide to Publishing for Children* (annual), published by SCBWI.

- *Writer's Digest Magazine* maintains a regular blog (Guide to Literary Agents) with frequent updates on literary agents (both new and established) and what they are looking for.

- *Guide to Literary Agents* (annual) has a listing of more than 1,000 agents who represent writers and their books.

What You Should Look For in an Agent

When you "selected" your spouse or your life's partner, you probably had some basic criteria in mind. You may have wanted someone with a sense of humor, someone who was intelligent and inquisitive, someone who showed compassion and empathy for others, or someone who enjoyed the outdoors. Whatever your criteria were, they helped you narrow the field and identify individuals most compatible with your personality or outlook on life.

Below I have listed some of the essential criteria you should consider if you are in the market for a literary agent. These items will help you identify those agents who will best serve your needs and represent your work appropriately.

1. Make sure any agent you consider is a member of The Association of Authors Representatives (AAR). This is a professional society of agents, all of whom embrace a strict code of conduct and ethical guidelines. One of those guidelines involves the issue of reading fees. Agents and agencies that are members of AAR typically do not charge writers a fee for reading their work.

2. Discover the books an agent has represented in the past. Oftentimes, an agent's name will appear in the Dedication of a book or in a brief acknowledgements section. You need to know if an agent handles the type of material you write. For example, if you write science fiction, you will need an agent that handles science fiction. If you write picture books for

early readers, you need an agent who handles those types of books. The references listed above will help you determine the type of material each agent handles.

3. Check out a prospective agent's usual compensation for representation. Most agents will require ten to fifteen percent of your total sales (fifteen percent is the standard). If they require more than fifteen percent, you should probably consider other agents.

4. How long has the agent been in business? Is the agent just starting out or has she been doing this for five, ten, or fifteen years? Do you need an agent with lots of experience (and thus lots of contacts within the publishing industry) or are you more comfortable with an agent who is just getting her career started.

Insider Tip

There is an advantage to new agents. Since they are just getting their career started, they may be more amenable to signing on new authors (particularly new authors with a very marketable manuscript) than might be the case with agents who currently have many authors under their wings. In other words, don't simply dismiss a new agent because of her inexperience; she may be looking for equally inexperienced authors to get her career off on the right foot.

5. Contact writer friends or colleagues and ask them for recommendations. One of the advantages of joining a local writing group (or an affiliate of SCBWI) is the opportunity to tap into the collective wisdom of the group. You may discover another writer who currently has an agent and would be willing to recommend her to you. You should feel free to ask a fellow writer for a letter of recommendation on your behalf. If

a fellow writer really likes her agent, that may be a sufficient recommendation in your quest for literary representation.

6. It used to be that if you really wanted an outstanding agent, you should look in only one place: New York City. That's no longer true. Good agents can be found all over the country. Their location is not as important as the contacts they maintain throughout the children's book publishing industry. An agent may live in the Badlands of South Dakota, the bayous of Louisiana, or the Sonoran desert of Arizona. That makes them neither good or bad. What you really need to know is how well do they know the market and how well do they know the editors at various publishing houses.

7. Something else you may want to consider in your search for an agent is whether a specific agent offers any kind of editorial guidance prior to submitting a manuscript to a prospective editor. Do they do any kind of line editing (and are there any additional fees for those services) or do they expect their authors to submit "perfect" manuscripts?

8. Most agents have contracts or letters of agreement that bind an author to the agent for a specified period of time. You need to know the specified period of time an agent requires on those legal documents as well as your degree of freedom in breaking with an agent should the relationship prove to be disharmonious or incompatible (sort of like a divorce).

Contacting an Agent

Contacting a prospective agent is very similar to applying for a professional job. For that job, you would submit two critical documents: a résumé and a cover letter. Your manuscript is your résumé and your query letter is your cover letter. You want to be sure that any manuscript you submit to a prospective agent is complete and finished. It shouldn't be a draft or a semi-complete story. It should be the best story you can craft—one that has gone through all the steps and stages (*see* Chapters 11 and 12) necessary for writing excellence. Never submit a work-in-progress; always submit a finished piece.

A query is your letter of introduction. From this one-page document, you will establish your "bona fides" for a prospective agent (or prospective employer, if you will). This letter should be no more than one page in length, straightforward, simple, and business-like. This is not the time to be cute or humorous. Nor is it the time to be boastful or arrogant. Above all, be professional.

Many agents will tell you that a good query letter consists of three parts:

1. A one-sentence description of your manuscript. This is known as the "pitch"—a high-level description of your book as you might explain it to someone you just met at a social function.

2. A brief one-paragraph description of the book. For good examples, take a look at the descriptions that appear on the back covers of novels (or on the inside flyleaf). Notice how each of those singular paragraphs encapsulate several hundred pages in a succinct, precise, and dramatic paragraph. You should do the same.

3. Offer some relevant information about yourself. This is not the time to write an extensive autobiography; limit your description to a single concise paragraph.

Insider Tip

For examples of outstanding queries (along with not-so-outstanding queries) you may wish to check out the following:

- Writer's Digest Successful Queries post on the Guide to Literary Agents blog (www.writersdigest.com/editor-blogs/guide-to-literary-agents/successful-queries)

- Query Shark (www.queryshark.blogspot.com)

As you are doing your research on prospective agents, you'll also want to pay attention to each agent's specific submission guidelines. Only send an agent exactly what she asks for: nothing more, nothing less. If an agent asks for a query letter and a complete manuscript, that's exactly what you should send. Don't include a letter of reference from your minister or rabbi, a cute note ("That was really a swell story, Author Person.") from a youngster at the local library where you read your story, or a list of all the vacation spots you plan to visit after the book is accepted. Some agents may want a query letter only, some may request the "query plus the first fifty pages of the manuscript," and others may ask for "a query letter, the first ten pages of the manuscript, and a one-page synopsis." Whatever an agent lists in her submission guidelines is exactly what you should submit.

A Conversation with a Children's Book Agent

Every once in a while, someone walks into your life and changes it—for the better! Sandy Ferguson Fuller is one of those individuals in my life. Sandy has been my agent for considerably more than two decades and, as a result, I have enjoyed significant success as a children's author. She is the CEO and sole agent for Alp Arts Company (www.alparts.com) in Vail, Colorado, an agency in business for more than thirty years. Sandy is also a children's author and thus, has a most unique and insightful view of the market. Throughout her years as a literary agent, she has worked with a wide range of editors, a sizable number of authors, many other agents, and innumerable publishers. Her knowledge of the field and sage insights offer you some unique perspectives about this engaging, curious, and challenging profession.

AUTHOR: What should authors know about agents?

SANDY FERGUSON FULLER: Authors have choices. They may choose whether or not to engage an agent, and they should be aware of a variety of available professionals. It is possible to negotiate/navigate the children's publishing field, to an extent, without an agent. Many publishers entertain unsolicited submissions and remain open to new authors who approach them sans agent. The majority of larger traditional publishers still request representation, but there are many small to mid-size publishers and alternative publishing models to pursue without an agent. Self-publishing or alternative publishing has become much more feasible and does not require an agent. There are a number of ways to submit a manuscript without engaging an agent.

If an author opts for representation, I believe the most important thing is to choose an agent who shares editorial tastes, personal compatibility, and expectations. Other than writing talent, that's exactly what I look to find in an author. Authors and agents should like each other! Do your homework—remember you have many choices. Don't sign with the first agent you meet or interview. Each agent has different focuses and specializations. Mine, for instance, has always been picture books. Know what excites your agent and what he or she is good at selling. Location is also a factor. I've always been based in Colorado, which has served me well, but occasionally it might have been advantageous to be in NYC. In the current market, location is less of a factor. It's possible to be effective from just about anywhere. Other considerations, I believe, are experience and style. I have never been an aggressive, demanding person, and I'm certainly not that type of agent, but I have a tremendous amount of experience in the industry to compensate. So authors, I invite you to go shopping, then enjoy your purchase.

A: What are some of your regular responsibilities?

SFF: Professional agents should expect to spend a lot of time keeping up with market trends, individual publisher acquisition focus, and the publishing personnel merry-go-round as editors and imprints come and go. This information flow is constant and ever-changing. It's a challenge to keep up. Also critical is staying current with social media. Maintaining an updated and informative web presence is important for any agency.

Receiving, screening, **and** soliciting manuscripts. I'm extremely selective but I try to respond to any author who sends me a manuscript, not just a "sorry, no thank you, this isn't right for us." Instead, I offer a few constructive comments with a rejection if the work doesn't float my boat. If I'm interested in a manuscript, editing is a large part of what I've always done. Editing is a controversial area as relates to agent accountability; customarily, agents are expected to edit at no charge. Agents who charge fees for editing are not recommended in the mainstream. To resolve this, I spend hours editing manuscripts both unpaid as an agent and as a paid editorial consultant. The "paid" portion of my work remains separate from my agent role. I expect to help my established authors with surface editing at no charge. However, if I'm "hired" to rewrite and revise a manuscript at length, I often negotiate a separate fee. I believe that this is a valuable, professional service that requires talent and time, and I think it is reasonable to charge a modest fee.

Sending out submissions is a careful, selective process, much more efficient now that most submissions are done online. Additionally, submission follow-ups are detail-oriented and time-consuming—it's extremely frustrating at times trying to get a final response. Some editors are quick and decisive; others require repeated follow-ups. The former is much appreciated!

Contract negotiations with publishers, and representing the best interests of the author or illustrator comprise part of the agent's role. Once a book is under contract, most editors prefer direct contact with the author regarding editorial matters. The agent often "gets in the way." However, if I'm needed and requested to do it, I will step in and try to help the author on editorial development with a book that is under contract. Once a book is published, I monitor royalty statements, payments, assist with additional sub-right sales, and coordinate publicity/marketing follow-up with the publisher depending upon their preference.

I also work as a foreign rights agent—not customary for a traditional literary agent.

In addition to my US authors and illustrators, I represent four foreign publisher groups for North American and/or English language rights. Meeting with publishers at Bologna Fiere, Frankfurt Buchmesse, and other rights fairs reinforces my relationships with US editors and other children's book publishing professionals and keeps me involved with the current international markets. Challenging and refreshing!

A: What are some common misperceptions about your job?

SFF: It's not easy street or easy money! Probably everyone in the outside circle assumes that children's book agents are rich. Rarely. Collectively, we all share the never-ending quest for the Holy Grail or the next J. K. Rowling! I have never made a sizeable fortune as an agent, and it's mostly "off-the-clock" work, but I love it!

I always try to be clear, upfront, that I can't devote all of my time to a single author. Sometimes I'm willing to be a counselor or cheerleader, but never a personal valet! Each author whom I represent deserves my attention and requires a share of valuable time; but, I'm not anyone's exclusive agent. Airing these concerns in advance—and working with authors who understand—is key to our successful collaboration.

A: How often do you take on a new client/author?

SFF: Rarely. This has evolved over years of experience. I've been an agent for over thirty years. At the outset, I needed to build a stable of authors and I wasn't as discerning.

I didn't yet have a clue what might work for us. Through trial and error, I've learned what works for me and for my authors. I find that shepherding a small group of authors and focusing on their work is most effective. Although I'm content with my established authors and have a full plate, my door remains ajar. Just recently, I signed a new, unpublished author. It still happens!

A: How many authors/clients do you represent? What is the ideal number for you?

SFF: Alp Arts Co. is specialized and small, currently representing twelve authors. Reviewing our years as an agency (established 1989), our largest number of clients capped out at forty. At that time, I employed a valuable administrative assistant, but even then, there were only two of us. Now working by myself, ten to fifteen authors is a comfortable group in order to maintain quality service. Again, I also work in foreign rights and provide separate manuscript development/editorial consultation.

A: What do you look for in a potential client (new author)?

SFF: The first thing I look for is a manuscript that I love—or that has the potential for me or others to love, either as is or with development. Equally attractive to me is an author who is talented, can write, and offers a unique voice or aspect. Generally, I prefer to take on an aspiring writer who has more than one manuscript available or ideas on the back burner—a writer or artist who is seeking a career instead of a one-shot deal. Publishers prefer that too! I also look for a manuscript that is timely in its message or entirely unique in the market; publishers are searching for the same. Something fresh, sustaining, but hasn't been done a hundred times over.

A: What mistakes do authors typically make when contacting you for representation?

SFF: Probably the biggest mistake is not doing homework in advance regarding what an individual agent does. For example, we get frequent requests to represent adult books that immediately tells me that my name has been pulled out of a hat with no idea what we do!

Research the agency, know what the agent's focus tastes are, identify their location and special markets. I'm in Colorado; I receive a lot of manuscripts because discerning authors have learned that I'm a mountain person, I live in Vail, I love picture books about nature, animals, outdoor life—and that's great. I *so* appreciate that an author has paid attention to preferences.

I receive manuscript queries in different ways. Phone is fine. Email with attachments fine. Snail mail works. Authors should consult available references to determine how an agent prefers to get queries and submissions. SCBWI, Literary Agents Guild, etc. However you send material, be sure to use the agent's correct name, address, and other contact information. And avoid misspelling! Also, please keep query letters or emails to a few succinct and well-composed paragraphs. Let the manuscript sing for itself.

Authors should expect and request a written agreement with their agent. I recommend a contract that is fairly easy to get out of for either of you, because circumstances may change, for whatever reason. My contracts are easy to dissolve, but they honor any transactions or contracts already acquired on behalf of the author

A: What can you **not** do for an author?

SFF: I will never "promise a contract" upfront. Children's book publishing is a competitive, subjective, often fickle business. For any author to believe that an agent guarantees a ticket to success is a misperception. So, from the beginning, our expectations must line up.

I won't stand behind a proposal or manuscript that I don't believe in or that doesn't resonate. Ultimately, this will tarnish our agency's reputation or alter an editor's perception of our tastes. Certainly a sticky wicket, because I've represented a few authors for a first book, but I've not been willing to commit to the next.

I won't edit, edit, re-edit, and edit again without compensation. That's the legitimate reason for portioning out the editorial consultation aspect of my business.

I can't negotiate terms that I respect—terms that are customary to a specific publisher. For example, some publishers never offer a list-based contract; their royalties are always based on net revenues. I respect that publisher's way of conducting business and I won't try to change it. If there's any wiggle room with a publisher, certainly I will suggest a larger advance, a different publication date, escalating royalties, etc. But, I respect individual publishers and their customary terms.

A: What makes a manuscript easy to pitch to an editor?

SFF: A manuscript must be well written. If the author can offer some specific points to pitch to the publisher (why they've written it, what's important about it, etc.), I will include this in my cover letter. If I can quote an author in a cover letter, even better. If an author has crafted a book proposal targeting a specific publisher's list, that is ideal. Those manuscripts have the best chance for publication.

A: If there is a secret to success in this very competitive business, what would it be?

SFF: Perseverance. For author, illustrator, and agent. Hang in there, to a fault. Believe in your work, then stick with it. If you get rejected, it's not over. Also, realize when to say,

"OK, let's try something different."

Savvy. Know the market—editorial tastes, with or without an agent. A more informed author is always a better author; most new authors aren't knowledgeable about current trends and events in the industry. Do your research.

Flexibility. Is your goal a six-figure advance with one of the big major publishers? Or, would you settle for a small advance with a smaller publisher? Do you prefer to be a small fish in a big ocean or a large fish in a tiny pond? What will serve you best in the end? The best strategy is to get started and to build your publishing portfolio. Consider your options carefully. A lucrative one-book deal can be seductive, but consider the larger, longer horizon. Try to establish a great relationship with an editor and a publisher with a solid, steady backlist. Who will market and distribute your book to the best advantage? More and more medium-sized publishers, small publishers, and different publishing models are available to give you an opportunity to launch your first book and your publishing career.

A: What is the best piece of advice you can offer new children's authors?

SFF: Hang in there. Research: get educated about the market and about the business. Don't quit your day job. Honor your writing passion. Take it seriously. For starters, don't rely on it to put bread on the table. That should come in time! Write as much as you can—wherever and whenever—on a regular basis, even if you're not creating a book every day. Always leave off in a place where it's easy to pick up again—know your next sentence—to jumpstart you the next time!

A: What do you enjoy most about your job as an agent?

SFF: That's a hard one. Over the years, reflecting on the many books introduced by Alp Arts Co., and having had the opportunity to introduce kids to those books means everything. That's what it's all about. Frequently I have this opportunity, because I work part-time at our local independent bookstore. I have the unique chance as an agent to share books from my authors with lots of kids and that's a lot of fun.

The friendships I've developed with authors over the years

have been sustaining and meaningful. I truly appreciate the authors who have stayed with me over the years, even though they might have been tempted to move to a larger agency. Their loyalty has culminated in rewarding results for Alp Arts Co.

I always enjoy working with new ideas with my authors, morphing a few phrases into something memorable and great! My forte is picture books; I love this unique genre. Looking to the future, I plan to get back to creating my own books as a published author and illustrator. That's how my career began, studying with Maurice Sendak at Yale in the early 1970s. I credit Maurice for the inspiration to pursue this career.

A: Is there anything else you'd like to add?

SFF: I'd like to emphasize that a good personal relationship and loyalty between author and agent is primary. I believe there is an unwritten code of ethics in this business which should be respected. If an agent has been strategic to an author's success (especially contracting his or her first book), and if the author has enjoyed a professional and cordial relationship with the agent, then I think it is the author's responsibility not to build on their success by moving forward without the agent. Especially this applies to signing new titles with a publisher originally engaged by the agent for the author. Some authors will never honor the agent's hard work and ultimate goal to build a signature group of clients. Bottom line, agents need our successful authors as much as they need us!

Why You Don't Need an Agent

While a literary agent can help "grease the wheels" for you in the very competitive children's book market, you don't need one to succeed. Many authors I have met over the years do not have an agent and they have done quite well. They have established a reputation for themselves writing books that grab the attention of specific editors as well as books that do very well in the marketplace. Other authors, such as myself, have chosen to have a literary agent to assist in getting publishable manuscripts directly into the hands of editors. My agent has personal relationships with several different editors and can target my work to two or three very specific publishers who specialize in the type of manuscripts I write. In that way, I can concentrate on the process of writing, leaving the business dynamics to my agent.

But, you don't need an agent to succeed as a children's author. Here are some instances when you may decide to "go it alone" and eschew the services of a literary agent.

- You may prefer to control all aspects of your writing career (writing, negotiations, monitoring royalty statements, dealing with an editorial/production team, etc.).

- You have plans to publish a single book. For that, you don't need an agent and all the long-term responsibilities that requires.

- You are comfortable in negotiating your contracts, including (but limited to), royalty rates, escalation clauses, due dates, manuscript lengths, editorial responsibilities, foreign rights, etc.

- You would rather keep all the money a book earns, instead of paying the usual fifteen percent commission to an agent over the life of the book.

- You like doing things on your own.

- You just don't have the time to research all those possible agents.

- You would rather not take the chance of getting the wrong agent—an individual who causes more problems than he solves.

- You are just starting out. You know that doing the necessary work and research on locating a reputable agent will detract from the time you need to perfect your craft. You'd rather spend your time now becoming the best writer you can. As you establish yourself (perhaps with a few published books), it might be appropriate to have someone represent you.

Caveat emptor

I'm sure it wouldn't surprise you to know that there are a lot of people out there who would love to have their hands on your wallet. In other words, there are probably more scammers out there (particularly in cyberland) than there is tea in China (to use an old, hackneyed phrase). To say there are con artists who would love to separate you from your hard-earned money would be to understate the obvious. And, yes, this holds true in the publishing industry as much as it does in selling used cars or any type of merchandise or service on the internet.

Let's just say that there are many people posing as "literary agents" who would be thrilled to separate you from your money. They aren't out there to steal your manuscript, but rather to offer you fictitious or imaginary services that cost a lot of money and produce nothing in return. Here are some clues that will help you spot these frauds before you ever think about signing over your children's inheritance or your retirement nest egg:

- If an "agent" has a display ad in a writing magazine, odds are they aren't legitimate. Real agents don't need to advertise.

- If an "agent" asks for any fees ("reading fees," "contract fees," "editing fees," or "contract fees") up front, there's a good chance you're about to be scammed.

- If you can't locate the titles of any books represented by an "agent" (on the agency's website, for example), then you should back away—far, far away.

- If an "agent" guarantees certain results ("You will be published!") then it's likely that a request for certain fees will be forthcoming soon. Don't fall for it.

- If an "agent" doesn't list a valid phone number or valid mailing address, then you can assume that they're only around for a short period of time (enough time to abscond with your money).

- If an "agent" tries to sell you lots of ancillary services (e.g. "Your very own business cards to share with all your friends," "A web site that will have editors beating down your door," or "A marketing plan that will knock your socks off") put both hands on your wallet and get away as quickly as you can.

Like any major financial decision, if it sounds too good to be true, then it probably is. **Buyer beware!**

Do you need an agent to succeed as a published children's author? ☐ YES ☐ NO

Which box did you check off? YES or NO? Guess what, either answer is correct. Please don't fall into the all too common trap of thinking that the only way you're going to succeed in this business is to have an agent working for you. As mentioned above, many authors don't have agents and have done very well for themselves. Other authors have signed on with an agent and they have enjoyed a long and very profitable relationship as a result.

When I was starting out, I got some very good advice: start with small publishers (those who publish a limited number of books in a very specific niche of the market). I wrote a manuscript that focused on an unusual physiological characteristic of several animals. I submitted it to several small publishers and waited. One of the publishers I approached dealt specifically with nature books for six to nine-year-olds, an area I wanted to specialize in at that time. They eventually accepted that initial manuscript. Then, they accepted another and another. After I had published five different books with them (negotiating all my own contracts), I felt I was ready to approach an agent and ask for representation. I was looking for a long-term career as a children's author and since I had proven I could write publishable manuscripts, the individual I contacted (Sandy Ferguson Fuller, whom you met in the interview above) was thus more than willing to take me on as a client.

It will be up to you to decide if an agent will be part of your goal(s) as a children's author. Talk with other children's authors and get their views and insights. Consult all the references listed in this chapter. Strike a balance between your short-term and long-term writing objectives and determine (just for you) the ultimate benefits of agent representation. Know that there is no single right answer for all writers. You are unique and you need to make a decision that works to your best interests.

Chapter 17

What About Self-Publishing?

Once upon a time, a thirty-five-year-old writer began a children's story about one of the animals she frequently cared for. A quiet naturalist by heart, she often had a menagerie of pets in her house: everything from bats to rabbits and frogs to hedgehogs. It was not unusual for her pet mice to run around the house at all times of the day—an event that must have detoured many a potential visitor to the home.

She especially enjoyed penning stories about her "zoo" and would often focus on one or two of the critters for starring roles in her fanciful tales. She was particularly enamored of her pet rabbit—a cherished "friend" she often took for walks on a leash. Not only did she write a story about her furry friend, she was also an accomplished artist and drew many drawings of her companion.

She decided that her story and drawings were good enough for publication and began to send them out to various publishers. However, one publisher after the other rejected her work. Frustrated at her inability to get commercially published, she eventually decided to self-publish her work. With some money from her savings account, she funded a very small print run of 250 books and began to distribute them to friends and family.

The book proved to be so successful that, within a year, it had been picked up by one of the publishers that had originally rejected it. Within a year of its commercial release, 20,000 copies of the book sold. Since its initial release many years ago, it has been translated into thirty-six languages and has sold well over forty-five million copies—becoming one of the best-selling children's books of all time.

And, it all began with 250 self-published copies.[8]

---

8. Who was the author (No, it's not J. K. Rowling.)? The answer is revealed at the end of this chapter.

For many writers, self-publishing is a path to publication that offers a great deal of control and the possibility of profits traditionally unavailable in the competitive world of commercial publishing. Authors who have experienced months (or even years) of rejection often turn to self-publishing as a way to take charge of their writing careers. It offers formerly unpublished authors an opportunity to have a book "out there," sharing a story with the reading (and buying) public.

Suffice it to say, self-publishing your children's book (either as an e-book or a POD) carries some risks and uncertainties. It's not for everyone, but it does offer a viable option to all those rejection letters you may have accumulated. But, it's important that you go into the world of self-publishing with your eyes wide open. For that reason, let's take a look at the positives and negatives of this burgeoning field.

Reasons for Self-Publishing

It offers a viable option for getting your manuscript into print.

When you consider the fact that as many as 95% of all manuscripts submitted to children's publishers are rejected, then the thought of taking charge of your story by publishing it yourself seems quite inviting. That pile of rejection emails and letters sitting on your desk may be calling out to you, "Hey, you know you can still get your book published without having to deal with all those people who don't know a good story when they see one." In many ways, self-publishing (an e-book, for example) offers you an "ace in the hole" that traditional publishers are not willing to provide: a viable option to seeing your book in print.

Everyone has a virtual library in their pocket.

As I write this, there are approximately five billion cell phones in use around the world. That means that more than sixty-three percent of the population of the planet has a cell phone. That's a fairly large audience for an e-book, don't you think? Self-publishing gives you the opportunity of reaching this very sizable audience at a very small cost. You can get your book out there and into the hands of a large segment of the reading public. The challenge, of course, is making the public aware of your book, but the possibilities are limitless.

Insider Tip

Publish Your Children's Picture Book (www.udemy.
com/publish-your-childrens-picture-book)—Step-by-
step video instruction guides you to write, revise,
illustrate, design, and publish your children's picture
book. Learn the indie-publishing process as you DIY
your first book right alongside the course instructor.

You have complete and total control over the production process.

With self-publishing, you are in total control. You manage all the editing, all the production, all the profits, all the marketing, and all the distribution. You are a total publishing company wrapped up in a single individual. All the decisions are yours; as well as all the risks. You don't have to rely on the whims of others: you are in total control of every facet of the publishing cycle. This can be a wonderful opportunity to become a company unto yourself.

Your profit margin is higher.

We'll get into the dollars and cents of traditional publishing in Chapter 20, but think about this: If you publish your book the traditional way, the finances and profits are heavily weighted in favor of the publisher. If a traditional children's picture book (hardback) sells for $16.95, you (as the author) will earn 5% of that sales price, or a mere eighty-five cents. If you do the math very quickly, you will see that you'll need to sell a ton of books to make any kind of decent profit. On the other hand, with a self-published book, all the profits are yours. Instead of 5% of the profits, you have the potential to take in 100% of the profits.

It can open doors to traditional publishing.

Every once in a while, lightning strikes and a self-published book is picked up by a traditional publisher and goes on to sell millions of copies. By the same token, by successfully selling a self-published book yourself, and building up a sizable audience, you now have some "ammunition" to approach traditional publishers with a well-established platform. By proving you have a viable audience, traditional publishers will be more apt to take a much closer look at any future manuscripts you may generate. You've proven yourself with a self-published book (eliminating much of the doubt that goes along with traditional submissions) and helped an editor make a publishing decision.

Insider Tip

Amazon opened the doors for the self-publishing boom with the introduction of Kindle Direct Publishing or KDP (kdp.amazon.com). This is a unique opportunity to "get your book out there" with very little time investment and absolutely no cost. I have used KDP to craft a few adult e-books and I can assure you it is easy to do, fast, and extremely efficient. In fact, even for "technophobes" such as me, this is one of the easiest programs to learn and most uncomplicated to execute.

There is a wide variety of e-book publishers.

With the popularity of e-books, a serious industry has sprouted to assist prospective authors in getting their books published. Offered below is a list of some of the more popular sites. If interested in this option, you would be well advised to do your homework and research each of these firms to determine the best one for you. You will note that the services and conveniences between these businesses vary widely. Take your time and select the one that best meets your needs.

- Amazon KDP (kdp.amazon.com)
- Blurb (www.blurb.com)
- Book Baby (www.bookbaby.com)
- Book Tango (www.booktango.com)
- eBookit (www.ebookit.com/tools/bp/Bo/eBookIt)

- iBooks Author (www.apple.com/itunes/working-itunes/sell-content/books)
- iUniverse (www.iuniverse.com)
- Kobo (www.kobo.com/us/en/p/writinglife)
- Lulu (www.lulu.com)
- Nook Press (www.nookpress.com)
- Scribd (www.scribd.com)
- Smashwords (www.smashwords.com)
- Trafford (www.trafford.com)

Insider Tip

Book Bridge Press (www.bookbridgepress.com) is a boutique book production company that specializes in producing children's books for independent authors. Their services include all aspects of book production from story development through the editorial process, hiring illustrators, art direction and design, and printing. Their team brings a wealth of direct industry experience (the owner is a former children's book editor who worked for several traditional publishers) and expertise to every project.

Reasons Against Self-Publishing

Self-published books are taken less seriously.

Unfortunately, self-published books are not taken as seriously as traditional ones. Far too many people in the book industry consider e-books as a low-grade option for authors who can't get their books published the traditional way—in other words: they're not good enough, they're second-rate, and they're less than adequate. True, there's a lot of junk being written and self-published every day, and the more that gets published the more people will discount you work as being legitimate and good. At times, this seems like an uphill battle, and it often is, simply due to the reality that self-publishing opens the doors for anybody and everybody with a computer to get their words into print. A lot of those words aren't worth reading and, as a result, getting folks to read your words becomes that much more challenging.

Low profits.

Many authors have the mistaken idea that if they can "just get my book on Kindle" they'll make trainloads of money, retire to some Caribbean resort, and bask in financial sunrises for the rest of their lives. Here's some hard facts:

- According to *Bowker* (September 2016), more than 700,000 e-books were self-published in the United States in 2015. Those books, in addition to the thirteen million previously published e-books still available, are competing for the reading public's money.

- The average self-published author can expect to sell approximately fifty to one hundred copies of their e-book over the lifetime of the title (Yes, you read those numbers correctly!). If your e-book is priced so that you make a profit of $2.00 on each one sold, that would give you a total overall profit of between $100 and $200 (a sum I believe to be considerably less than one night at most Caribbean resorts).

Self-published children's books are not purchased by librarians.

One of the largest audiences for your children's book is school and public librarians. These folks have considerable influence over whether a book will either be successful or will gather dust in the back of some publisher's warehouse. One of the critical criteria that helps librarians determine which books to buy and which books to ignore is whether or not a book has garnered any awards, prizes, or commendations. There are many different awards that children's books compete for every year: everything from the "biggies" such as the Caldecott Medal and Newbery Award to citations such as the International Reading Association's Teacher's Choice Award and the ForeWord Reviews Book of the Year. Librarians rely on these awards to determine the few books they will purchase each year from the more than six thousand traditional children's titles released each year. Self-published e-books, since they do not come from well-established traditional publishers, are never considered for these awards. Without the awards, librarians won't purchase your book.

Publicity and Promotion are time-consuming.

Take it from someone who has self-published a few titles, publicity and promotion will consume large qualities of your time (and a sizable chunk of your wallet) leaving you precious little time for writing new books. Getting some positive reviews of your e-book from family and friends is relatively easy (particularly if your book is posted on websites). However, bringing that book to the attention of a buying public takes lots of time and dedication—and it's a process that never stops. You can't just send out one or two announcements via Facebook and sit back to collect buckets of cash. Publicity and promotion are 24/7 jobs requiring attention, devotion, and dedication over an extended period of time.

You can get scammed.

There are a lot of folks out there who are well aware of how desperate some authors are to get their books into print. And they are willing to quickly separate you from your hard-earned money with all manner of promises and guarantees that are nothing more than smoke and mirrors. Be careful—be very **very** careful—about who you enlist to assist with the self-publishing process. Many an unknowing author has paid a great deal of cash for a great deal of nothing in return. Watch out!

Print on Demand (POD)

Print-on-demand is a digital process that takes care of the multitude of production issues and provides you with a viable product for distribution to bookstores and other buyers. It's important to keep in mind that POD publishers offer a variety of services at a variety of costs that will transform your story into a printed book. Their primary responsibility is to create a finished product—one that rivals the traditional books you find in your local bookstore. For that, they will charge an escalator of fees depending on the quality of services you require for the design (of the cover and interior), layout, and production of your masterpiece.

Insider Tip

A few years ago, a colleague and I did a POD book specifically designed for middle school and secondary teachers (*The Gettysburg Address: The Complete Teaching Guide*, 2012). We knew our market was small and felt that a POD would be the best way to get our information into the hands of classroom teachers. Traditional education publishers would have been reluctant to take on this project due to the limited market size. We found a suitable POD publisher and worked with them closely throughout the production cycle. Our book was released and within a year we were able to recoup all our costs. Although the book is still available, we have seen very little profit. Would we do it again? Yes. It was fun to work together and share our ideas with a receptive, but small, audience. It was also a great learning experience into this ever-growing faction of self-publishing.

The primary purpose of a POD publishers is to sell you, the children's author, publishing services. These services—and their costs—will vary from company to company, and they offer you, the author, differing levels of involvement. To illustrate this, here are some of the services offered by one Print-on-Demand publisher for children's books.

To give you an idea of the costs involved, here are the posted prices for four print-on-demand publishers. As illustrated in the chart above, each publisher has different levels of involvement depending on the services you require. Please note that these prices are current as of the writing of this book (2018) and are subject to change in the future.

As you can see, there is a lot of variation in pricing, depending on the specific services, packages, or design features you want to include in your children's book. If you are considering POD publishing, you would be well advised to carefully review the services and prices offered by

	Entry Level	Basic Level	Advanced Level	Diamond Level
Digital formatting & distribution	✓	✓	✓	✓
Paperback publishing	✓	✓	✓	✓
Cover	✓	✓	✓	✓
Image insertions	40	40	40	50
Image manipulation— simple			10	20
Illustration service— personal touch		6	10	
Illustration service— fine detail				10
Electronic proofs of book	✓	✓	✓	✓
Interior revisions	✓	✓	✓	✓
One-on-one author support	✓	✓	✓	✓
Bookstore availability	✓	✓	✓	✓
Online distribution	✓	✓	✓	✓
ISBN assignment	✓	✓	✓	✓
US Copyright		✓	✓	✓
ISBN		✓	✓	✓

	Entry Level	**Basic Level**	**Advanced Level**	**Diamond Level**
Paperback author copy	✓	✓	✓	✓
Paperback package books	5	5	15	20
Amazon "Look Inside"	✓	✓	✓	✓
Google preview	✓	✓	✓	✓
Barnes & Noble "Read Istantly"	✓	✓	✓	✓
Social media setup guide	✓	✓	✓	✓
Booksellers return program				✓

several companies to be sure you are getting a product that meets your specific needs and is within your budget.

One of the questions new POD authors frequently ask is, "How many books will I need to sell in order to recoup my original investment?"

	Level 1	**Level 2**	**Level 3**	**Level 4**	**Level 5**	**Level 6**
Publisher A	$1500	$2800	$5500			
Publisher B	$1400	$2000	$3100			
Publisher C	$900	$2600	$4000	$6000		
Publisher D	$900	$1500	$2100	$4000	$7800	$15,300

This is an excellent query and in order to answer it, let's assume you are getting the least expensive production package available from a company. Please keep in mind that most POD publishers offer a wide range of upgrades and will try to upsell authors on those features (see the two charts above) during the publishing process. If you purchase any of those upgrades, you will need to sell considerably more books than reported here.

Based on the least expensive package offered by each of nine randomly selected POD publishers, you will need to sell anywhere from 160 to 730 copies in order to recoup your original investment. Add in any costs involved with promotion and publicity (or those extra upgrades), and you will quickly see the need to sell considerably more books before you begin to break even.

A Few Print-on-Demand Publishers

- Author's House (www.authorshouse.com)
- Book Baby (www.bookbaby.com)
- Hillcrest Media (www.hillcrestmedia.com)
- Ingram Spark (www.ingramspark.com)
- iUniverse (www.iuniverse.com)
- Lightning Source (www.ingramcontent.com)
- Lulu (www.lulu.com)
- Mill City Press (www.millcitypress.net)
- Outskirts Press (www.outskirtspress.com)
- Thomson-Shore (www.thomsonshore.com)
- Xlibris (www.xlibris.com)

Please keep in mind that self-publishing is not for everyone. It is an option, not the ultimate answer. There are risks as well as opportunities, so you need to enter this field with both eyes wide open. Do all your homework before investing any money. The amount of research you do early on will be a significant factor in deciding whether self-publishing is a viable option for your book.

Insider Tip

Take advantage of review sites such as Writer Beware (www.sfwa.org/for-authors/writer-beware) and Predators & Editors (www.pred-ed.com) to carefully evaluate the legitimacy of any firm offering publishing options.

Check resources specifically geared for self-publishers, including the Independent Book Publishers Association (www.ibpa-online.com), Dan Poynter's highly informative website (www.parapublishing.com), and the Independent Publisher online magazine (www.independentpublisher.com).

Hybrid Publishing

There's a new kid on the block, and it's called hybrid publishing. As the name suggests, hybrid publishing is a combination of two familiar publishing options. Hybrid publishers are those who have married elements of a traditional publisher (who takes on all the financial responsibilities of getting a book into the marketplace) and self-publishing (in which the author assumes all the financial risks of publication and distribution). Instead of financing all the production and marketing costs themselves, a hybrid publisher uses an author-subsidized business model. In exchange, they return a higher than industry standard share of sales to the author. In other words, by covering some of the costs of publishing a book, an author reaps greater financial rewards (higher royalties) than would be the case with a more traditional publishing house. Similarly, a publisher benefits because their profits stem from a combination of publishing services (offered directly to an author) and book sales (offered directly to the reading public).

What clearly differentiates hybrid publishers from typical "author subsidizes everything" models—often known as vanity presses or vanity publishing—is that hybrid publishers embrace a strict set of professional publishing standards.

Insider Tip

A vanity press (often known as a subsidy publisher) is a publishing house in which authors pay all the costs associated with their book's publication. Typically, vanity publishers have no selection criteria and will publish anything an author is willing to pay for. It should be noted that books published by vanity presses never make it into bookstores or online. It is up to the author to distribute and sell the books printed.

The standards (drafted in February 2018 by the Independent Book Publishers Association) comprise a list of nine criteria that clearly and explicitly define the responsibilities of any professional hybrid publisher. It is expected that all reputable hybrid publishers will adhere to these standards. The nine criteria (along with a brief explanation of each) are as follows:

1. Define a mission and vision for its publishing program. Just like a traditional publisher, any hybrid publishing house must have a clearly defined goal, a definitive mission statement, and industry-appropriate principles.

2. Vet submissions. Similar to a traditional publishing house, a hybrid publisher doesn't publish every manuscript that is submitted (as opposed to a vanity publisher). Every book manuscript must go through a rigorous and clearly defined vetting process.

3. Publish under its own imprint(s) and ISBNs. A hybrid publisher, like a traditional publisher, typically has a publishing team dedicated to developing and distributing a select number of books. Each of those books is recorded (via ISBNs) and catalogued.

4. Publish to industry standards. The caliber of books published by a hybrid publisher must be equivalent to those released by a traditional publisher

5. Ensure editorial, design, and production quality. Just like traditional houses, the books published by a hybrid publisher must evidence professional editing, design, and production values consistent with traditional books.

6. Pursue and manage a range of publishing rights. Authors have the opportunity to negotiate their rights. These include domestic, foreign, audio, electronic, and video rights (among others).

7. Provide distribution services. A hybrid publisher actively promotes and publicizes books (rather than simply offering them online). Each book released has a marketing and sales strategy that ensures it will come to the attention of the largest possible audience.

8. Demonstrate respectable sales. Hybrid publishers must show evidence that their publicity efforts result in a consistent and regular pattern of sales. Reasonable quantities of books must be sold within each of the publisher's market niches.

9. Pay authors a higher-than-standard royalty. Since there is a financial investment on the part of the author, a hybrid publisher must offer their authors a royalty rate that is greater than that expected from a traditional publisher (who does not rely on an author's financial contribution). For the most part, these royalty rates are negotiable; however, the IBPA strongly suggests that an author's royalty be greater than 50 percent of net on both print and digital books.

The Good, The Bad, and The Ugly

Suffice it to say, there are a lot of people out there determined to get their hands on your wallet, your children's inheritance, or that retirement nest egg you've been contributing to for all these years. Some companies will market themselves as a "Hybrid Publisher" when they are nothing more than a "wolf in sheep's clothing," so to speak. Their ultimate goal is to siphon as much money as they can from your pockets with little chance of publishing or promoting a quality book. How can you tell the good ones from the bad? Here are some critical factors you need to investigate and consider:

Insider Tip

The Independent Book Publishers Association is defining the hybrid publishing model as follows: "A hybrid publisher makes income from a combination of publishing services [sold to an author] and book sales."

- A reputable hybrid publisher doesn't publish everything (or nearly everything) that is submitted. A good hybrid is selective in the manuscripts they accept. They have strict standards for the manuscripts they decide to publish and will often reject many more manuscripts than they accept.

- A reputable hybrid offers a clearly defined distribution program. They actively try to get their books into brick-and-mortar stores (something a vanity press will not do). They also have a regularly issued catalog available to marketers as well as the general public.

- A good hybrid will offer or provide editorial services just as a traditional publisher does. They are interested in selling lots of books, just as you are, and will give your manuscript a commensurate level of editorial attention. All books (including this one) need some level of editorial attention. No reputable publisher publishes a first draft!

- A good hybrid will designate a traditional print run. That is, they will print a specific number of books in anticipation of projected sales figures. Their sales department actively works towards the success of each book, ensuring that every book generates appropriate sales figures (Note: vanity publishers do not have sales teams; they will print books, but have no means to get those books into the hands of buyers.).

- A reputable hybrid has an active and robust marketing plan for each title. As such, review copies are submitted for evaluation to select publications, press releases are provided to newspapers and other media, and media outlets are notified of a book's publication.

- A good hybrid will give you the opportunity to communicate with recent authors. One of the best ways you can research a hybrid publisher is to interview (in person, via a phone call, through a Skype interview, or with a series of emails) one or more current authors about their experiences with a specific company. Listen carefully and you will undoubtedly learn a lot of valuable information about a publisher's mission, philosophy, and goals (as well as their professional relationships with authors).

Insider Tip

Here are a few select hybrid publishers for your consideration:
Greenleaf Book Group (https://greenleafbookgroup.com)
She Writes Press (https://shewritespress.com)
Inkshares (https://www.inkshares.com)
Matador (https://www.troubador.co.uk/matador)
Unbound (https://unbound.com)
Evolved Publishing (https://evolvedpub.com)

Interview with Brooke Warner

In order to give you some insight into the dynamics of hybrid publishing, I took advantage of a unique opportunity to interview Brooke Warner, who is the publisher for **She Writes Press** in Berkeley, California (www. shewritespress.com). According to Brooke, **She Writes Press** exists to "provide women writers with a professional publishing platform that rivals traditional publishers." I talked briefly with Brooke about the dynamics of hybrid publishing in general, as well as how her company works with authors.

AUTHOR: What do you see as the distinguishing features of hybrid publishing?

BROOKE WARNER: I worked on helping to craft the nine criteria for hybrid publishing by the Independent Book Publishers Association (IBPA). Basically, hybrid publishers are distinguished by the following: all submissions are vetted, the publisher has a mission, there is a process of distribution in place, there is an incentive to sell books, and there is a set of high standards.

A: How does this distinguish you, say, from a vanity publisher?

BW: By and large, a vanity publisher engages in "mill publishing," that is, they will publish anything. They have no mission statement, there is no vetting, and they are primarily a service provider. They really don't care about selling books.

A: What kinds of royalties do you offer authors?

BW: At **She Writes Press,** authors get a royalty of 60 percent; and the publisher keeps 40 percent. On e-books, the author gets 80 percent and the publisher gets 20 percent.

A: What is the financial commitment of the author?

BW: The author pays $5,900.00 for our services. For that amount, they have their manuscript proofread and they get a professional cover. That fee also covers the interior design, e-book conversion, an ISBN, a copyright, any project management, work with a developmental editor, an updating of information, and ongoing management of the book.

A: What is your acceptance rate?

BW: Roughly, we get about 40 − 50 submissions a month. We accept about seven to eight percent of the manuscripts submitted.

A: How many books do you publish each year?

BW: We publish about one hundred books a year.

A: How would you distinguish **She Writes Press**?

BW: We do a lot of things that a traditional publisher would do. We are selective, we edit, we have a sales force, and we promote our books. We like working with authors who want a fighting chance in the market.

A: What advice would you offer authors considering hybrid publishing?

BW: Be careful! It's important to keep your eyes wide open.

It's clear that hybrid publishing offers authors a unique and distinctive way to get their words into print. I know I've said it before, but it surely bears repeating: Please do your homework and research any publishing firm—whether traditional, hybrid, or self-publishing—before you invest either money or time into securing a publishing arrangement. Many readers will discover lots of advantages with hybrid publishing, but only if they are clearly knowledgeable about its parameters and possibilities.

Insider Tip

Take advantage of review sites such as Writer Beware (www.sfwa.org/for-authors/writer-beware) and Predators & Editors (www.pred-ed.com) to carefully evaluate the legitimacy of any firm offering publishing options.

The author profiled at the beginning of this chapter was Beatrice Potter, who penned (and initially self-published) *The Tale of Peter Rabbit* in 1902.

Part VI

Reality Check

Chapter 18

From the Editor's Desk

Imagine having a job with all these daily responsibilities:
- Staff meetings
- Meetings with the top management
- Meetings with the Art Department
- Meetings with the Editorial Department
- Meetings with printers and production people
- Meetings with sales representatives
- Phone calls/emails to authors
- Phone calls/emails to agents
- Phone calls/emails to staff
- Phone calls/emails to distributors
- Preparing the next catalog
- Preparing "Profit and Loss" statements for any new books accepted
- Contracts to write, review, and approve
- Sales presentations
- Corporate training sessions
- Copyediting manuscripts
- Managing editorial staffs
- Designing promotional campaigns

AND

- Reading tons of submissions

Yup, that's just a small sample of what book editors face every day. It's almost like a circus performer who is juggling eight bowling balls, ten flaming torches, five spinning hoops, and three chainsaws while walking a tightrope over an open cage of very hungry lions (Oh, and she's carrying two clowns and a somersaulting dog on her back, too).

To say that most children's editors are busy would be to understate the obvious. While, as an author, you would like to have an editor spend an extraordinary amount of time reading your carefully prepared manuscript, that's just not going to happen. Reviewing manuscripts is just one small part of their everyday responsibilities. What's important to remember is that publishing is a business and the editor was hired in order to help the business make money. If she doesn't contribute to the publisher's bottom line, then she is soon out the door looking for other employment.

What Editors Wish Writers Knew

Wouldn't it be nice if you could sit down with a children's editor and ask her anything you wanted? What if you could dig into an editor's mind and find out what she looks for in a good manuscript? If you could ask an editor about some of the biggest mistakes writers make (so you wouldn't make them, too), what would you like to know?

When I began writing professionally, I, too, thought about those questions. If I could crawl inside an editor's head and discover some of the things that would help my manuscripts get out of the slush pile and into production, then that would be an enormous bonus in my favor.

And, so, over the course of my writing career, I've read, interviewed, and listened to many editors. I've met them through the columns and articles they write for professional publications and blogs, I've chatted with them and listened to their presentations at writing conferences, and I've spoken with them on the phone and through countless e-mails as we have worked together to revise and improve various manuscripts slated for publication. Their thoughts and philosophy have given me an education available nowhere else. I thought you might enjoy some of their sage advice as you begin this incredible journey.

The list below is a compilation of some of the most common flaws of children's manuscripts as shared by the editors who read them. As I do, you should consider these items as critical to the acceptance or non-acceptance of any manuscript you write. You will quickly note that most of the items on this list are topics previously discussed in this book—and that was intentional. Much of the inspiration for selected chapters came about as a result of input from a wide range of children's editors. I wanted to offer you the most critical and most pertinent tips and techniques for a successful writing career, so I began with insights from the folks who are on the front lines of children's literature: the editors themselves.

Use these items as "tools" for your own publishing success. Know that many other writers will continue to make traditional mistakes and errors, thus sending their work on a short trip to the trash can. Know, also, that avoiding these mistakes won't guarantee acceptance of your manuscript, but you certainly will be helping your work stand out (in a very positive way) from the competition.

- **Not Following Submission Guidelines**—Far too many authors neglect to follow the submission guidelines of a specific publisher. They assume that submission guidelines are universal across the industry. They aren't. It's important that you follow each house's guidelines explicitly.

- **Bad Spelling/Bad Grammar**—Spelling and grammar count on both the cover letter as well as throughout the manuscript. Many editors, when they encounter a misspelled word or a grammatical miscue, will toss the manuscript without reading farther.

- **Moralistic Stories**—Don't write stories with morals or lessons to be learned. They are a dime a dozen and most of them are far too heavy-handed to be any good.

- **Unknowing**—Writers who haven't read a lot of contemporary children's books stand out like a sore thumb. Know what's being published and what kids are reading; don't try to write something similar to what you read as a child, it won't work!

- **Improper Manuscript Format**—A manuscript should be set up in a professional manner. Don't invent something new just to be different. You'll stand out for all the wrong reasons.

- **Unprofessional Writing**—It is quite easy to determine of a manuscript has had a great deal of time and effort invested in it. Hastily written stories can be spotted very easily. Write like a professional; write like it's your job (Please re-read Chapter 3)!

Expert Quote

"If I'm reading a manuscript and I miss my subway stop, then I know it's a good book. That's my ultimate test."

—Tiffany Liao, children's book editor

- **Untargeted Submissions**—Editors bemoan the tendency of authors to submit anything: science fiction to a publisher that only produces nature books, rhyming stories to a publisher who has never, once, published a rhyming book, or a picture book to a house that specializes in Young Adult (YA) novels.

- **Bad Rhyming Books**—Far too many first-time authors think the way to a published book is to write one in rhyme. Mostly the rhyming is poor, hackneyed, and trite—and very dull! Yes, yours truly has written several rhyming books, but they were not the first books I tried to get published. They came about only after I had published several other books in advance.

- **Illustrations**—Don't include any illustrations from yourself, your dear Aunt Susie who lives in Orlando (right down the road from Disney World), or your favorite niece who's thinking about selling real estate but may go to art school instead. Make the words create pictures in the mind of the reader. If your manuscript is accepted for publication, it will be up to the editor or art director to select an appropriate illustrator

- **No beginning, middle, and/or end**—Editors constantly wail about all the stories that come in without a beginning, middle, or end. For the most part, they are "stream of consciousness" tales that are better left recorded in diaries or personal journals. Spend considerable time reading all the children's books you can to determine how published authors deal with this oft-forgotten element.

- **Trends**—Don't write a story about a current trend (e.g. vampires, robots, a third grade teacher who is a vampire by night and has a robot as her best friend). Your book won't be published for at least two years, and by then, the trend has died. Instead, create a new and original trend.

- **Cute/Alliterative Names**—Bucky Beaver, Timmy the Turtle, Wally W. Walrus, Henrietta Hippo, and Silly Sally Salamander are not character names, they are names that make editors regurgitate their lunch.

- **Anthropomorphic animals**—Animals don't talk. Editors don't want to read about talking animals, or animals wearing the latest ensemble from Tommy Hilfiger, or animals who have been in a bad relationship and are now attending regular counseling sessions with a Zen master in Sedona, Arizona.

- **Unprofessional Cover Letters**—Re-read Chapter 15. Write it right!

- **Too Long**—Picture books of more than 1,000 words will seldom see the light of day; neither will YA novels of 150,000 words. Keep it down—way down.

- **Boring**—Don't write about A) "A Day in the Life of . . ."; B) how a very shy girl taught the school bully a lesson that changed his life forever; C) my favorite dog, cat, mouse, iguana, kangaroo, or dinosaur; D) grandpa died and we're so sad, but we'll make some lemonade and get over it eventually; or E) my mom is the best mom in the whole wide world and all my friends come over to our house every day after school to have her famous chocolate chip cookies and learn a lesson about sharing. Those have been done a thousand times—no, a million times! Write something that's never been written before.

Most children's book editors have personal pet peeves. Although the items on any single editor's list may vary from every other editor, the list below represents some of the most disrespectful miscues shared with me by a variety of editors. Unbelievably, these are not one-time events; they happen more frequently than you might imagine. But, they do represent the (inappropriate) lengths some authors will go to in order to get published. Use these quotes as templates for what you shouldn't do—or, better yet, what you should never do!

- "There are many novice authors who expect and request a full evaluation of their unsolicited manuscript. This includes requests for numerous suggestions on how to make their work publishable by that particular publisher."

- "Although the Submission Guidelines state that it often takes three to four months to make an evaluation of a manuscript, many authors expect an instant reaction from the publisher. Unbelievably, they will follow up by phone or email the day after the manuscript arrives."

- "Thinking that editors spend the day twiddling their thumbs, many authors call or query with an idea they want help in developing. Then there are the authors who call and want to talk through their plot before they even begin a manuscript."

- "We get far too many submissions from authors who blindly submit their work with absolutely no idea about the titles that normally appear on our list."

- "The submission rules are quite clear; yet, we see numerous authors who submit several manuscripts in the same envelope."

- "I don't know how to be any clearer—no sample illustrations!"

- "I'm frustrated by the number of prospective authors who don't know, understand, or respect children. They have no idea of the audience for whom they are writing."

Expert Quote

"Knowing you can work with someone on revision is the most important part of the editor/ author relationship."

—Caitlyn Dlouhy, children's book editor

A Conversation with a Children's Book Editor

Below is a transcript of a conversation I had with Carol Malnor, the editor-in-chief of Dawn Publications (dawnpub.com), a children's book publisher that has been "connecting children and nature since 1979." As a children's author herself, Carol has a unique perspective on the industry from both sides of the desk. In the business for many years, she has garnered a plethora of insights and reflections about children's books and the authors who write them. I sincerely hope her words of wisdom offer you some perspectives and instruction on your own unique journey to publication.

AUTHOR: What are some of your everyday responsibilities?

CAROL MALNOR: Every day is different because I'm simultaneously working on books that are at different stages of the development process. On a weekly basis, I'm reading manuscripts, looking for that special one that perfectly fits our niche; working with authors to revise their text; fact checking information to prepare manuscripts for vetting; and working with illustrators and our book designer. Writing for the business is also a part of my regular responsibilities— creating promotional materials, press releases, catalog information, online lesson plans and activities, a weekly blog, and a quarterly article for our website. And, of course, there is the continuous stream of emails to respond to!

A: What's the biggest misconception people have about children's book editors?

CM: (laughs) It's such an easy job that anybody can do it. Most people think, "There are so few words, it can't be hard to edit a kids' book."

A: What do you wish all authors knew about your job?

CM: I wish authors knew that publishing a book is a huge financial investment for publishers, and also a big risk. Publishers have tremendous upfront costs, and we depend on successful sales to recoup those costs and continue in business. No matter how much I may personally like a manuscript, we're only able to publish it if our team believes that it has wide appeal in the marketplace—the bottom line is that we have to have confidence that the book will be a good seller. Unfortunately, that means we're not able to publish all of the worthy manuscripts that come across my desk. I would also like authors to know that every submission I receive is handled with respect. I honor and appreciate the author's creative expression even if we can't publish their work.

A: What's one of the biggest misconceptions new authors have about children's books?

CM: A big misconception is that writing a children's book is easier than writing a book for adults. Many new children's book authors think, "Children's books are just simple stories. It will be easy to write one." That's just not the case. It's a real challenge to communicate an interesting story or meaningful concept using just a few words, in short sentences, with simple vocabulary. I've written for adults, and I know first-hand that it's much harder writing for children.

A: What would you like to tell every potential author?

CM: Before submitting a manuscript, it's imperative that you find out as much as you can about the publisher. Check out their website and peruse their catalog. Get to know the kinds of books they publish—understand the scope and variety of their books. You'll save yourself a lot of rejections if you put in the time to get to know the publisher **before** you submit. Once you determine that your work is a good match with the publisher, carefully read their submission guidelines, and follow them to the letter.

A: What do you look for in a submission?

CM: First of all, I'm looking for manuscripts that fit the parameters stated in our Submission Guidelines. We clearly spell out what we want, and also what we don't want. Because our niche is creative nonfiction, the manuscript must connect with the school curriculum, usually meeting one or more elementary science standards. Beyond that, I'm looking for an emotional hook that grabs me and pulls me in. Something that has a special spark—maybe it's an endearing character or an unusual plot twist that makes me want to know "what's next." I often receive a manuscript that's well-written and meets our guidelines, but it just doesn't have a special quality that will delight the reader. It's difficult to describe, but I recognize it when I see it.

A: What makes a manuscript stand out (from the slush pile)?

CM: A manuscript that touches my heart and tickles my funny bone always stands out from the pile! An endearing main character is also a big factor. Manuscripts that make their way out of the slush pile and into the "potential manuscripts pile" must have a creative element, address a unique topic, or take a really fresh or unusual look at a topic. And a catchy title gets my attention, too. A clever title in the subject line of a submission email entices me to open it right away.

A: What's missing from most manuscripts?

CM: An engaging element that surprises and delights the reader.

A: What's one of the biggest mistakes writers make when writing picture books?

CM: Writing nonfiction that is creative and entertaining is a real art. Not many people can do it. I often receive manuscripts that are well-written, but that wouldn't be exciting for children. And many authors make the mistake of being didactic or preachy. They tell children what to think and how to feel rather than weaving the message into a story for children to discover on their own. I also receive beautiful, heartfelt manuscripts that I can't publish because they're written for an adult's sensibilities rather than for a child's—the vocabulary is too complex or the concept is too abstract. While we should never underestimate what children are capable of understanding and feeling, the writing needs to reflect the language realities of young children.

A: And, how do you tune into that child's energy at the appropriate age with the right words?

CM: Spend time getting to know the age-group you're writing for—discover what they find interesting and fun. Talk to teachers. I had an "Aha moment" when I received this comment from a first-grade teacher: "This is a question that my students often ask me when I'm going to read a new book to them, 'Is this a story or just talking?' They strongly prefer a story! If a book is mostly information, it must have a main character they can connect with."

A: What single piece of advice would you give all authors (new and experienced)?

CM: I don't have any advice. But I will quote Maurice Sendak who has excellent advice for authors: "You cannot write for children. They're much too complicated. You can only write books that are of interest to them."

A: What should writers do (that they don't) before submitting a manuscript?

CM: Get feedback from children **not** related to you. Ideally, become a fly on the wall while someone else reads your manuscript to children so you can see how kids react to it. Then keep editing until kids love it.

A: What do you see as the future of picture books?

CM: Changes in technology are going to continue to influence the future of picture books, and it's hard to know where tech will take us. Books about diversity with diverse characters, including female main characters, is a trend that I think will be continuing. STEM (Science, Technology, Engineering, and Math) remains a hot topic in education, and picture books have a huge potential to fill that niche. On a personal level, I'm hopeful that there will be an increasing demand for books that focus on social-emotional skills, as well as mindfulness skills.

Words of wisdom? You bet!

Chapter 19

Rejection is Just Another Fact of Life

What do Judy Blume, Dr. Suess, J. K. Rowling, and the author of this book all have in common? That's right—we've all been rejected. Each of us has been rejected more than once in our professional writing careers, and you will be too. The sun will rise tomorrow morning, your children will grow up, New York taxi drivers will drive like madmen, California will fall into the ocean as the result of a major earthquake, and you and I and a million other writers will have our manuscripts rejected. It's a fact of life!

I've been writing professionally for more than three decades. Hardly a month goes by that I don't receive a rejection letter or email of some sort or another. Am I angry, frustrated, miserable, upset? You bet I am! But, I also know that not every editor or editorial assistant is going to like everything I write and that everything I write may not be appropriate for that particular market at that particular point in time. Here's something you may want to keep in mind: When a manuscript is rejected, it's often because one person, *one person*, didn't like it. Not an audience, not a school district, not a country—just one person.

Although rejection is a "given" for every writer, it's what you do about rejection that will ultimately determine the success you will enjoy as a published author. Treat rejection as just another event in your writing life and you will undoubtedly go on to enjoy a successful career. Treat it as a major obstacle or major stressor and it will become a proverbial anchor weighing you down and preventing you from moving forward in your authorial pursuits.

Expert Quote

"A published author was once an unpublished author who didn't quit submitting."

—Lee Masterson, author

Insider Tip

The Realities:
1. **If you write, you will be rejected.**
2. **Rejection sucks!**
3. **Get over it.**
4. **Move on.**

When I first began writing professionally, I was fearful of rejection letters. After all, I had devoted considerable time, effort, and creativity to each and every manuscript. Shouldn't an editor recognize all my "mental investments" and reward me with a contract? I certainly didn't deserve, or earn, a form rejection letter. Of course not! But, still the rejection letters kept coming. I brooded. I moped. I fretted. I purchased way too many bottles of California wine.

But, then I realized that the rejection letters were actually an incentive to keep trying. Each rejection letter was simply one person's opinion about my work at a specific point in time. Each person is certainly entitled to his or her opinion and I don't necessarily have to agree with that opinion.

So, I began to rethink my reaction to rejection. I came to the conclusion that excessive worrying about rejection wasn't going to get my work out to those people whose opinions I sought and whose opinions I needed—in essence, those people who wanted my work and were willing to see it through to publication. So, I initiated a new personal policy regarding rejection:

Publication is not just to the few, but rather to the persistent.

Yes, I still get rejections, but now I just see them as another opportunity to submit a work to someone else.

It Happens to Us All!

- J. K. Rowling received fourteen rejections for the first Harry Potter book. She's now one of the richest women in the world!

- After completing A Wrinkle in Time, Madeleine L'Engle received over thirty rejections. When published, the book won the prestigious Newbery Award.

- Dr. Seuss's first book—And to Think That I Saw it on Mulberry Street—was rejected by twenty-seven different publishers.

- Judy Blume received rejection letters for two years before her first book—The One in the Middle is the Green Kangaroo— was accepted and published.

- Shel Silverstein was told by one editor that The Giving Tree was "too sad and too simple;" by another that it was "neurotic." Yet, it went on to sell 8.5 million copies.

- "Too radical of a departure from traditional juvenile literature" was what one editor said about The Wonderful Wizard of Oz. The book went on to sell fifteen million copies.

- One of the first children's books I wrote was initially rejected by eleven different publishers. The twelfth publisher decided it was perfect for their list. Since its initial release, it has been re-published in Spain, Brazil, and India and has been anthologized in several collected works. If I had stopped circulating that manuscript after the first or third or eighth rejection, the book never would had sold the more than 100,000 copies that it did.

A Personal Story

In early 2001, I began work on a children's book: *The Tsunami Quilt: Grandfather's Story* (a book you met in Chapter 11). The book is a fictionalized account of a horrific tsunami that struck the Big Island of Hawaii on April 1, 1946. Specifically, it is the story of the students and teachers at Laupāhoehoe School and how their lives were tragically altered that day. I wanted to tell the story through the eyes of a young boy whose grandfather was one of the students that fateful day.

In the course of preparing the manuscript, I took two trips to Hawaii to conduct my research at the Pacific Tsunami Museum and at the former site of Laupāhoehoe School. I talked with survivors, tsunami experts, and consulted numerous documents. To say that I really "got into" the story would truly be an understatement; it consumed me with its intensity and its tragedy. I sincerely wanted to honor the memory of those who lost their lives that day as well as those who ultimately survived.

I began crafting the manuscript and went through about twenty-seven drafts over the course of a two year period. Although this was only a thirty-two-page children's book, it was a story that required attention to every historical detail as well as the two main characters—a grandfather and his grandson. Finally, the manuscript was completed in Summer 2003 and was sent into the market.

The first editor took eight months to review the manuscript and sent it back with a terse note that it was "slightly melodramatic." It was sent to another house and was rejected within two months. Editor after editor rejected the manuscript with comments such as "doesn't fit our needs at this time," "not likely for our list," "not strong enough," and "the grandfather should be telling the story." There was also the usual collection of form letters with "Thanks, but no thanks." Undaunted, it was resubmitted to a new editor each time it was rejected by another. I was convinced the story was solid and that the tragedy of the tsunami had been effectively detailed through the eyes of a young boy. I knew I had written a good tale and just wouldn't take "no" from editors.

Throughout most of 2004, all through 2005, and into the early part of 2006, the manuscript gathered rejection letter after rejection letter—a total of twenty in all. Finally, in March of 2006, an editor called and said she wanted the manuscript. In fact, she said she "fell in love with the manuscript." Fifteen months later, the book was released and has now become one of my best-selling children's books.

Incidentally, as the editor and I were working on the manuscript during the editing process, we modified just three short sentences in the entire manuscript—everything else remained as it was originally written. I refused to believe those editors who rejected this book because "the young boy was not fully developed" or "there was no dialogue for the grandfather." I was committed to the story and the way in which it had been written; I just wasn't about to accept the rejections I received. Each time I got one, my agent just put the manuscript back in circulation. "Dumb Persistence" is what I call it. If we had stopped after the first, the tenth, or the nineteenth rejection, I may never have seen my story in print—or in the hands of young readers!

"Why Was I Rejected?"

Authors often wonder why a manuscript is rejected. Very rarely will you get an explanation as to the specific reasons for a rejection. Suffice it to say, there are an incredible array of reasons why manuscripts are dismissed. The following (partial) list of reasons/excuses is not meant to be exhaustive. Rather, it is intended to showcase the infinite variety of reactions that a proposed book may engender.

- The manuscript was too long.

- The manuscript was too short.

- Your cover letter was terrible.

- The writing isn't strong enough.

- The characters are weak or poorly developed.

- There is a considerable lack of detail.

- The dialogue is ho-hum.

- You included a letter of recommendation from your Aunt Louise. The editor doesn't know your Aunt Louise.

- Let's face it: your title ("Unknown Secrets of the United States Internal Revenue Code") is not particularly exciting.

- That editor only buys historical fiction. You submitted poetry.

- Somebody didn't think the story would sell more than four or five copies.

- Your manuscript was addressed to the wrong editor.

- You spelled the editor's name wrong.

- The manuscript was "anti-cat." The editor loves cats.

- The manuscript wasn't double-spaced.

- That story has been done a thousand—no, a million— times before!

- The manuscript was about antiferromagnetism. No one in the office knew what that was.

- The person you sent the manuscript to no longer works there.
- You sent out your first draft rather than the best draft.
- Your cover letter had 593 misspellings.
- The main character is not very interesting.
- The manuscript swarms with all sorts of grammatical "boo-boo's" ("'They're, they're,' she said. 'You won't get their until you read there directions.'").
- You ended each sentence with an exclamation mark! The editor isn't fond of exclamation marks!

Suffice it to say, there are more reasons for rejection than there are grains of sand on a beach. I once had a manuscript rejected because "Your writing is too intelligent." Some of the reasons are matters of practicality; while others are beyond logic. The key is to know that rejection is inevitable[9]; but it doesn't have to be accepted.

Expert Quote

"Prepare for the possibility that your work will be rejected. Your work. Not you. This is terribly important to remember. If that form letter that you can barely stand to open tells you that your short story isn't being accepted for an anthology, remind yourself that it's the story, not you, that didn't make it in."

—Carol Whiteley, author

Nine Reasons Why Manuscripts Are Rejected (Unrelated to the quality of your work)

You may have written the best YA novel since *The Hunger Games*, penned the picture book destined to outsell *Goodnight Moon*, or crafted a book of poetry guaranteed to leave *Where the Sidewalk Ends* in the proverbial dust. You may have gone through fifty-three drafts, spent more time in your public library than you did at home, and spit-polished a manuscript that would dazzle any child in the Western hemisphere and

9. Even mainstream authors such as John Grisham, William Faulkner, John Updike, and Kurt Vonnegut (among many others) have all been rejected.

still wind up with a fistful of rejection notices. You could have followed every tip, suggestion, and idea in this book and still have a barrel full of rejections sufficient to wallpaper your garage (and the garages of all your neighbors). The fact that you did everything right doesn't guarantee you publication. In many cases, the reasons why your manuscript wasn't accepted has more to do with factors outside your control than you could possibly imagine. Let's take a look:

1. **We're Overbooked.** You may be rejected simply because a publisher has way too many "lost in the Arctic + senior citizen romance + demented landscape architect + hairless orangutan + drunken cowboy + gay parents" books already accepted and they need to get all those published first before they can consider any more. Your submission was just one book too many in that genre. It may be good, but it had to be rejected.

2. **Won't Make Money.** When a book is seriously considered for publication, someone needs to do a "Profit and Loss" projection. This is an assessment of all the costs involved in publishing a specific book including printing, distributing, storing, overhead, royalties, and publicity. It's also an assessment of the projected profits such as bookstore sales, online sales, eBook sales, and foreign rights.

   For example, before *Writing Children's Books* was accepted for publication, my editor spent several weeks doing a "Profit and Loss" profile. In short, would the book make sufficient profit for the publisher to offset any and all costs involved with its publication and release? After all her calculations, she contacted me with the good news, "Yes, we'd love to publish your book." If your children's book (or any book, for that matter) flashes red after those calculations, then it will be rejected—not because there was something wrong with it, but more because there was something wrong with the numbers.

3. **Sheer Ignorance.** The first reader of your manuscript had limited experience with your topic—and, well, let's face it, "he's really a few fries short of a Happy Meal." He sent your manuscript back out of sheer ignorance ("He's one brick shy of

a load," "He's not the sharpest knife in the drawer"). Anyway, you get the picture.

4. **The Sales Guys.** The Sales Department of every publisher always gets into the act whenever books are being considered for publication. Essentially, they are the ones who have to sell the book to bookstores, book clubs, school and public librarians, and all those other outlets tasked with offering the book to the reading public. The Sales Department might say that children's books about a pygmy hippopotamus and his giraffe-with-a-thyroid-problem friend marooned with a troop of Boy Scouts on a remote island on Lake Reallyuglyspiders just won't sell the way they used to, so they're just going to have to reject this latest offering even though they really like books about a pygmy hippopotamus and his giraffe-with-a-thyroid-problem friend marooned with a troop of Boy Scouts on a remote island on Lake Reallyuglyspiders.

Expert Quote

"A . . . rejection is an opinion, not a judgement."
—Paul Raymond Martin, author

5. **I Wasn't in the Mood.** Keep in mind that editors (just like you) have "bad hair days." They get flat tires on the way to work, their babysitter cancelled out at the last minute, they got into an argument with the dry cleaner, somebody cut them off in traffic, they just got rejected by an on-line dating service, and/or a splot of grape jelly the size of Mongolia showed up on their new silk tie. They may get to the office in no mood to accept a manuscript—and yours is the first one they see that morning. "Sorry, I just wasn't in the mood."

6. **Clash of the Genres.**

- The publisher only publishes nonfiction nature books, but you sent them a manuscript about a fairy princess in the Witness Protection Program living in Tucumcari, New Mexico.

- The publisher only publishes picture books for preschool and/or Kindergarten kids, but you sent them a manuscript about a dwarf bank robber and his heavily tattooed sister on the run through the Florida Everglades (oh, and don't forget the pygmy alligators and the approaching hurricane).

- The publisher only publishes religious titles and you submitted a book with the title "How to Scam Your Neighbors, Deceive Your Relatives, and Get Away with Murder."

7. **Money, Money, Money.** The company has a cash flow problem and is under orders (from the boss whose job is on the line) not to accept any new manuscripts. Sorry, bad timing.

Expert Quote

"Rejections are a sign that you're working hard. Be proud that you actually wrote something, polished it, researched your markets, and mailed it out. That, in itself, is an accomplishment. Most people will go to their graves with the unrealized intention of getting this far!"

—Jennifer Minar, author

---

8. **Great Topic, But ...** You have a terrific topic, but it just happens to be one that offends the editor.

- You sent a manuscript about hunting to an animal rights advocate.

- You sent a manuscript about classical music to someone who only listens to hip hop.

- You sent a manuscript about bacon to a vegetarian.

- Your name is Lorraine. The editor once dated a girl in high school named Lorraine who dumped him—hard! To retaliate, he's vowed never to accept *any* manuscript from *any* woman named Lorraine.

9. **Reorganization Blues.** The company has been acquired, sold, refinanced, reorganized, or merged with some other conglomerate and are trying to establish a new identity and not quite ready to accept any new manuscripts for publication. And, oh, by the way, about half of the original company's staff has been let go (although they are all receiving occupational retraining on how to get a job in the "real world"). The new staff has absolutely no idea what they are doing and probably won't know what they are doing for quite some time. Your manuscript arrived at absolutely the wrong time. Sorry!

Expert Quote

"You can't take rejection personally. There are multitudes of factors that go into decisions about whether or not to sign a book. Good writing? Yes. Motivated author? Yes. But also: salability into various markets, competition, shelf life, timing, and so much more. The editor has to answer to the publisher, who has to answer to the sales and marketing teams, who have to answer to the bottom line. Remember: it's not personal—it's just business."

—Aimee Jackson, children's book editor

What Not to Do

When you get rejected (and you surely will), there are some things you shouldn't do. Yes, it's OK to throw a plate of pancakes at the kitchen wall, and it's fine if you want to shout lots of four-letter words at your computer screen, but please don't ever, no never, do any of the following after your prized manuscript has been rejected (in fact, don't even *think* about doing any of the following after getting rejected):

- Send a barrage of emails back to the editor commenting on the mutated gene pool from which he arose.
- Threaten to present the editor's first-born child as a sacrificial offering to the volcano gods.
- Rough up the editor's cat.

- Impale a voodoo doll of the editor with 666 needles (well, maybe that one is OK).

- Call the editor fourteen times in one day and leave voice mail messages about her obvious lack of backbone and/or brain cells.

- Send the editor a plain brown package filled with fossilized animal droppings (an obvious reference to what resides between his ears).

- Call the editor's secretary and cry uncontrollably.

- Call the editor's mother and cry uncontrollably.

- Call the editor's children and cry uncontrollably.

- Promise to slash the tires on the editor's car, bicycle, and lawnmower.

You may want to keep this in mind: editors frequently change publishing houses. If you bug, annoy, offend, or in some other way pester a certain editor (especially after being rejected), she or he may remember. Then, one or two years later when you send another manuscript to another house, that same editor (who was just hired by the new publisher) may be the one who reads it. She or he will certainly remember you. And, she or he will certainly know just what to do with your manuscript.

Personal Note

Ironically, as I was working on the first draft of this chapter, I received the following message from a children's book editor to whom my agent had sent a new manuscript:

"I publish so few picture books and really am not looking to expand. This is a strong text, but not what I'm needing for the list. Thanks for thinking of me."

Yup, even authors who write chapters on rejection still get rejected.

Chapter 20

Dollars and Sense

Which of the following two anecdotes is fiction?

☐ A.

Once upon a time, Tony wrote a children's book. It was published to great acclaim and began receiving a plethora of awards. In very short order, it rose to the top of the New York Times Best Seller list (where it stayed for over three years). Tony appeared on all the morning talk shows and was interviewed by every major newspaper from the Los Angeles Times to the Washington Post. Every library in the country purchased the book. Tony made so much money that he was able to retire early, purchase condos in Key West, Maui, and Aspen, and began collecting a fleet of BMWs, Aston Martins, and Lamborghinis. He and his wife bought two enormous yachts—one based on the east coast and one on the west coast. He was on the cover of *Time* Magazine (Person of the Year) and was frequently seen with Hollywood celebrities. His book went on to sell millions of copies and became a classic in children's literature.

☐ B.

Once upon a time, Tony wrote a children's book. It was published by a small publisher in the Midwest and was included in their fall catalog. The first year after its publication, the book sold a few hundred copies earning Tony about $250 in royalties. It continued to sell for several years after that; although fewer copies sold each successive year. Tony continued to write several more books for that publishing company, each one earning between $300 and $500 per year. Tony continued his career as a teacher with writing as a most pleasurable side occupation. The money he made from his children's books was used to buy new shoes for his children, an occasional night out at a local restaurant, and some repair work on the family's aging car. Although never getting rich, he continued to write for the sheer joy of putting books in the hands of an appreciative audience.

Anecdote B. is my own story, and for most children's authors, it will be their story, too. If you are entering this field to make a ton of money, may I respectfully request a reality check—chances are you won't! With more than 6,000 new children's books released every year, the competition is intense. Surprising as this fact may seem, less than 10% of all the books published will produce a substantial income for the author. If you think you will be making tons of money as a children's author, I would invite you to reassess your reasons for writing in the first place. Writing for money will be a very painful, frustrating, and unsatisfying process. Writing for kids, on the other hand, will bring you great joy and satisfaction. No Key West condos, oversized yachts, or BMWs—but lots of joy.

Expert Quote

"Most writers don't write for money or fame, they write from this longing to share what's in their hearts."

—Joanna Penn, author

Sure, there have been children's authors who hit the big time. They wrote a children's classic, sold a ton of books, and made so much money that they could give up their day jobs and be a full-time author. Here are a few examples:

- For ten years Jon Scieszka was an elementary teacher at the Day School in New York City. He loved to make kids laugh and came up with the idea of a story about the three little pigs as told from the wolf's point of view. The resulting book—*The True Story of the Three Little Pigs*—was published in 1989. It quickly captured the attention of kids, librarians and teachers. It sold so well that Jon was able to leave his teaching position and write full time. Since that early success, he has published numerous other notable titles such as *The Stinky Cheese Man and Other Fairly Stupid Tales, Math Curse, Science Verse, Squids Will Be Squids*, and *The Time Warp Trio*. And, yes, he makes a lot of money from his books!

- The story of J. K. Rowling, the author of the Harry Potter series, is well known. A single mother, jobless, on welfare, living in a small flat and writing in coffee house and cafes, she had almost every conceivable obstacle thrown her way. But, she persevered with her story about a young boy who attended a school of wizardry. The manuscript, typed on an old manual typewriter was submitted to twelve publishers, all of whom rejected it. It was eventually accepted by Bloomsbury, a small publishing house in London. The rest is history. Incidentally, in 2017 Rowling was named (by Forbes magazine) as the most highly paid author in the world with earnings of ninety-five million dollars per year.

- Born in the US, Eric Carle and his family moved to Germany in the early 1930s. Homesick for the US, Eric moved to New York City in 1952 with only seven dollars in his pocket. He landed a job as a graphic designer with the New York Times. Recruited by author Bill Martin Jr. to illustrate *Brown Bear, Brown Bear, What Do You See?*, he decided that writing and illustrating children's books might be a more satisfying career move. In 1969, he wrote and illustrated *The Very Hungry Caterpillar*, perhaps his most popular children's book. Since, he has created scores of books that have garnered numerous awards and accolades. In 2002, The Eric Carle Museum of Picture Book Art (44,000 square feet) opened in Amherst, NH.

The stories above are exceptions to the rule. For most of us, myself included, writing children's books will not result in bulging bank accounts, hordes of screaming fans (children and adults), or down payments on ancient castles and tropical resorts. Like me, you too will be able to walk through an airport or have dinner at your local Italian restaurant without being pestered by autograph hounds or crowds of reporters. Trust me, there is some solace in anonymity.

So, how much can you expect to make as a children's author? Let's take a look.

Somewhere buried in the legal language of a book contract is information about your royalty statement(s). A royalty statement is an accounting of how well your books are selling. You will be able to see how many books sold during that royalty period. Most publishers designate two royalty periods: January 1 through June 30, and July 1 through December 31. I work with one publisher who issues their royalty statements four times a year—quite unusual. The royalty statement contains information about how many books were sold during the royalty period as well as how many copies have been sold to date (since the book was published).

Also included on the royalty statement is the total amount of sales for a specific book, your royalty rate, and how much you earned as the author on each book published by that publisher. In most cases, the royalty rate on a children's book is 10%. On a picture book, that 10% is split between the author and the illustrator. Typically, the author gets 5%, and the illustrator gets 5%. So, let's say that your picture book racked up $2,000 in sales during the previous six months. Your profit, as the author, is 5% of those sales. The illustrator also gets 5% of those sales. As a result, the royalty statement will indicate that you earned $100.00 for that royalty period. You should find a check in the amount of $100.00 in the same envelope as your statement. If not, scream loudly!

Right now, you may be inclined to say, "Hey, Tony, are you kidding me? You mean that after all that time, toil, and trouble to write that picture book, get it accepted, go through an extensive editing process, and usher it into the world, all I get is a lousy 5%?"[10] Sorry, but my answer is "Yes." One of the great realities of this business—one seldom considered by folks who want to get a book into print—is that you will, most likely, not get rich. You may be able to take that royalty check and take your significant other out to dinner, or pay the electric bill, or buy a new outfit, but I think it's safe to say that a European cruise, two weeks in Cabo San Lucas, or a flashy new sports car are definitely out of the question. Most children's authors don't make a lot of money, they must be in it for other reasons.

---

10. If, on the other hand, you write a young adult novel (one without illustrations), you can anticipate a full 10% royalty for that book.

Insider Tip

If you'd like some inside information on what authors earn, as well as background data about the issues and concerns regarding payments for published works, please check out www.authorearnings.com.

Now, let's take a look at one of my own royalty statements.[11] This particular publisher would be considered a small publishing house (less than ten children's books released each year). Their royalty statements are issued twice a year and reflect sales from January 1 to June 30 and from July 1 to December 31. So far, I have published two children's picture books with this publisher: *Surfer Girl* (which was published six years prior to the date of this royalty statement) and *Buffalo Boy* (which was published three years prior to the date of this royalty statement).

Let's examine this statement in a little more detail. You'll note that this publisher provides information for each month of the reporting period (something I like). That way, I can see the ebbs and flows of a book over time. You'll also note that one book (*Surfer Girl*) consistently sells more copies than does the other (*Buffalo Boy*). Over this reporting period, *Surfer Girl* sold 2,091 copies and *Buffalo Boy* sold 769 copies—an indication that one book is doing much better in the marketplace than the other.

---

11. On the advice of counsel, and for reasons of confidentiality, I have created a fictitious name and address for this publisher. In addition, the titles of the two books as listed on this statement have also been altered. However, be assured that everything else reported here are the exact figures from the original royalty statement as received from the publisher.

Sample Royalty Statement A

Blue Daisy Press
1234 Garden Lane
Flowertown, NY 09876

Royalty Statement

Anthony D. Fredericks Title(s):   Surfer Girl

Address   Buffalo Boy

City, State, Zip

Statement Date: 7/10/20XX
Statement Period: 1/1/20XX to 6/30/20XX

Editions & Printings
Royalties from sales of the publisher's editions

Date	Edition	Quan.	Sales	Rate	Royalty
Jan	Surfer Girl	219	$1,915.39	6%	$114.92
	Buffalo Boy	81	$690.40	5%	$34.52
Feb	Surfer Girl	394	$3,548.28	6%	$212.90
	Buffalo Boy	103	$943.66	5%	$47.18
Mar	Surfer Girl	308	$2,802.55	6%	$168.15
	Buffalo Boy	72	$662.82	5%	$33.14
Apr	Surfer Girl	413	$3,935.64	6%	$236.14
	Buffalo Boy	171	$1,549.00	5%	$77.45
May	Surfer Girl	276	$2,595.73	6%	$155.74
	Buffalo Boy	160	$1,456.53	5%	$72.83
Jun	Surfer Girl	481	$4,347.76	6%	$260.87
	Buffalo Boy	182	$1,651.55	5%	$82.58
TOTALS	Surfer Girl	2,091	$19,145.35	6%	$1,148.72
	Buffalo Boy	769	$6,953.96	5%	$347.70

Net Royalties Payable for the Period $1,496.42

You'll also note two different royalty rates (5% for one book; 6% for the other). With this publisher, my agent was able to negotiate "escalator clauses"—segments of the contract that give me increased profits when a book does particularly well. For example, the contracts for these books state that when a book sells more than 20,000 copies (over its lifetime) my royalty rate increases from 5% to 6%. Also, when any book sells more than 50,000 copies (over its lifetime), then my royalty rate increases to 7%. At the time this statement was issued, *Surfer Girl* had sold a total of 21,677 copies (since its publication), thus entitling me to the 6% rate. *Buffalo Boy*, on the other hand, had only sold 14, 983 copies (since its publication) thus earning me the 5% rate. In essence, the more books that sell, the more I'm able to make on any future books that sell.

While I love escalator clauses, there's also another reality: the longer a book is in print, the more its sales diminish. Books tend to sell the most copies shortly after their publication, and sales often tend to drop off the longer a book is around. When a book is no longer profitable for a publisher, it goes OOP (out of print). This, as you might guess, means no more royalties. I have had several of my children's books go OOP. If you're really interested, you can locate them on the used book market. The decision to yank a book off the market is the publisher's, and there's no way of knowing when that might happen. I had one book go OOP in less than two years. Although my editor was very excited about it, it sold very few copies. I have another children's book, published in 2001, which is still selling quite well and according to a recent report from my editor, it remains one of their top five best-selling books. And, yes, I still get statements (at a 7% royalty rate) every reporting period.

Before I cash in my royalty check from this publisher, however, there is another reality. My agent is entitled to 15% of everything I make on the sales of my children's books. That means I owe her $224.46 on my royalty of $1,496.42.

Let's look at another one of my royalty statements.[12] This publisher typically publishes about twenty-five to thirty new children's books each year. As is customary, their royalty statements are issued twice a year and reflect sales from January 1 to June 30 and from July 1 to

---

12. As in the previous example, I have created a fictitious name and address for this publisher. In addition, the titles of the three books as listed on this statement have also been altered. However, be assured that everything else reported here are the exact figures from the original royalty statement as received from the publisher.

December 31. So far, I have published three children's books with this house: *Behind the Rainbow* (which was published seven years prior to the date of this royalty statement), *Magical Insects* (published ten years prior to the date of this royalty statement), and *Tree of Life* (published five years prior to the date of this royalty statement).

Sample Royalty Statement B

You will quickly note that this royalty statement is set up a little differently from the first one. This publisher doesn't break down their sales on a month-by-month basis. They only provide information on the accumulated totals for the previous six months of sales. Something else you'll note is that this particular publisher only issues children's books in two formats: hardcover copies and eBooks. They do not release any of their children's books in a paperback format.

Once again, you'll note two different royalty rates. For the hardback picture books, the royalty rate is 5%. There is an escalator clause in the contracts for all three books, but none of the titles has exceeded 20,000 books in sales (19, 237 books sold of *Behind the Rainbow*; 11,223 books sold of *Magical Insects*; and 8,513 books sold of *Tree of Life*). The eBooks have a different royalty rate altogether (12.5%). This royalty rate is common for eBooks as many publishers are releasing electronic versions of their books. However, at the time of this writing, children's eBooks are in their infancy (no pun intended), and the number of eBooks sold is a relatively minor part of the children's book publishing industry.

You may look at this statement and say, "Hey, Tony, you put a lot of blood, sweat, and tears into writing those three books and all you made was a lousy $280.57! (Not to mention the $42.09 [15% of $280.57] that I owe my agent.) Are you crazy or what?" True, my profits on these three books is relatively small. But, here's something to consider: as noted above, one book is seven years old, another is ten years old, and the third is five years old. In short, this particular publisher has kept my books in print for extended periods of time. As you might surmise, I earned much more on each of these books shortly after they were first published. Over time, as was to be expected, the sales for each of the books diminished. But one of the things I enjoy about this publisher is that they keep books in their catalog for a long period of time; in short,

Purple Bear Publishing
9876 Forest Road
Chicago, IL 59209

Royalty Statement
Statement period: 1/1/20XX to 6/30/20XX

Anthony D. Fredericks   Title(s): Behind the Rainbow
Address   Magical Insects
City, State, Zip Code   Tree of Life

Statement date: 8/8/20XX

Editions & Printings

Summary

Net royalties $280.57
Royalties earned this period $280.57
Net royalties payable for the period $280.57

Title	Frmt	Price	Copies	Revenue	Rate	Royalties
Behind the Rainbow	H	$17.95	421	$3,179.11	5%	$158.96
Behind the Rainbow	e			$141.98	12.5%	$17.75
Magical Insects	H	$17.95	116	$1,124.98	5%	$56.25
Magical Insects	e			$131.40	12.5%	$16.42
Tree of Life	H	$16.95	59	$504.98	5%	$25.25
Tree of Life	e			$47.56	12.5%	$5.94

they continually support their authors. I made much more money when these titles were initially released; and, even now, I still relish getting the semi-annual royalty statement, knowing there will be a check (small, to be sure) inside for me.

Sample Royalty Statement C

Here's another royalty statement[13], this time for a publisher with whom I have a single picture book (*Magnificent Monkeys*). This publisher releases about six new books each year and focuses on a very specific area of the children's book market: animal books. You will note that there are two separate editions of this single title: a hardback edition (H) and a paperback edition (P). For each edition, there is a separate report.

In comparing the two editions, you will note that during this six month reporting period, significantly more hardback (H) copies (1,017) were sold than were paperback (P) copies (539). For me, this is important information. Typically, hardback editions are purchased by both school and public libraries (paperback books have a considerably shorter shelf life). This seems to indicate that the library market for this book may be stronger than the retail market. I can't be absolutely sure of that, but previous experiences suggests that that may be the case here.

For both the hardback edition and the paperback edition you will note the inclusion of two interesting bits of information: "Sales at <60% discount" and "Sales at 60+% discount." In most cases, a publisher will offer a bookseller (your local independent bookstore, for example) a discount of 45 – 50% off the cover price of a book (45% is usual).

Thus, a children's picture book priced at $16.95 would be purchased by that bookstore for $9.32 (45% discount). That book is then sold at the cover price and the author gets the usual 5% royalty rate.

In rare cases, a bookseller may purchase a large quantity of books (for example, more than 500 books). In those instances, the publisher may offer the seller (Ingram, for example) a larger discount—more than 60%. Sellers will sometimes make those large purchases when they know a

---

13. As with the previous two examples, I have created a fictitious name and address for this publisher. In addition, the title of the book as listed on this statement has also been altered. However, be assured that everything else reported here are the exact figures from the original royalty statement as received from the publisher.

Anthony D. Fredericks
Big Blue Frog Press
Address: 9274 Swamptown Lane
Lilypad, SC 23958

Royalty Statement for Period Ended
June 30, 20XX

Title: MAGNIFICENT MONKEYS (H) Pub date: 9/20XX

	Sliding Scale Level	Copies Sold	Royalty Rate	Net Proceeds	Earnings
Sales:					
Sales at < 60% discount	thru 10,000	1001	5.00%	8402.02	420.10
Sales at 60+% discount	thru 10,000	6	2.50%	40.68	1.02
Mail Order Sales	thru 10,000	10	5.00%	127.10	6.16
SUBTOTAL (H)					427.28

Title: MAGNIFICENT MONKEYS (P) Pub date: 9/20XX

	Sliding Scale Level	Copies Sold	Royalty Rate	Net Proceeds	Earnings
Sales:					
Sales at < 60% discount	thru 20,000	426	5.00%	1865.10	93.26
Sales at 60+% discount	thru 20,000	106	2.50%	379.48	9.49
Mail Order Sales	thru 20,000	8	5.00%	53.68	2.68
SUBTOTAL (H)					105.43

TOTAL PAYMENT DUE:					532.71

book will be "hot" (the latest John Grisham novel, for example). Since there is a lower profit margin for the publisher, the author of those books gets a lower royalty rate (although there is the possibility of selling many more books).

And, as was the case with the previous two royalty statements, there is also the 15% ($71.91) due to my agent.

If the only reason you want to write a children's book is to make a lot of money, you will be very disappointed—and probably very frustrated. However, if your goal is to put good literature in the hands of children without regard for any subsequent profits, then you may be, as I am, a very satisfied author. The opportunity to influence a new generation of readers and the possibilities to refine and improve my writing skills are what continually drives me. Ultimately, a passion for writing and a passion for kids is what truly "floats my boat."

Expert Quote

"I have never set a single word down on paper with the thought of being paid for it. I have written because it fulfilled me. Maybe it paid off the mortgage on the house and got the kids through college, but those things were on the side—I did it for the buzz. I did it for the pure joy of the thing. And if you can do it for joy, you can do it forever."

—Stephen King, author

Chapter 21

Becoming a Successful Children's Author

"What do some authors do that makes them so successful?" That may be a question you asked when you decided to read this book. Indeed, it's a question many novice writers frequently pose. You, along with many of your contemporaries, are looking for the "holy grail" of authorship: the principles and practices that can lead to lots of published books and lots of adoring fans. Early in my writing career, that was a question I asked at several writing conferences or whenever I bumped into a published author at a bookstore or book fair. I, too, wanted to know the secrets of success. What I discovered was not a collection of secrets, but rather a bank of principles embraced by many of the children's authors I admired, read, and collected. I "borrowed" these ideas and made them part of my own writing philosophy. In doing so, I have been privileged to write over fifty children's books, sign tens of thousands of autographs, visit more than 150 schools throughout North America, conduct numerous workshops and seminars, and thoroughly enjoy the opportunity to touch the lives of countless children.

I offer these principles to you as beacons for your own writing ventures. I sincerely urge you to embrace them and make them part of your personal routines. What you will discover will be eye-opening, transformative, and evolutionary. You will be changed!

Reading Books

In Chapter 4, I shared the biggest mistake you could ever make as a prospective children's author. That is, never (or seldom) reading children's books. The lesson is that the more children's books you read, the more style, content, language, and pacing of children's books gets into your head—and ultimately onto your computer screen or paper.

Well, guess what, you can expand all the good things about reading children's books exponentially by also reading a plethora of other books—adult books. Read business books, science fiction novels, bodice-ripping romances (if you must), gung-ho adventure stories, fascinating biographies, travelogues to distant countries, murder mysteries, gardening tomes, or even backyard barbeque cookbooks. The more words you can pass through your subconscious, the more you will begin to see the various ways in which words can be used to convey ideas and excite imaginations.

For example, I read lots of fast-paced adventure novels (e.g. Clive Cussler, Robert Ludlum, Preston & Child, etc.), because the authors can create scenes that keep me on the edge of my chair turning page after page. I also read business books, not because I'm interested in how the business world works, but because I want to see how other writers use the same words I do to convey compelling information. I also read nature books so I can catch the subtleties of words and phrases that build an empathetic connection to inanimate objects.

A diversity of reading materials provides me with insights into good writing: I learn (as will you) about the power of narration, the intricacies of plot, the beauty of characterization, and the elements of style. As a prospective author, you begin to understand that writing is both an art and a craft; it is more than simply recording some words on a computer screen; it is an incentive to grow and expand as a writer. It gives you perspective; it opens your eyes to the possibilities of language beyond the mundane, trite, and hackneyed. Like me, you too will discover that a variety of reading material offers you a wealth of insights into the English language and a wealth of opportunities to strengthen your writing as a result.

Expert Quote

"You must read dreadful dumb books and glorious books, and let them wrestle in beautiful fights inside your head, vulgar one moment, brilliant the next. You must lurk in libraries and climb the stacks like ladders to sniff books like perfumes and wear books like hats upon your crazy heads."

—Ray Bradbury, author

Discipline

Every morning I brush my teeth. Every morning I tie my shoelaces. Every morning I feed the cat. These are things I do automatically, I don't even have to think about them: they are a natural and normal part of my morning routine. They are ingrained habits. Oh, there's also one other ingrained habit: I write every morning—each and every morning—no exceptions (OK, maybe I make an exception on my birthday). I'm at my desk by seven a.m. typing away at my computer on some sort of writing project or creative endeavor. No excuses. No apologies. No change.

For me, writing is part and parcel of what I do every day. It doesn't matter whether I have a cold, I have errands to run, I have bills to pay, or I have emails to draft. That early morning session with my computer is a clear and definite element of my morning routine. It's called discipline!

Are there times when I just don't feel like writing? You bet there are—times when I'd rather have root canal, do my income taxes, or be tied into my recliner and forced to watch a home decorating show for seventeen hours nonstop. What about you? Are there times when you can think of a thousand other things you'd rather be doing than staring at your computer screen and drafting a manuscript for a future children's book. Sure there are. It happens all the time. But, here's a little secret that you need to know: the successful writers are those who push through those "I don't feel like writing today" emotions. The successful writers push themselves into their chair, implore themselves to turn on the computer, and urge themselves to craft some words, perhaps some paragraphs, perchance a new chapter for a work in progress. They have learned, as have I, that it is far easier to give up and give in, than it is to put in the time and effort needed to be successful in this business. The best writers are those who see every writing opportunity as a learning opportunity. Is everything that comes out of our head (or on to the computer screen) worthy of a Pulitzer Prize or Newbery Award? Of course not. That's not the point. Rather, it is the act of placing our fanny in a chair, our fingers on a keyboard, and our brain in motion that creates books. You can't write a book if you don't write words—and you need to write words whether you feel like it or not.

If undisciplined, your tenure as a writer may be short. You gain that discipline by making writing a regular, normal, and daily habit. Anything less and you may be cheating yourself of the opportunity to succeed.

Expert Quote

"On writing, my advice is the same to all. If you want to be a writer, write. Write and write and write. If you stop, start again. Save everything that you write. If you feel blocked, write through it until you feel your creative juices flowing again. Write. Writing is what makes a writer, nothing more and nothing less."

—Anne Rice, author

Passion

One of the great pleasures of the writing life is the opportunity to travel around the country presenting writing workshops or visiting schools to share the joys of authorship. I always enjoy responding to questions from the audience—whether they be young or old. But, the query that got me thinking about the true craft of writing was the one posed by a woman in Portland, Oregon a few years ago. She asked, "What is the one ingredient you try to include in all your books?" After some thought I responded, "The most important feature for any book—fiction or nonfiction—is *passion!*"

Now, I'm not talking about our inherent passion for writing. After all, if we didn't have that we wouldn't have a reason for sitting in front of a blank computer screen every morning (or even reading this chapter). The passion I'm talking about is the writing that engages the reader through personal connections, links with background knowledge, common experiences, and engaging emotional bonds. Whether we write fiction or nonfiction, the factor that determines whether our writing will be embraced by readers is not necessarily the passion *for* the writing (focus on the writer), but rather the passion *in* the writing (focus on the reader).

While it's certainly important for me to share my enthusiasm *with* readers, it's even more important for my writing to engender enthusiasm *within* readers. Whether I write a nonfiction book about trees or a fictional story about a devastating tsunami, the words must be chosen carefully and woven into a narrative that invites a connection between the reader and the material. My excitement for the writing is immaterial if the reader isn't given an opportunity to build a personal, reflective, and passionate bridge between what is read and what can be felt.

> **Expert Quote**
> "At the end of the day I ask, 'Is it a well-told story?'"
>
> —Marietta Zacker, children's book agent

In my children's book *Tall Tall Tree* (2017), I wanted young readers to experience the majesty, awe, and wonder of a redwood forest. I knew how important it was to give youngsters the opportunity for an emotional response. The theme of this book revolves around the creatures that live high in the redwoods. Presented as a counting book, the design is invitational—encouraging preschool and kindergarten students to actively and enthusiastically participate in the sharing of the story.

7

Seven

Seven busy Bumblebees

Zig and zag and wait.

They flash in black and yellow,

And now comes number . . .

8

Eight

Eight sleeping Bats

Roosting in a line,

Waiting for the moon to rise,

And now comes number . . .

A reviewer on Amazon wrote, "My family really enjoyed this book, and it was read three times in a row in the first hour (I said no to the 4th). We are definitely fans of this book and will revisit it often—5 stars." It was then I knew I had tapped into the passion of the intended audience.

Too many authors define passion as a personal drive or incentive for writing. That's all well and good, but it's a narrow definition. Writing is not just about you. It's about respecting your readers, giving them an opportunity to become intimately connected with your characters or with your information. It is a respect for their passion, for what drives them, for what "floats their boat." Just because you like to write, doesn't mean that readers like to read what you scribe. If you can't give them a passion for reading (a reader-centric approach to writing) your success may be quite limited. To offer anything else is to deny your audience the joy of a personal connection and the opportunity of an impassioned response.

Expert Quote

"Find your originality of vision—your own voice. This is one of the toughest things I've had to deal with—to develop my writing 'voice.' But voice will set you apart from everyone else and define why you write and what you ultimately care about."

—Lindsay Barrett George, children's author

Writer's Block

I don't get "writer's block!" Never have, never will.

Why? Because I believe writer's block is a personal exemption—a "get-out-of-jail free" card. It's an all-too-common fallback, a walled defense against discipline, and a self-imposed pardon for the sins of inaction. It's a cheap way to justify a writer's lack of incentive, drive, or passion.

It's an escape clause for the unmotivated.

Wikipedia defines writer's block as "a condition, primarily associated with writing, in which an author loses the ability to produce new work, or experiences a creative slowdown." I'm OK with that definition as it offers the uninitiated (the non-writer) with a way to compartmentalize and clarify an apparently common affliction of the writing class. My degree of uncomfortableness comes from the overt tendency of many writers to give in to this disease. As stated above, it's an excuse the brain buys into—a way to justify that what you are facing is insurmountable, unconquerable, or unimaginable.

Writer's block may be something dancing among the brain cells of other writers; but it's something I refuse entrance into my cranium. I do that by engaging in any number of creative measures that prevent either its birth or its influence (*see* Part III of this book).

The list below includes a few strategies I've incorporated into my writing regime. Some of these are done on a regular and systematic basis as elements of my daily activities, rather than at times when I might be struck with this insidious disease. In short, I take a proactive stance to writer's block, believing that an ounce of prevention is worth a pound of cure. My secret: make some of these suggestions a regular part of your time in front of the computer well in advance of any potential onset of the disease. Use them before you get the disease, not when you might be face-to-face with this monster.

Twenty-Seven Tricks to Eliminate Writer's Block Before It Ever Occurs

1. Visit a bookstore—spend some time and read the good, the bad, and the ugly.
2. Take a walk—focus on the details in the world around you.

3. Write in a different place—the laundry room, a closet, the basement, in your car: it doesn't matter. A new environment always stimulates new thoughts.
4. Start in the middle of your story, not the beginning—beginnings are always tough, middles are much easier.
5. Use a different writing tool—a pencil, a crayon, a paint brush: anything that takes you out of your comfort zone
6. Play with a child's toy—I like simple wooden building blocks.
7. Set the timer—write as much as you can about anything for two minutes, five minutes, ten minutes.
8. Read a really lousy book, then read a super book—What did you notice?
9. Free write—Write about anything bouncing around in your head.
10. Reward yourself—Give yourself a chocolate chip cookie after 299 words, a slice of key lime pie after twenty-three minutes, a night out after finishing a chapter.
11. Browse photos—Access those photos from your vacation last year. Any book ideas there?
12. Copy and type the first paragraph from a favorite book—close the book and pretend that that paragraph is yours. Now write the rest of the story.
13. Listen to two different types of music—Jazz and classical always energize my brain cells.
14. Do some different kind of writing—Write a memoir, a racy narrative, a letter to the president, a complaint to the electric company, a science fiction tale.
15. Read some quotes about writing—Go to www.brainyquotes. com and look for writing quotes.
16. Call an old friend—talk about the last book you read.
17. Watch some funny You Tube videos—laughter always changes your mindset.
18. Write at a different time—very early in the morning, very late at night, just after dinner, during commercials on TV, while folding laundry.
19. Take a trip—around the block, to a new city, the beach, a mountain retreat, a new country
20. Paint—pick up a paintbrush and paint a picture of your story. It doesn't have to be pretty; no one will see it.

21. Write a letter to your audience—tell them why you are writing this story.
22. Stand in front of a mirror—read some of your writing out loud.
23. Move—do some easy exercises before writing, during a writing session, and after you're done for the day.
24. Talk to an imaginary character—make sure no one is around to hear you.
25. Write something for yourself instead of for your readers—a shopping list, a love poem for your sweetheart, a note to your neighbor reminding him to return your lawnmower, a letter to the editor.
26. Read strange books—there's plenty in your local library.
27. Have a long conversation with someone under the age of sixteen.

Expert Quote

"I don't believe in writer's block. Think about it: when you were blocked in college and had to write a paper, didn't it always manage to fix itself the night before the paper was due? Writer's block is having too much time on your hands. If you have a limited amount of time to write, you just sit down and do it. You might not write well every day, but you can always edit a bad page. You can't edit a blank page."

—Jodi Picoult, author

Write Garbage

Here's one of the most valuable lessons I've ever learned. It comes from Natalie Goldberg, the author of one of the best writing books around—*Writing Down the Bones: Freeing the Writer Within* (1986). She says that in order to get (and keep) writing in your blood, you need to give yourself permission to write garbage. She actually used another word, but since this is a G-rated book, I'll use a G-rated synonym. That's right, allow yourself the opportunity to write lousy stuff, stuff that will never see the light of day, stuff that will never, ever find its way into the pages of a children's book. Garbage—plain and simple garbage!

Expert Quote

"For me and most others writers I know, writing is not rapturous. In fact, the only way I can get anything written at all is to write really, really [lousy] first drafts. The first draft is . . . where you let it all pour out and then let it romp all over the place, knowing that no one is going to see it and that you can shape it later."

—Anne Lamott, author

Take a look at this:

> The cactus stood all alone in the desert. There wasn't anything around it except for a few rocks and lots of sand. The sun was hot overhead and so was the day. The temperature kept rising as the day got longer. It was so hot there weren't any animals around.

I will be the first to tell you that that short paragraph is downright crummy—in short, it's trash! It was part of the first draft of a book I was working on several years ago—a children's book eventually titled *Around One Cactus: Owls, Bats and Leaping Rats* (2003). My initial task was to get words out of my head and on to the computer screen. In so doing, I also gave myself permission to pen some pretty worthless stuff. I knew that my initial draft was, most likely, going to be just short of awful and just this side of terrible. And, I was okay with that.

But, then, my real work started. After getting my first thoughts down, I then had to revise, edit, and alter those words into a paragraph that would convey all the magic of desert life in an engaging way. And, after twenty-six drafts and ten months of work, that's what evolved. Here are the first six lines—considerably different from that first (and very rotten) draft:

> This is the desert wild and free,

A place of sun-baked majesty,

With shifting dunes and rocky edges

And bushes gripping ancient ledges.

Here stands a cactus, tall and grand,

A haven for creatures in a waterless land.

But, I couldn't have done that if I hadn't allowed myself to write some really second-rate stuff (actually, it was fifth-rate) in the first place. The dreadful stuff was an impetus to craft a story that would engage children through the magic of words well-chosen and well-ordered. Those efforts paid off when the book was selected to receive the International Reading Association's Teacher's Choice Award as well as Learning Magazine's Teacher Choice Award, both in 2004.

Give yourself permission to write garbage. Then, make it better.

Expert Quote

"I know some very great writers, writers you love who write beautifully and have made a great deal of money, and not one of them sits down routinely feeling wildly enthusiastic and confident. Not one of them writes elegant first drafts. All right, one of them does, but we do not like her very much."

—Anne Lamott, author

Kill the Editor

Lurking in the back recesses of your brain is an evil, demented, and warped being who is secretly undoing all the things you are trying to accomplish as a writer. It's a maniacal creature who wants to crush your spirit and squash your creativity. In essence, this creature wants to challenge you on every front. Whenever you put down a rambling thought on a piece of paper, the creature steps in to tell you what's wrong with it. Whenever you establish a seemingly plausible plot line, the creature wants to tear it apart. Whatever you do, the creature tells you, "Hey, hot shot, you don't have any idea what you're doing, do you?"

The creature is your mental editor!

In fact, there's a battle going on inside your head between the Editor and the Creator (a very nice soul). The Creator wants to generate a plethora of ideas while the Editor wants to censor everything you put down. Your Creator is active, involved, and dynamic; the Editor, on the other hand, wants to jump in every chance it gets to tell you what's wrong, what you shouldn't write, and that you would be better off embroidering place mats for the local senior citizen center than you would in trying to write a children's book. "Hey you," the Editor shouts. "You are absolutely crazy for thinking that you'll ever be an accomplished children's author. Your work stinks—in fact, it's absolutely putrid! It's ridiculous. It's beyond ridiculous. It's downright idiotic. I'm totally embarrassed with what you're doing and, what's more, your spelling sucks."

The problem with the Editor is that if you listen to it, it will slow down or even stop your writing. It will take over your brain cells and slowly turn them into a pile of rancid gruel. You need to kill your editor when you write. Get the ideas down on paper (or your computer monitor) without regard for their quality, impact, or intent. Just write: good stuff, bad stuff, garbage! Know that the real act of writing is not the recording of words, but rather in their revision. The voice you hear in your head doesn't know that; it's trying to stop you before you create anything worthwhile; it's judging you.

Ignore it!

Silence it!

Kill it!

Fermentation Time

Let's assume you're making preparations for a weekend party. Lots of your friends are coming over, and you want to be sure you have some great food and their favorite beverages. So, you drive on over to your local liquor store and ask one of the employees to suggest a good wine. She takes you over to a display area of new wines and points out two different possibilities:

A. **El Vino de Hoy** (Hoboken, NJ): this Cabernet Sauvignon has been fermenting in industrial drums since last Tuesday.

B. **Fleur Élégante** (Sonoma Valley, CA): this Cabernet Sauvignon has been fermenting for at least four years in fine old oaken casks.

Which one do you select?

Here's one of the most difficult things I do as a writer: I give my manuscripts some fermentation time. After I've gone through a couple of drafts with a book idea, I put the manuscript in a desk drawer and let it sit. I don't disturb it, I don't re-read it, I just let it sit there—fermenting. It begins to mellow; it begins to age. But, most important, I move on to another project and just allow that manuscript to sit.

While I work on my new project, the former one is now exiting my consciousness. It is receding from view and is becoming a distant memory. Perhaps four weeks go by, five weeks, six. My thoughts have been elsewhere, my brain cells have been purged of its memory, and my mind has been cleansed. I resist all temptation to take it out and peruse it just for the fun of it. After all, would I disturb a fine wine aging in an oaken casket while it is still fermenting? Of course not.

After sufficient time (for example, six weeks) I retrieve that manuscript and read it through. I now have a new perspective and the realization that I'm looking at this product as though it was brand new. I begin to see some things I hadn't noticed before: I see some vocabulary that must be replaced, I see a character that is not particularly well-developed, I see some dialogue that now sounds silly. In short, I see the manuscript through new eyes. I know there will (and should) be changes, and now I'm ready to address those needs with a fresh viewpoint. That "fermentation" has offered me something quite different than what I started with and the resultant editing is precise and concise.

Feedback

Writers often work in isolation. It's just us in front of a computer screen trying to craft a story that will amaze an editor and engage a host of readers. Unlike our day jobs, we do this work alone. There is little interaction with other humans (or cats who like to sleep the morning away under the desk of a certain writer). Yet, in order to grow and evolve as a writer, we need feedback. We need the perceptions of real live human beings: their insights, reactions, and criticisms.

- Volunteer as a storyteller at your local library. Read your story to a group of youngsters. Watch their faces; they'll let you know if you touched them in some way.

- Do what I do: read your story into a mirror (OK the reflection "listening" to my story doesn't really count as an audience, but stick with me here). By doing this, I get a sense of the pacing and structure of my manuscript.

- Share the story with family members and friends. But, be aware that they will tell you what you *want* to hear, not necessarily what you *need* to hear ("Oh, Aunt Betty, your story about the neurotic dinosaur and the flirtatious chipmunk was just so special. I loved it!"). Take their review(s) with the proverbial grain of salt.

- Join SCBWI (The Society of Children's Book Writers and Illustrators). You will have the opportunity to attend their conferences and regional meetings to chat with fellow writers, editors, and agents. In addition, you will be automatically enrolled in a regional chapter. These chapters offer critiquing opportunities, seminars, and other unique sessions for feedback

- Take a writing course at your local college. A writing course gives you the opportunity to make your writing available to a professional writing instructor as well as the other students in the class.

Set a Writing Goal Each Day

Stephen King writes a minimum of 2,000 words a day—every day of the year. While you're probably not trying to support yourself by writing supernatural fiction, you do need to have a target in mind. That is, you will find it most advantageous to set a goal each and every day. That goal becomes something to aim for, something to focus on that can keep you motivated and keep you focused.

Your daily writing goal will be dependent on several factors: your day job, family obligations, recreation time, hobbies, and many other events that take up your time during an "average" day. You need to determine how much time you're going to be able to devote to writing each day and craft a writing goal for each of those days. For example, you may only be able to devote fifteen minutes a day to writing. If so, then perhaps your writing goal will be 300 words per day, or 150 words each day. The amount of words written is not the critical issue, the fact that you have tasked yourself to write on a regular basis is.

A regular writing goal gives you both perspective and discipline. As mentioned earlier, it becomes part of your daily routine, part of your everyday schedule, part of who you wish to become: a successful author. Sure, there will be unexpected events (a flat tire, a sick child, an unexpected visitor) that will alter your schedule, but knowing that you

have established a regular pattern of goal-setting keeps you focused on your ultimate mission: writing a children's book.

Continue Your Education

One of the things I enjoy most about the writing life is that there is always something new to learn—always some new strategy, technique, or insight that will help me expand my education and improve my authorial skills. You see, for me, learning is never a product, it's always a process. That is to say, it is always ongoing, always taking place, always in motion. To stop learning is to stop growing. And when you stop growing, you stop living.

Here are some ideas to consider for your own literary education:

- Attend writer's conferences. The Society of Children's Book Writers and Illustrators (SCBWI) has two annual conferences (one on the west coast; one on the east coast). There are also several regional conferences held throughout the year. Other writers, agents, editors, and writing professionals present a wealth of workshops and seminars on how you can improve your writing. Be sure to attend.

- Check out a local college or university. Many institutions of higher education have writing programs and courses available.

Many have adult education programs for folks in the local community. Check out your local institution for any offerings they provide throughout the year.

- Local writer's groups. Many communities (both urban and rural) have formal or informal writing groups. These groups often meet once a month to discuss and critique members' writing. Look for postings on community bulletin boards, on the web, or in the local paper. Your neighborhood bookstore or library may have information on these groups as well.

- Online communities. Take a look at the various online communities that exist to assist writers in honing their craft. Here you'll have an opportunity to get the latest tips, ideas, and strategies that will keep your creative batteries energized and charged.

Insider Tip

Subscribe to or read professional journals. Two of the best journals are Writer's Digest and The Writer. Each one offers articles and columns that can be useful in your overall education. They often include specific information for children's authors. Other periodicals include:

- Children's Book Insider (www.write4kids.com)
- Children's Writer (www.childrenswriter.com)
- The Horn Book (www.hbook.com)
- School Library Journal (www.slj.com)
- SCBWI Bulletin (www.scbwi.org)

Teachers and librarians. If you have kids in school, take the time to talk with teachers and school librarians about the books kids are reading. Who are the "hot" authors? What are the "hot" titles? What are the "hot" themes and/or topics kids gravitate towards? If possible, take some time to talk with kids about what they like to read and what they don't.

Hard Work

Of all the suggestions I've proffered in this book, this might be the most important: being a writer is hard work! Being a good writer is even harder! Being a successful writer may be the most difficult and challenging task any of us faces.

Hard work? Count on it!

> ### Expert Quote
> "Easy reading is damn hard writing."
>
> —Maya Angelou, author

Postscript

At this particular point in most writing instruction books, the author wishes you "good luck." I'm not going to do that! Writing a publishable children's book is not a matter of luck; it is not a matter of chance or fortune or circumstances beyond your control. This is not the Powerball Lottery we're talking about here.

This is real life!

This is your future; this is what you have been dreaming about for a long time; this is one of your significant and important goals in life. Do you want to leave your success to the elements of chance, fortune, or just plain luck? I hope not!

I do, however, wish you great success. That success will come from extended and sufficient preparation, extended and sufficient homework, and extended and sufficient time. The more you invest in your writing career the more you will reap. I wrote this book to give you an edge in an extremely competitive and demanding business. I have seen what happens when a new children's author submits a "knock your socks off" manuscript—a manuscript where a powerful synergy evolves between a storyteller and an audience; a manuscript where an editor knows, long before she finishes reading, that this is a book "we must have in our catalog"; and a manuscript where a brand new author is offered a contract and a unique opportunity to touch the lives of youngsters.

You now have the tools to make that manuscript your manuscript!

Here's to your success!

Appendix

Sources and Resources

Books

If you are looking for additional books (other than this one) on writing for children, here are some possibilities. Please note that all of the listed books have been awarded four or more stars (out of five) by readers at Amazon, Barnes & Noble, or Goodreads. In addition, I have placed an asterisk (*) after several selected titles. These are books I often recommend to prospective children's authors and those that are a vital part of my own professional library.

Writing for Children

- *Adventures in Writing for Children*, Aaron Shepard, Shepard Publications
- *Children's Writers & Illustrator's Market*, Chuck Sambuchino, Writer's Digest Books*
- *How to Create a Successful Children's Picture Book*, Bobbie Hinman, Best Fairy Books
- *How to Write a Children's Book and Get It Published*, Barbara Seuling, Wiley*
- *How to Write a Children's Book*, Katie Davis, Institute of Children's Literature
- *How to Write a Children's Picture Book*, Andrea Shavick, How To Books
- *How to Write a Children's Picture Book*, Darcy Pattison, Mims House
- *How to Write a Children's Picture Book*, Eve Heidi Bine-Stock, E & E Publishing
- *How to Write a Great Children's Book*, Robyn Opie Parnell, Magellan Books
- *How to Write and Publish a Successful Children's Book*, Cynthia Resser & Lisa Michaels, Atlantic Publishing Group
- *How to Write and Sell Children's Picture Books*, Jean Karl, Writer's Digest Books
- *Picture Books: The Write Way*, Laura Purdie Salas, Create Space
- *Picture Writing*, Anastasia Suen, Writers Digest Books.
- *The Business of Writing for Children*, Aaron Shepard, Shepard Publications*
- *The Complete Idiot's Guide to Publishing Children's Books*, Harold Underdown, Alpha*
- *The Everything Guide to Writing Children's Books*, Lesley Bolton, Adams Media

- *Writing Children's Books for Dummies*, Lisa Rojany Buccieri & Peter Economy, For Dummies
- *Writing for Children and Teens*, Cynthea Liu, Pivotal Publishing
- *Writing Picture Books*, Ann Whitford Paul, Writer's Digest Books
- *Writing with Pictures*, Uri Shulevitz, Watson-Guptill
- *You Can Write Children's Books*, Tracey Dils, Writer's Digest Books*

Writing in General

- *Bird by Bird*, Anne Lamott, Anchor*
- *On Writing Well*, William Zinsser, Harper Perennial*
- *On Writing*, Stephen King, Pocket Books*
- *The Forest For the Trees*, Betsy Lerner, Riverhead Books
- *The Midnight Disease*, Alice Weaver Flaherty, Mariner Books
- *The Tao of Writing*, Ralph Wahlstrom, Adams Media
- *Thinking Like Your Editor*, Susan Rabiner, W.W. Norton
- *Thunder and Lightning*, Natalie Goldberg, Shambhala
- *Wild Mind*, Natalie Goldberg, Shambhala
- *Word Painting*, Rebecca McClanahan, Writer's Digest Books
- *Writing Begins with the Breath*, Laraine Herring, Shambhala
- *Writing Down the Bones*, Natalie Goldberg, Shambhala*
- *Writing on Both Sides of the Brain*, Henriette Klauser, HarperOne*
- *Writing Open the Mind*, Andy Couturier, Ulysses Press
- *Writing the Natural Way*, Gabriele Lusser Rico, TarcherPerigee
- *Writing to Change the World*, Mary Pipher, Riverhead Books

Writing Mechanics

- *Do I Make Myself Clear*, Harold Evans, Little, Brown & Co.
- *Words Fail Me*, Patricia O'Conner, Mariner Books
- *Writing Tools*, Roy Peter Clark, Little, Brown & Co.*

Organizations

There are a variety of professional organizations which can assist you on the road to publication. The premier organization is the Society of Book Writers and Illustrators (SCBWI) - one all children's authors (or prospective authors) should join. You are invited to check out other groups as a way of establishing some vital networks to support your writing.

- Alliance of Independent Authors - https://www.allianceindependentauthors. org
- American Association of School Librarians - http://www.ala.org/aasl
- American Christian Fiction Writers - https://www.acfw.com
- Association of Booksellers for Children - http://www.abfc.com
- Children's Book Council - http://www.cbcbooks.org
- Institute for Writers - https://www.instituteforwriters.com/account/login

- Institute of Children's Literature - https://www.instituteforwriters.com/about/institute-of-childrens-literature
- National Association of Independent Writers and Editors - https://naiwe.com
- National Association of Science Writers - https://www.nasw.org
- National Writers Union - https://nwu.org
- Nonfiction Authors Association - http://nonfictionauthorsassociation.com
- PEN America - https://pen.org
- Society of Children's Book Writers and Illustrators (SCBWI) - https://www.scbwi.org
- The Author's Guild - https://www.authorsguild.org
- Western Writers of America - http://westernwriters.org
- Women's Fiction Writers Association - http://womensfictionwriters.org/index.php
- Writer's Relief - http://writersrelief.com

Newsletters & Periodicals

Staying up to date on the latest information in the field of writing children's books is critical to your success. Here are some publications that offer a wide range of inside information for your continuing and ongoing education. Check them out.

- Children's Book Insider - http://cbiclubhouse.com
- Children's Publishing - www.childrenspublishing.blogspot.com
- The Purple Crayon - http://www.underdown.org
- Write for Kids - http://writeforkids.org
- Writer's Digest (blog for children's authors) - http://www.writersdigest.com/editor-blogs/guide-to-literary-agents/childrens-writing

Resources on the Internet

This list is a brief compilation of additional resources that can both inform and educate you on the dynamics of this ever-changing endeavor. You'll discover lots of valuable information and insightful tips.

- Aaron Shepard - www.aaronshep.com/kidwriter
- Children's Book Clubhouse - http://cbiclubhouse.com/clubhouse
- Children's Writing - http://people.ucalgary.ca/~dkbrown/writlist.html
- How to Write a Children's Book - https://bookriot.com/2017/11/16/how-to-write-a-childrens-book
- Kid Lit - www.kidlit.com
- Kids Reads - https://www.kidsreads.com
- Resources for Children's Writers - http://resourcesforchildrenswriters.blogspot.com
- The Children's Literature Web Guide - http://www.underdown.org
- Writing for Children - http://www.writing-for-children.com
- Writing for Children (articles) - http://www.writing-world.com/children/

index.shtml
- Writing World - www.writing-world.com/children

Blogs

There are literally hundreds of writing blogs online. The following list is a compilation of some of the best blogs for writers - both novice and experienced.

- Copyblogger - https://www.copyblogger.com/blog
- Daily Writing Tips - https://www.dailywritingtips.com
- Helping Writers Become Authors - https://www. helpingwritersbecomeauthors.com
- Inky Girl: Reading, Writing, and Illustrating Children's Books - http:// inkygirl.com
- KidLit411 - http://www.kidlit411.com
- Terrible Minds - http://terribleminds.com/ramble/blog
- The Creative Penn - https://www.thecreativepenn.com/blog
- The Write Life - https://thewritelife.com
- The Write Practice - https://thewritepractice.com
- The Writers' Academy - http://www.thewritersacademy.co.uk/blog
- Write to Done - https://writetodone.com
- Writer's Digest - http://www.writersdigest.com/editor-blogs
- Writers in the Storm - http://writersinthestormblog.com
- Writing for Kids - https://taralazar.com

Of course, the one essential book EVERY writer or aspiring author should read is *The Elements of Style* by William Strunk, Jr. and E.B. White. It is the best advice on the "rules" of writing and should be re-read at least once a year. Best of all, it's a full composition course in only 85 pages.

Trivia Note: E.B. White is the same E.B. White who wrote the classic children's book *Charlotte's Web.*

Index

A
achievement p
accuracy, 79–81
lots, 154
active writing, 55, 174
adults, purchase of juvenile books, 5
adults who save the day (mistake), 55–56
age, selecting, 160–64
AgentQuery.com, 233
agents, 6, 231–48
    contacting, 236–38
    criteria for, 234–36
    Fuller, Sandy Ferguson, 238–45
    function of, 231–32
    reason not to hire, 245–46
    scams, 246–47
    searching for, 232–34
Alexander, Kwame, 71
Alp Arts Company, 238. *See also* Fuller,
    Sandy Ferguson
The Amazing Bone (Steig), 65
Amazon.com, 5, 6, 252
    See also self-publishing
American Booksellers Association (ABA),
    5
anthropomorphism, 48
Arial font, 185
Around One Cactus: Owls, Bats and
    Leaping Rats (Fredericks), 313
attitude, self-exam, 7–12
authors
    expectations of, 26–30
    mistakes, 35–46, 47–48 (*see also*
        mistakes)
    occupation as, 23–31
    success (*see* success)
awards, 254
B
barnesandnoble.com, 6
beginning of stories, 41, 154–55
The Best Christmas Pageant Ever
    (Robinson), 73
biographies, 140
Blume, Judy, 281
board books, 145, 195
Book Bridge Press, 253
book markets
    growth of, 4, 6

opportunities, 6
books
    facts about children's, 4
    number of published in the United
        States, 3
    opportunities to publish, 3
    purchase of, 4–5
    reading (for success), 303–4
    religious, 4
bookstores, 5, 6
The Book: The Essential Guide to
    Publishing for Children, 202,
    234
Bowker, 3
The Bridge to Terabithia (Patterson), 53,
    72–73
C
Cannibal Animals: Animals That Eat Their
    Own Kind (Fredericks), 74
capitalization, 176
Captain Underpants, 38
Carle, Eric, 293
catalogs, 204
categories of fiction, 4
chapter books, 148
    determining number of pages, 195
    formatting manuscripts, 191–93
characters
    mistakes, 51–52
    no main character (mistake), 56
checklists, 157–60, 179–81
Cherry, Lynne, 53
Children's Book Council (CBC), 203
children's books
    agents (*see* agents)
    are easy to write (myth), 14
    elements of good books, 61–81
    facts about, 4
    formats, 144–50 (*see also* formats)
    genres, 135–44
    not reading, 35–46
    popular titles, 38–39
    reading widely in all genres, 44
    rejection, 279–90
    revision, 165–82
    self-publishing (*see* self-publishing)
    starting to write, 151–64
    as tools, 204–5
children's magazines, 128
Children's Writer's & Illustrator's Market,
    202–3, 212, 233
Children's Writer's Word Book (Mogilner
    and Mogilner), 172

Chrysanthemum (Henkes), 64
coincidences, 58
comparing good and bad stories, 41–42
comparisons, 67. *See also* similes
conferences, 24, 318–19
confidence, 30
conflict, 53–54, 156
contact information, 186, 189
continuing education, 318–19
copyrighting myths, 19–20
cover letters, 219–22, 225
cover sheets, 187
creativity
    generating ideas, 105–21
    searching for ideas, 123–32
    writing prompts, 85–103
Creech, Sharon, 44
criticism
    comparing good and bad stories,
      41–42
    taking, 29
Crossover (Alexander), 71
D
daily newspapers, 123–24
daily walks, 128
daily writing goals, 317–18
Dave the Potter: Artist, Poet, Slave (Hill),
    76
Dawn Publications, 3
descriptive words, 157
dialogue, 51, 69–71
Dig, Wait, Listen (Sayre), 76
Dinosaur Ghosts: the Mystery of
    Coelophysis (Gillette), 75–76
discipline, 305–6
Dixon, Franklin W., 38
double-spacing manuscripts, 185
drafts
    guidelines, 45
    phase five, 173–75
    phase four, 171–73
    phase one, 169
    phase seven, 177–79
    phase six, 175–76
    phase three, 170–71
    phase two, 169–70
dream endings, stories with, 58
E
Each Kindness (Woodson), 54, 66
early readers, 146–47
easy-to-read books, 195
e-book publishers, 252
editing services, 178–79. *See also* revision

editors, 6
    calling after submitting to, 230
    Malnor, Carol (conversation with),
      275–79
    mistakes writers make, 270–75
    responsibilities of, 269–79
education, 27
Ehlert, Lois, 78
electronic submissions, 212, 217–18. *See
    also* submissions
elements of good books, 61–81
    accuracy, 79–81
    dialogue, 69–71
    fascinating facts, 75–76
    fiction, 62–73
    metaphors, 67–69
    nonfiction, 73–81
    powerful lead/hook, 62–63
    rhythm of language, 66–67
    similes, 67–69
    special insights, 71–73
    topic selection, 73–75
    unusual viewpoints, 78–79
    vocabulary choices, 63–67
Elephants for Kids (Fredericks), 77, 113
ending of stories, 41
end of stories, 156
errors. *See* mistakes
expectations of authors, 26–30
    confidence, 30
    cultivating relationships, 30
    education, 27
    learning new skills, 27–28
    productivity, 29–30
    professionalism, 28
    taking criticism, 29
    work habits, 26
F
family loves your stories (myth), 16
fantasy books, 138
fascinating facts (nonfiction books), 75–76
feedback, 316–17
fiction books
    categories, 4
    dialogue, 69–71
    elements of good books, 62–73
    metaphors, 67–69
    powerful lead/hook, 62–63
    rhythm of language, 66–67
    similes, 67–69
    special insights, 71–73
    vocabulary choices, 63–67
    See also genres

figures of speech, 67. *See also* similes
financial benefits of writing (myth), 20
first person, 57
fishbowl idea strategy, 116–17
fonts, 185
formats, 144–50
    board books, 145
    chapter books, 148
    early readers, 146–47
    middle grade books, 148–49
    picture books, 146
    selecting, 150
    young adult novels, 149
formatting manuscripts, 183–95
    chapter books, 191–93
    cover letters, 219–22, 225
    cover sheets, 187
    determining number of pages, 194–95
    general manuscript formats, 185–90
    picture books, 190–91
    second sheet formats, 189
    third sheet formats, 190
    young adult novels, 191–93
Fredericks, Anthony D., 74, 75, 77, 80, 106,
        113, 152, 154, 157, 161, 313
Fuller, Sandy Ferguson, 238–45, 248
G
general manuscript formats, 185–90
generating ideas, 105–21
    fishbowl idea strategy, 116–17
    The Leonardo Strategy, 105–9
    picture portfolios, 119–21
    random thoughts, 117–19
    What If idea strategy, 109–14
    word chains, 114–16
    writing prompts, 85–103
genres, 135–44
    biographies, 140
    historical fiction, 141–42
    informational books, 142–43
    modern fantasy, 138
    picture books, 137
    poetry, 143
    reading widely, 44
    realistic fiction, 144
    resources, 136
    traditional literature, 139
Gillette, J. Lynett, 75–76
goals, 7–8, 317–18
Goldberg, Natalie, 312
good books
    accuracy, 79–81
    dialogue, 69–71

    elements of, 61–81
    fascinating facts, 75–76
    fiction, 62–73
    metaphors, 67–69
    nonfiction, 73–81
    rhythm of language, 66–67
    similes, 67–69
    special insights, 71–73
    topic selection, 73–75
    unusual viewpoints, 78–79
    vocabulary choices, 63–67
grammar, 175
The Great Kapok Tree (Cherry), 53
grocery stores, 130–32
growth of book markets, 4, 6
guidelines for drafts, 45
Guide to Literary Agents, 234
H
habits, work, 26
hard copy submissions, 215–16
Hardy Boys mysteries, 38
Hatchet (Paulsen), 70
headers, formatting, 188
Henkes, Kevin, 64
Hill, Laban Carrick, 76
historical fiction, 141–42
Holes (Yelnats), 72
honest truths, 13–21
hook, writing, 62–63
How Much Is a Million? (Schwartz), 77
hybrid publishing, 260–66
    determining publisher reputations,
        263–64
    Independent Book Publishers
        Association (IBPA)
        standards, 261–62
    Warner, Brooke (conversation with),
        265–66
I
ideas
    children's magazines, 128
    daily newspapers, 123–24
    daily walks, 128
    fishbowl idea strategy, 116–17
    generating, 105–21
    grocery stores, 130–32
    junk mail, 125
    The Leonardo Strategy, 105–9
    magazines, 127
    mistakes, 7
    online communities, 126
    outlining, 152–57
    picture portfolios, 119–21

random thoughts, 117–19
searching for, 123–32
talking with kids, 126
talking with librarians, 125
talking with teachers, 125
talking with writers, 126
theft of (myth), 19
vacations, 129–30
watching TV, 126–27
What If idea strategy, 109–14
word chains, 114–16
writing prompts, 85–103
If You Give a Mouse a Cookie (Numeroff), 53
I Have Heard of a Land (Thomas), 80
illustrations, 48–50
illustrators, finding (myth), 17
impact, adding, 69. *See also* metaphors
inanimate objects, stories of, 50
Independent Book Publishers Association (IBPA), 261–62
informational books, 142–43
Ira Sleeps Over (Waber), 70
J
junk mail, 125
K
kids, talking with, 126
Kindle Direct Publishing (KDP), 252. *See also* self-publishing
Konigsburg, E. L., 64
L
lack of conflict, 53–54
language
examples of precision, 65
patterns, 40
rhythm of, 66–67
vocabulary choices, 63–67
lead/hook, writing, 62–63
Leaf Man (Ehlert), 78
learning new skills, 27–28
L'Engle, Madeleine, 281
length of time to write (myth), 18
The Leonardo Strategy, 105–9
librarians
purchase of self-published books, 254
talking with, 125
literary classics, 43
Literary Marketplace, 203, 234
literature
formats, 144–50 (*see also* formats)
genres (*see* genres)
traditional, 139
long time periods (mistake), 58

love and friendship plots, 154
M
magazines, 127, 128
main characters, 174
Making the World (Wood), 79
Malnor, Carol, 275–79
manuscripts
agents (*see* agents)
chapter books, 191–93
cover letters, 219–22, 225
cover sheets, 187
determining number of pages, 194–95
electronic submissions, 212, 217–18
fermentation (give it time), 315–16
formatting, 183–95
general manuscript formats, 185–90
hard copy submissions, 215–16
mistakes (submission), 222–24
number received by publishers
annually, 205–6
picture books, 190–91
rejection, 279–90
second sheet formats, 189
self-publishing (*see* self-publishing)
simultaneous submissions, 226
submissions, 209–30 (*see also* submissions)
third sheet formats, 190
waiting for answers (to submissions), 227–30
writer's guidelines (publishers), 210–15
young adult novels, 191–93
See also children's books
margins, formatting, 185–86, 189
markets. *See* book markets
metaphors, 67–69
middle grade books, 148–49, 195
middle of stories, 41, 155–56
Missing May (Rylant), 62
mistakes, 47–48
active writing, 55
adults who save the day, 55–56
anthropomorphism, 48
characters, 51–52
coincidences, 58
dialogue, 51
heavy-handed morals, 54
illustrations, 48–50
lack of conflict, 53–54
long time periods, 58
multiple points of view, 57
no main character, 56

not reading children's books, 35–46
passive writing, 55
proofreading, 58–59
rhyming stories, 52–53
self-editing, 314–15
single settings, 58
stereotypes, 57
stories of inanimate objects, 50
stories with dream endings, 58
submissions, 59–60, 222–24
telling instead of showing, 50
writers make, 270–75
writing, 7
See also success
modern fantasy, 138
Mogilner, Alijandra, 172
Mogilner, Tayopa, 172
Mojave (Siebert), 79
money, 291–302, 294–302
morals
heavy-handed, 54
stories need a moral (myth), 15
multiple points of view (mistake), 57
myths, 13–21
children reading levels, 18–19
children's books are easy to write, 14
copyrighting, 19–20
family loves your stories, 16
financial benefits of writing, 20
finding an illustrator, 17
length of time to write, 18
picture books are easy to write, 14–15
promotion by publishers, 20–21
publisher theft of ideas, 19
rhyming stories have more appeal,
15–16
stories need a moral lesson, 15
success of subsequent books, 21
trends, 18
N
National Science Foundation, 13n1
Naylor, Phyllis Reynolds, 72
newspapers, 123–24
no main character (mistake), 56
nonfiction books, 5, 73–81
accuracy, 79–81
fascinating facts, 75–76
topic selection, 73–75
unusual viewpoints, 78–79
See also genres
Numeroff, Laura, 53
O
occupations, authors, 23–31

online communities, 126
online newspapers, 123–24
The Other Side (Woodson), 54, 66–67
outlines, 151, 152–57
overcoming writer's block, 308–12
P
pages, determining number of, 194–95
paper, types of, 185
passion, 306–8
passive writing, 55
patience, 11–12
patterns, language, 40
Patterson, Katherine, 53, 72–73
Paulsen, Gary, 70
periodicals, subscribing to, 24
picture books, 137
are easy to write (myth), 14–15
determining number of pages, 195
formats, 146
formatting manuscripts, 190–91
submission mistakes, 48–50
picture portfolios, generating ideas, 119–21
planning outlines, 152–57
plots, 61
achievement, 154
love and friendship, 154
outlining stories, 152–57
survival, 154
poetry, 143
point of view (POV), 57
popular titles (children's books), 38–39
postage, 212
precision language, examples of, 65
preparing to write, 3–12, 7–12
print newspapers, 123–24
print-on-demand (POD), 256–66
processes
checklists, 157–60
formats, 144–50
formatting manuscripts, 183–95
genres, 135–44
outlining, 152–57
revision, 165–82
self-publishing, 251 (*see also* self-publishing)
production, 251
productivity, 29–30
professionalism, 28
profits, self-publishing, 251, 254
promotion by publishers (myth), 20–21
proofreading, 58–59, 176
publicity, self-publishing, 255
publishers

e-book, 252
number of manuscripts received, 205–6
print-on-demand (POD), 256–66
promotion by (myth), 20–21
searching for, 199–207
subsidy, 261
targeting, 199–201
theft of ideas (myth), 19
writer's guidelines, 203, 210–15
Publisher's Weekly, 3, 4, 203
publishing
facts about children's books, 4
hybrid, 260–66
myths, 13–21
odds of getting published, 6
opportunities to publish books, 3
preparing to write, 3–12
self-publishing (*see* self-publishing)
punctuation, 175
purchase of books, 4–5
Q
query letters to agents, 236–38
R
random thoughts, 117–19
reading
books (for success), 303–4
children's books regularly, 39
influence on what to read, 4
levels, children (myth), 18–19
literary classics, 43
selections, 43
as training to write, 37, 38
realistic fiction, 144
rejection, 279–90
how to react to, 289
reasons for, 283–89
relationships, cultivating, 30
religious books, 4
resolution, 156
resources, genres, 136, 266
revision, 165–82
checklists, 179–81
phase five, 173–75
phase four, 171–73
phase one, 169
phase seven, 177–79
phase six, 175–76
phase three, 170–71
phase two, 169–70
rhyming stories, 15–16, 52–53
rhythm of language, 66–67
The River (Paulsen), 70

Robinson, Barbara, 73
Rowling, J.K., 138, 241, 281, 293
royalties, 265, 294–302
Rylant, Cynthia, 62
S
Sayre, April Pulley, 76
scams
agents, 246–47
self-publishing, 255
schedules, work habits, 26
Schwartz, David, 77
Scieszka, Jon, 292
searching for ideas, 123–32
children's magazines, 128
daily newspapers, 123–24
daily walks, 128
grocery stores, 130–32
junk mail, 125
magazines, 127
online communities, 126
talking with kids, 126
talking with librarians, 125
talking with teachers, 125
talking with writers, 126
vacations, 129–30
watching TV, 126–27
See also generating ideas
second person, 57
second sheet formats, 189
selecting formats, 150
self-addressed, stamped envelope (SASE), 212
self-editing, 314–15
self-exam, 7–12, 9–10
goals, 7–8
hard work, 8–9
patience, 11–12
self-education, 9–10
seriousness, 10–11
talent, 9
self-publishing, 249–66
awards, 254
print-on-demand (POD), 256–66
reasons against, 253–55
reasons for, 250–53
stigma of, 253
seriousness, 10–11
settings, mistakes, 58
She Write Press, 265–66
Shiloh (Naylor), 72
showing, instead of telling, 50, 64, 174
Siebert, Diane, 79
Silverstein, Shel, 281

similes, 67–69
simultaneous submissions, 226
skills
    learning new, 27–28
    productivity, 29–30
    professionalism, 28
    taking criticism, 30
Slugs (Fredericks), 75
Society of Children's Book Writers and
    Illustrators (SCBWI), 202, 233,
    318, 319
starting to write, 151–64
    checklists, 157–60
    planning outlines, 152–57
    selecting age to write for, 160–64
statements, royalties, 294–302
Steig, William, 65
stereotypes, mistakes, 57
stigma of self-publishing, 253
stories
    beginning of, 154–55
    comparing good and bad, 41–42
    with dream endings, 58
    end of, 156
    family loves your stories (myth), 16
    of inanimate objects, 50
    middle of, 155–56
    need a moral lesson (myth), 15
    outlining, 152–57
    rhyming, 52–53
    rhyming stories have more appeal
        (myth), 15–16
    structures of, 41
    themes, 42–46
    See also children's books
structures
    outlining stories, 152–57
    of stories, 41
submissions
    agents (see agents)
    cover letters, 219–22, 225
    electronic, 212, 217–18
    formatting manuscripts, 183–95
    hard copy, 215–16
    to hybrid publishers, 260–66
    manuscripts, 209–30
    mistakes, 59–60, 222–24 (*see* mistakes)
    rejection, 279–90
    searching for publishers, 199–207
    simultaneous, 226
    targeting, 199–201
    waiting for answers, 227–30
    writer's guidelines (publishers),
        210–15
subsidy publishers, 261
success
    continuing education, 318–19
    daily writing goals, 317–18
    discipline, 305–6
    feedback, 316–17
    fermentation (give it time), 315–16
    guidelines for authors, 23–31
    passion, 306–8
    reading books, 303–4
    stop self-editing, 314–15
    strategies, 303–19
    of subsequent books (myth), 21
    write garbage, 312–14
    writer's block, 308–12
Suess, Dr., 281
Surprising Swimmers (Fredericks), 106
survival plots, 154
T
talent, 9
targeting publishers, 199–201
Taylor, Mildred, 44
teachers, talking with, 125
telling instead of showing, 50, 63, 174
The Tenth Good Thing About Barney
    (Viorst), 55
themes, 42–46
third person, 57
third sheet formats, 190
Thomas, Joyce Carol, 80
Times New Roman font, 185
titles, formatting, 186
tools
    AgentQuery.com, 233
    The Book: The Essential Guide to
        Publishing for Children,
        234
    catalogs, 204
    checklists, 157–60
    Children's Book Council (CBC), 203
    children's books as, 204–5
    Children's Writer's & Illustrator's
        Market, 202–3, 212, 233
    feedback, 316–17
    Guide to Literary Agents, 234
    Literary Marketplace, 203, 234
    outlines, 151, 152–57
    overcoming writer's block, 308–12
    Publisher's Weekly, 203
    searching for agents, 233–34
    Society of Children's Book Writers
        and Illustrators (SCBWI),

202, 233
success (*see* success)
Writer's Digest Magazine, 234
writer's guidelines (publishers), 203
topic selection, 73–75, 105–9. *See also* ideas
transitions, 173
trends, myths, 18
Tsunami Man: Learning About Killer
        Waves with Walter Dudley
        (Fredericks), 80
The Tsunami Quilt: Grandfather's Story
        (Fredericks), 124, 152, 154, 157,
        161, 282
TV, watching, 126–27
U
United States, number books of published,
        3
V
vacations, 129–30
vanity publishers. *See* hybrid publishing
The View From Saturday (Koningsburg),
        64
viewpoints, unusual, 78–79
Viorst, Judith, 55
vocabularies, 61
    choices, 63–67
    sophistication of, 53
    using metaphors, 68
W
Waber, Bernard, 70
Warner, Brooke, 265–66
Weird Walkers (Fredericks), 77–78
What If idea strategy, 109–14
Williams, Mo, 44
The Wonderful Wizard Oz, 281
Wood, Douglas, 79
Woodson, Jacqueline, 54, 66, 67
word chains, 114–16
work habits, 26
write garbage, 312–14
Writer Beware website, 266
writers, talking with, 126
writer's block, 308–12
Writer's Digest Magazine, 234
writer's guidelines (publishers), 203,
        210–15
    See also submissions
writing
    active, 55, 174
    checklists, 157–60
    elements of good books (*see* good
            books)
    financial benefits of (myth), 20

mistakes, 7
myths, 13–21
passive, 55
planning outlines, 152–57
preparing to, 3–12
revision, 165–82
selecting age to write for, 160–64
self-exam, 7–12
starting to write, 151–64
work habits, 26
Writing Down the Bones: Freeing the
        Writer Within (Goldberg), 312
writing prompts, 85–103
    examples of, 88–103
    types of, 86–88
Y
Yelnats, Stanley, 72
young adult novels, 149
    determining number of pages, 195
    formatting manuscripts, 191–93